D0842409

Praise for *China's Great Migration*

"Economic growth requires large migrations of workers from unproductive agriculture to more productive industrial and service jobs, and China is no exception. The size of that country and its very fast economic growth since the 1980s has necessitated and been supported by a vast internal migration of workers and their families. Bradley Gardner's book *China's Great Migration* documents this 'great migration' with plenty of examples of real-life experiences, explains its origins and how it was intimately connected with Chinese Communist ideology, and draws lessons both for China and the rest of the developing world. *China's Great Migration* is timely and makes good reading at a time when political forces in the developed world are turning against migration and its benefits."

—**Sir Christopher Pissarides**, Nobel Prize Laureate in Economic Sciences; Regius Professor of Economics, London School of Economics

"*China's Great Migration* is a fascinating book. What the author Bradley Gardner calls 'the great migration of China' is an important engine and an integral part of the extraordinary Chinese market transformation. The whole story brings home the wisdom of the ancient Chinese dictum, 'migration breeds vitality' (人挪活, 树挪死 or Ren Nuo Huo, Shu Nuo Si). Moreover, as Gardner suggests, what has worked in China can work even better globally, if we change our entrenched views about international migration. An open, global labor market can make the 21st century more prosperous and peaceful."

—**Ning Wang**, Fellow, Coase Institute of Law & Economics, Shanghai Jiao Tong University; author (with Nobel Laureate economist Ronald Coase), *How China Became Capitalist*

"Bradley Gardner's book *China's Great Migration* offers an insight on every page. Even if you don't want to read a definitive account of China's modernization or about the widely ignored immigration dynamic that drives economic growth, you should read this book because Gardner is a gifted writer and an even better storyteller. I have not read a better book about China's economic transformation, and I doubt there is one."
—**Timothy J. Kane**, J.P. Conte Fellow in Immigration Studies, Hoover Institution, Stanford University

"Using the Chinese experience, Bradley Gardner beautifully demonstrates that it is less capital formation, tax reform or a strengthening of property rights (all good things) that has eliminated most of the world's poverty, but more the free, unimpeded movement of people seeking better lives. *China's Great Migration* makes a powerful case against heavy-handed government restrictions on migration."
—**Richard K. Vedder**, Distinguished Professor of Economics Emeritus, Ohio University; author (with Lowell E. Gallaway), *Out of Work: Unemployment and Government in Twentieth-Century America*

"Economic growth is about far more than just numbers. In *China's Great Migration*, Gardner weaves a masterful account of how China's modest and haphazard liberalizations have emboldened hundreds of millions of Chinese to seek out better lives in China's urban centers. His book puts a human face on China's impressive economic growth statistics."
—**Robert A. Lawson**, Jerome M. Fullinwider Endowed Centennial Chair in Economic Freedom and Director, O'Neil Center for Global Markets and Freedom, Southern Methodist University

"Bradley Gardner's understanding of regional dynamics in China is unparalleled amongst his peers. He does an excellent job laying out the dynamics of the force powering China's economic rise from the micro-level to the macro-level, and draws thought-provoking comparisons with migration patterns elsewhere in the world. Highly recommended read."
—**Victoria Lai**, co-head of Young China Watchers New York

"*China's Great Migration* is an excellent book on how liberty is the key for Chinese economic development. The Chinese migration movement, 260 million strong, is the largest freedom movement in the world and the key for Chinese development. The book is also great in terms of comparative value. It will further be a good book for college students to use, and I will use it in the future."

— **Kate Xiao Zhou**, Professor of Comparative Politics and Political Economy of China, Department of Political Science, University of Hawaii at Manoa; author, *How the Farmers Changed China: Power of the People* and *China's Long March to Freedom: Grassroots Modernization*

"By skillfully employing primary data and secondary sources in his book *China's Great Migration*, Bradley Gardner sheds a bright light on China's great liberal leap forward. It is a free-market story of how China removed the chains from human capital and how that facilitated an explosion of entrepreneurship and the greatest migration in world history—a migration from unproductive work and misery to productive private work and prosperity."

— **Steve H. Hanke**, Professor of Applied Economics, Johns Hopkins University

"The greatest anti-poverty program in the history of the world was driven by the greatest migration in the history of the world, from rural to urban China. *China's Great Migration* combines on-the-ground reporting with significant economic and historical scholarship, and it's a great read. Gardner has written an important book for anyone interested in understanding China, migration, or the economics of development. Highly recommended!"

— **Alexander Tabarrok**, Bartley J. Madden Chair and Professor of Economics, George Mason University

"In his outstanding book, *China's Great Migration*, Bradley Gardner reminds us that arguably not only the greatest achievement of China, but one of the greatest for humanity generally, was the reduction of the population living in absolute poverty between 1981 and 2010 by a staggering 753 million people. In great part, he argues convincingly, this is due to the Great Migration, as per the title of the book. The size and thrust of this Great Migration is comparable only to the experience of the United States at the time of Manifest Destiny. In both the American and Chinese cases, migration constituted a key driver of economic growth. What are some of the implications? For China, the Great Migration reached its peak a decade ago and therefore can no longer serve as a growth driver. To sustain the trajectory, China needs some radical reforms. Whether these are undertaken remains to be seen. In the meantime, for all those countries in Asia, notably India, and in Africa and Latin America where poverty remains stubbornly high as strict policies impeding migration persist, the lessons should be obvious. The strengths of this book lie not only in the quality of research and analysis, but also in it being a 'living testimony' as the author was present to see with his own eyes the process, progress and impact of China's Great Migration. It marks a major contribution to the understanding of China's spectacular growth, to the literature on development and especially to the ongoing global elusive quest for poverty-reduction."

—**Jean-Pierre Lehmann**, Emeritus Professor of International Political Economy, IMD Singapore; Visiting Professor of Business and Economics, Hong Kong University; Founding Director, The Evian Group

"In *China's Great Migration*, Bradley Gardner has written an outstanding book that shows how China's internal migration into the relatively freer cities fueled much of China's growth and led to a massive reduction in poverty. All people who are serious about understanding how migration can create prosperity need to read Gardner's excellent book!"

—**Benjamin Powell**, Director of the Free Market Institute and Professor of Economics, Jerry S. Rawls College of Business, Texas Tech University; editor, *Making Poor Nations Rich* and *The Economics of Immigration*

CHINA'S
GREAT
MIGRATION

INDEPENDENT INSTITUTE is a non-profit, non-partisan, public-policy research and educational organization that shapes ideas into profound and lasting impact. The mission of Independent is to boldly advance peaceful, prosperous, and free societies grounded in a commitment to human worth and dignity. Applying independent thinking to issues that matter, we create transformational ideas for today's most pressing social and economic challenges. The results of this work are published as books, our quarterly journal, *The Independent Review*, and other publications and form the basis for numerous conference and media programs. By connecting these ideas with organizations and networks, we seek to inspire action that can unleash an era of unparalleled human flourishing at home and around the globe.

FOUNDER & PRESIDENT
David J. Theroux

RESEARCH DIRECTOR
William F. Shughart II

SENIOR FELLOWS
Bruce L. Benson
Ivan Eland
John C. Goodman
John R. Graham
Stephen P. Halbrook
Robert Higgs
Lawrence J. McQuillan
Robert H. Nelson
Charles V. Peña
Benjamin Powell
William F. Shughart II
Randy T Simmons
Alexander Tabarrok
Alvaro Vargas Llosa
Richard K. Vedder

ACADEMIC ADVISORS
Leszek Balcerowicz
WARSAW SCHOOL OF ECONOMICS

Jonathan J. Bean
SOUTHERN ILLINOIS UNIVERSITY

Herman Belz
UNIVERSITY OF MARYLAND

Thomas E. Borcherding
CLAREMONT GRADUATE SCHOOL

Boudewijn Bouckaert
UNIVERSITY OF GHENT, BELGIUM

Allan C. Carlson
HOWARD CENTER

Robert D. Cooter
UNIVERSITY OF CALIFORNIA, BERKELEY

Robert W. Crandall
BROOKINGS INSTITUTION

Richard A. Epstein
NEW YORK UNIVERSITY

B. Delworth Gardner
BRIGHAM YOUNG UNIVERSITY

George Gilder
DISCOVERY INSTITUTE

Nathan Glazer
HARVARD UNIVERSITY

Steve H. Hanke
JOHNS HOPKINS UNIVERSITY

James J. Heckman
UNIVERSITY OF CHICAGO

H. Robert Heller
SONIC AUTOMOTIVE

Deirdre N. McCloskey
UNIVERSITY OF ILLINOIS, CHICAGO

J. Huston McCulloch
OHIO STATE UNIVERSITY

Thomas Gale Moore
HOOVER INSTITUTION

Charles Murray
AMERICAN ENTERPRISE INSTITUTE

Michael J. Novak, Jr.
AMERICAN ENTERPRISE INSTITUTE

June E. O'Neill
BARUCH COLLEGE

James R. Otteson, Jr.
WAKE FOREST UNIVERSITY

Charles E. Phelps
UNIVERSITY OF ROCHESTER

Daniel N. Robinson
OXFORD UNIVERSITY AND GEORGETOWN UNIVERSITY

Paul H. Rubin
EMORY UNIVERSITY

Bruce M. Russett
YALE UNIVERSITY

Pascal Salin
UNIVERSITY OF PARIS, FRANCE

Vernon L. Smith
CHAPMAN UNIVERSITY

Pablo T. Spiller
UNIVERSITY OF CALIFORNIA, BERKELEY

Joel H. Spring
QUEENS COLLEGE, CITY UNIVERSITY OF NEW YORK

Rodney Stark
BAYLOR UNIVERSITY

Richard L. Stroup
NORTH CAROLINA STATE UNIVERSITY

Arnold S. Trebach
AMERICAN UNIVERSITY

Richard E. Wagner
GEORGE MASON UNIVERSITY

Walter E. Williams
GEORGE MASON UNIVERSITY

100 Swan Way, Oakland, California 94621-1428, U.S.A.
Telephone: 510-632-1366 • Facsimile: 510-568-6040 • Email: info@independent.org • www.independent.org

CHINA'S GREAT MIGRATION

How the Poor Built a Prosperous Nation

BRADLEY M. GARDNER

INDEPENDENT
INSTITUTE

OAKLAND, CALIFORNIA

China's Great Migration
Copyright © 2017 by the Independent Institute

All Rights Reserved. No part of this book may be reproduced or transmitted in any form by electronic or mechanical means now known or to be invented, including photocopying, recording, or information storage and retrieval systems, without permission in writing from the publisher, except by a reviewer who may quote brief passages in a review. Nothing herein should be construed as necessarily reflecting the views of the Institute or as an attempt to aid or hinder the passage of any bill before Congress.

Independent Institute
100 Swan Way, Oakland, CA 94621-1428
Telephone: 510-632-1366
Fax: 510-568-6040
Email: info@independent.org
Website: www.independent.org

Cover Design: Shanti Nelson
Cover blue sky photo: Zazastudio © 123RF.com
Cover bamboo rafting photo in Li River, Guilin—Yangshou China:
    Alberto Rigamonti © 123RF.com

Library of Congress Cataloging-in-Publication Data

Names: Gardner, Bradley, author.
Title: China's great migration : how the poor built a prosperous nation / Bradley Gardner.
Description: Oakland, California : Independent Institute, 2017. | Includes bibliographical references.
Identifiers: LCCN 2016042324 (print) | LCCN 2016043469 (ebook) | ISBN 9781598132229 (hardcover) | ISBN 9781598132236 (paperback) | ISBN 9781598132243 (ePub) | ISBN 9781598132250 (Mobi) | ISBN 9781598132267 (Pdf)
Subjects: LCSH: Rural-urban migration—China—History. | Migration, Internal—Economic aspects—China—History. | Economic development—China—History. | Social change—China—History. | China—Economic conditions—1949- | China—Social conditions—1949-
Classification: LCC HB2114.A3 G27 2017 (print) | LCC HB2114.A3 (ebook) | DDC 307.2/40951—dc23
LC record available at https://lccn.loc.gov/2016042324

Contents

Acknowledgments

THIS BOOK WOULD not have been possible without the contributions and help of numerous people. At the top of this list should be David J. Theroux, Roy M. Carlisle, Alexander Tabarrok, William F. Shughart II, and the others at the Independent Institute who supported this project and helped develop it into what you read here.

Much of the content in this book stems from research projects I worked on for the Economist Intelligence Unit, and I am indebted to my supervisors, Alexander Van Kemenade and Victoria Lai, for much of my understanding of how China works. I also owe a debt of gratitude to J. C. Ning, who gave me my first job in China and was indulgent of my interests and larger story ideas. Additional thanks to Jagadish Upadhyay for providing comments on the completed manuscript.

Countless people in China helped me research this book. I would like to particularly thank Zhang Hong, Helen Feng, Zeo Niu, Meng Xiaodong, Jia Lingmin, Weng Wenbiao, and the Wenzhou businesspeople who will remain nameless. I would also like to thank Kam Wing Chan at the University of Washington for help wrapping my head around China's migration data.

And, of course, Zdenka, for twelve years together, three continents, two beautiful daughters, and many late nights typing.

This book is dedicated to my grandfather, Archie Lee Frazer, who witnessed the Chinese Civil War firsthand as a US soldier in Chongqing during the last months of World War II. He was born in rural Missouri in 1923, and spent several years, both before and after the war, traveling the country looking for work. Over fifteen years, he lived in Chicago, Memphis, and San

Francisco, working as a taxi driver, a building manager, a dispatching agent, and a tax adviser.

He eventually found a job as a manager with the multinational construction firm Bechtel, where he earned enough to buy a house and raise seven children in what would later become Silicon Valley. He celebrated his 92nd birthday while this book was being written and the birth of his fourth great-grandchild. I hope this book contributes to other migrants having the same opportunities and the same successes that he had.

Introduction

OVER THE PAST three decades, the world has become a much
better place for the poor. Between 1990 and 2015, the percentage of the world
living in absolute poverty declined by 72 percent despite the worst economic
crisis since the Great Depression. Today hundreds of millions of people have
access to opportunities that would have been denied to them a generation
ago—opportunities to invest in themselves and improve the lives of their
families and their children.[1]

The scale of this success was almost entirely unexpected. In 1990, two out
of every five people in the world lived in poverty, and in Latin America and
Africa the situation was getting worse. Ten years later, the decline in poverty
was visible, but still few people predicted the scale of progress that would be
seen over the next decade. The United Nations Millennium Development
Goals, announced in 2000, aimed to lower the developing world poverty rate
by half by 2015, a far more modest improvement than what would eventually
be achieved.

Why this happened is still a matter of some debate. The decline in poverty
has happened globally, in countries with varying economies and political
environments. Each affected country benefited from different local reforms,
as well as changes to the global economy brought about by new technologies
and globalization. Untangling which of these changes contributed the most to
the success of a country's poor, and which had negligible or negative long-term
effects, is often both challenging and politically controversial. Were Latin
America's poor helped more by reforms to social services that helped fight
income inequality, or by a succession of market-friendly political leaders that
opened the continent to the global economy?[2] To what degree have Africa's

improvements over the past decade been due to high commodity prices, and what will happen if commodity prices drop?[3] Does Western aid ever help a country's development, or is it all "dead aid," causing more problems than it solves?[4]

At the center of this debate is China. From 1981 to 2011, the size of the Chinese population living in absolute poverty declined by 753 million people—a number roughly twice the population of the United States. The Chinese economic miracle accounted for 50 percent of the total decline in poverty levels globally, and almost the entirety of the net decline in poverty levels, as population growth in other countries ate away at their progress. If we want to understand how the world has been so successful at reducing poverty, and how we could move forward to eliminating poverty, it is important to understand what China has done to transform itself from the worst performing major economy in the world to a middle-income economy and a global economic power.

Unfortunately, China's growth story inspires as much, if not more, debate as other developing countries. On the one side, China's free market reforms have been substantial. The Chinese economic miracle happened alongside China's transition from a brutally enforced communist system to a market-based economy. China's first wave of growth in the 1980s was spurred by the decollectivization of agriculture and the legalization of private employment. In the 1990s, China moved from a primarily state-controlled economy to a primarily private economy, with the state's share of employment dropping from 60.5 percent in 1998 to 19.4 percent by 2010.[5] These private sector companies would quickly come to dominate global export markets for light-manufactures and electronics, passing on wealth to their workers who invested in new homes and new businesses.

But past these points, the typical Washington consensus argument runs into trouble. While employment has been increasingly dominated by the private sector, the Communist Party still controls many strategically important industries, including finance, telecoms, oil, coal, and steel. Chinese farmers still don't have full ownership of the land they work, and China's booming real estate market is tied up with China's byzantine land-use regulations and its backward financial markets. For some, these distortions are indications of an intelligent guiding hand that has allowed China to succeed where other developing countries have failed. For others, they are a sign that China's economy is a Potemkin village, full of empty high-rises and factories producing for nonexistent consumers, waiting for financial reality to catch up to it.

• • •

When I found my first job in China in 2007, it was easy to have the sense that China's economy was too good to be true. I had previously worked as a reporter covering banking and monetary policy in Europe. I had a decent idea of how the commanding heights of the economy were supposed to work, and China's economy didn't work that way. Chinese banks lent to state-owned enterprises (SOEs) that were chronically inefficient and often loss making, while the country's robust export sector was severely underfinanced. I would learn that the need to prop up its state sector was the basis of China's much maligned currency policy, with the government tightly controlling outflow in order to keep money in the state-controlled banking system. Major government projects, like China's high-speed rail system, would end up poorly functioning and wildly over budget. Yet despite all this, the economy was growing 10 percent a year. At some point, the system had to break down.

Then, it didn't. Over the next two years, the population of China living in poverty dropped by 50 million people. Some of these people were my neighbors—the woman who worked at the dumpling restaurant by my house, the family who sold me vegetables, the men working on the building site outside my window. A decade earlier these people were living in rural villages, worrying about having food to eat, heat for the winter, and proper sanitation. Now they were trying to figure out what sort of phone they could afford and how they could sell their skills to a more competitive buyer. There was a qualitative change in these people's lives, and arguing that it would go away because Europe was going to buy fewer iPhones suddenly seemed absurd.

I knew what China was doing wrong, but at the same time China was doing something profoundly right. I wanted to know what that something was. China had its economic problems, but it had 753 million success stories, and those were stories that weren't being told. Luckily, as an economics journalist and researcher, I was being paid to write about it.

So I started asking people. Not just the economists, businesspeople, lawyers, consultants, and government officials that are the bread and butter of an economic researcher's job. I started asking shopkeepers, factory workers, taxi drivers, and waiters how they came to be making money the way they were making money, and why they had made the economic decisions that they had made. These were people who could tell me objectively how their lives had changed—how little they had before, what their plans for the future were, and how they were spending the USD 300 a month they made making iPhones, the USD 200 a month they made in a dumpling restaurant, the USD 250 a month they made sewing clothes. I met farmers who could talk about the lengths to which they went in order to get their children to succeed at school and what their children were doing in the cities. I talked to factory owners who told me about not having enough to eat growing up. These were real people leading real lives, and despite pundits' repeated predictions of China's coming collapse, their lives had been consistently getting better for more than thirty years.

And every one of their stories was about migration.

• • •

For forty days at the beginning of every year, China's cities empty out. The Chinese Ministry of Railways calls these days "the Spring Festival travel season," the weeks surrounding the Spring Festival holiday where travelers queue up for train tickets, often camping out for days to get a ticket home to see their family. These forty days are the closest thing to a snapshot of the Great Migration—the process that saw the population of China's cities swell by half a billion people in a little over thirty years.

In 2012, approximately 40 percent of the population of Shanghai left the city during the Spring Festival travel season, with 1.3 million people going through the city's three train stations on a single day. The country's transport infrastructure struggles under the weight of all these people. In 2016, 100,000 people became stranded in Guangzhou's main train station due to snow, requiring more than 5,000 police officers to maintain order. In cities across the country, parking lots surrounding major train stations are turned into waiting rooms filled with thousands of people, while security in subway stations is doubled to protect passengers from pickpockets.[6] The trains are packed full, with the railroad company opening up standing-room-only tickets to those who couldn't get a seat. There is a mix of students, factory workers, janitors, and construction workers, filling the trains with the smell of ramen noodles and pickled vegetables, and the noise of people playing cards, snoring, and spitting sunflower seeds.

The Chinese economy is built around the Spring Festival travel season. Industrial output surges in the weeks before as companies try to meet their contracts before their workers disappear for the following month. The travel season ends with a rush of hiring, as factories fill jobs left by those who didn't return and take advantage of the surge of new workers trying their luck in a new city. Every February, tens of millions of people move from the country to the cities, and millions more move from one city to another looking for new opportunities. Rental costs spike, not unlike a giant college town during the last weeks of summer vacation.[7]

There is robust competition for the best jobs, but also enough jobs to go around. Major foreign-owned factories hire by the busload, taking nearly every employee willing to work for the sum they're willing to pay. Better connections or better skills allow workers to find jobs in smaller factories, producing more specialized products. Whatever jobs migrants get, the wages are multiple times higher than what they would earn working on the farm. And over the long run, they might, like their bosses, find a way to get in on the ground floor of a new business and earn their place in China's manufacturing economy.[8]

• • •

Between 1978 and 2012, the population of China's cities grew by half a billion people, swollen by more than 260 million economic migrants moving to urban centers to look for new opportunities. To put this number in some perspective, only 13.6 million people are currently taking advantage of the European Union's single labor market to work outside of the country of their birth. The United States, by far the largest recipient of immigrants globally, is home to 41.3 million people from other countries.[9] China's internal migrants outnumber the 232 million international migrants worldwide, as well as the entire population of every country except for China, India, and the United States.[10]

In many countries, policy discussions about migration focus on the question of how to stop it. At a time when concerns about refugees, stagnant wages, and underemployment have bred animosity toward migrants in countries rich and poor, discussion about the role of the Great Migration in China's economic development is politically inconvenient and easily ignored. This is no less true in China, where the government continues to implement policies to restrict and redirect migration away from the country's largest urban centers. For many government officials, supporting migration has seemed like a quick road to ruin. Migrant families need homes, spots in schools, hospitals, and space in public transport, all of which need to be built before migrants can start contributing to tax revenue.

If we look at the situation from the migrant's perspective though, then the role of migration in economic growth is hard to debate. A Chinese worker moving from the farm to a factory could see his or her income grow by 500 percent. Though the extra 8 to 9 dollars a day that migrants earn may not seem like much to the average city dweller, for China's poor, the difference is life changing. An extra 8 to 9 dollars a day is the difference between struggling to buy clothes and struggling to buy a phone; between an empty field and a flush toilet; between illiteracy and a technical education.

Once workers have made the transition from rural farms to urban factories, there are many more opportunities for economic growth. Migrants need a place to live and a way to get around. They earn money that can be spent on entertainment, better quality clothes, and better quality food. Workers living in urban areas trade advice on how to best do their jobs, they compete to get jobs in the best-run factories, and some, once they've learned the trade, set up new factories so they can make money on some underserved corner of the supply chain. Most importantly, they work—they make goods that otherwise would not have been made, and they provide services that otherwise would not be provided.

These economic gains are what the economist Michael Clemens calls the "trillion-dollar bills on the sidewalk." In his paper of the same name, Clemens found that the gains from eliminating global barriers to migration would be in the realm of 50 to 150 percent of global gross domestic product (GDP). Most of this money would go to the people who need it, the poor, who would be able to sell their labor in places with better technology and higher wages. Clemens estimates that emigration of less than 5 percent of the population of the poorest countries would increase global GDP more than the elimination of all barriers to trade and financial flows combined.[11]

One of the simplest explanations for the Chinese economic miracle is that someone decided to pick up these trillion-dollar bills. The consensus estimate among economists is that labor reallocation—that is, the transfer of workers from agriculture to industry—accounted for more than 20 percent of Chinese GDP growth between 1990 and 2010, a period when the Chinese economy grew from USD 400 billion to USD 6 trillion. In other words, simply allowing Chinese people to move to cities where they could find factory jobs added USD 1.1 trillion to the Chinese economy over twenty years—growth equivalent to an economy roughly the size of Mexico.[12]

Migration is by no means the only reason for the Chinese economic miracle, but it is an incredibly useful tool for understanding how China works, and particularly how China has managed to defy many of the basic tenets of free markets, yet maintain a growth rate well in excess of anything the world has seen before. Besides the straightforward gains from expanding the industrial workforce, migrant workers learn new job skills, compete for jobs, and share information. Their farmland is redistributed to the workers who stay behind, increasing the productivity in the countryside. Though these gains are more difficult to measure than the gains from labor reallocation, they are likely just as substantial, if not more so.

Migration is also a useful framework for understanding China's political economy. Once the Great Migration began, the government was forced to make sweeping changes to how the economy was run in order to maintain fiscal solvency and, in the words of Hu Jintao, to "create 25 million jobs a year."[13] The Great Migration was a direct impetus for the country's opening to private enterprise, and has created an ongoing incentive for China to reform its fiscal system in a way that is friendlier to private enterprise and urban development. Though many of these reforms have been problematic and halting, the Great Migration has forced the Chinese government to take action on problems that it could have otherwise ignored.

For other developing countries, the political consequences of migration can make implementing migrant-friendly policies difficult. The liberalization of China's labor market during the Great Migration led to the collapse of "iron rice bowl" jobs in state-owned enterprises (jobs from which workers couldn't be fired), increased demand for real estate in China's urban areas, and strained the social services system to the point of collapse. While the average urban resident would see their income increase significantly from the Great Migration, migrants remain unpopular in most urban areas of China, and a deeply difficult problem for bureaucrats in those cities. China found ways to deal with its migrant population because it did not have any other choice, but for most countries, barriers to migration are politically popular because there are real political issues associated with migration.

This book attempts to explain why China has embraced an idiosyncratically pro-migrant development policy and what the consequences of those policies have been, as a way for policymakers elsewhere to consider solutions to some of the problems associated with large scale migration and capture the substantial economic benefits. Specifically, the book looks at how the Great Migration started (Chapter 1), how the Chinese government adapted to the Great Migration (Chapter 2), how much the Great Migration has contributed to economic growth in China (Chapter 4), and what we can predict about the future of the Chinese economy based on current migration trends (Chapters 5 and 6). Chapter 3 and Chapter 7 look at the past and future of the Great Migration through the history of two cities: Wenzhou (Chapter 3), the first city to embrace private employment in response to the Great Migration, and Zhengzhou (Chapter 7), which has grown significantly over the last five years as migrant workers have returned from coastal cities to inland provinces. Finally, the book concludes with a discussion of labor market restrictions outside of China, and how other countries could benefit from some of the lessons China learned during its thirty-year struggle with migrant workers (Chapter 8).

The answers to these questions largely turn on four ongoing reform programs: rural land reform, *hukou* reform, private enterprise reform, and tax reform. Let's consider each of these briefly now.

Rural Land Reform

Prior to the Great Migration, China dealt with unemployment and underemployment by increasing the labor density on collective farms. Reforms to the collective labor system in the early 1980s allowed land to be tended with fewer workers, creating a pool of "excess labor" that started to look outside the farm for employment. These workers were a political liability for the Chinese government, which at the time had neither the resources to employ them through state-owned enterprises and provide them with social services, nor the political control to stop them from looking elsewhere for work. Over the next thirty years, the Chinese government would explicitly tie rural land reforms to the country's progress on urbanization, a process that continues today.

Hukou Reform

China's household registration system, or hukou, assigns Chinese citizens a residence at birth, based on the residence of their mother. Since 1960, this system has been used explicitly to bar migration between rural areas and cities, and between cities in different regions. The hukou system has been enforced through a variety of mechanisms, including subjecting migrants to arbitrary arrest and fines, barring them from receiving social services outside their home areas, and, during the Maoist era, barring them from working and purchasing food in urban areas. During the reform period, these barriers slowly broke down, until the costs associated with disobeying hukou laws were overcome by the benefits. Despite significant progress in this area, some social services are still tied to a person's hukou, making migrants effectively second-class citizens in their adopted cities.

Private Enterprise Reform

The need to create employment for this pool of migrant labor has been the driving force behind many of China's more dramatic economic reforms. First, when sent-down youth (see Chapter 2) were returning to the cities from the countryside, China legalized "self-employment" as a means to take pressure off of overburdened state-owned enterprises. As the Great Migration picked up, these small businesses expanded while their state-owned competitors collapsed. Competition from private enterprise would force the government to embrace a more liberal labor market, which resulted in the laying off of more than 40 million people from the state sector between 1997 and 2004.[14] The companies that remained began hiring and firing workers at a similar rate as the private sector, increasing the overall efficiency of state-owned enterprises, and pushing more workers into the private sector.[15]

Tax Reform

The collapse of SOEs undermined China's Mao-era taxation system. After a number of piecemeal reforms, the government overhauled the entire taxation system in 1994 in a way that provided specific incentives for urbanization and reduced the costs associated with migrating. There were substantial negative effects to this reform that China is still wrestling with today, with consequences for migrants, farmers, and China's overall economy.

While the Great Migration has contributed enormously to China's success over the past three decades, it is also a finite resource. Rural-urban migration peaked in 2007, and is likely to continue slowing until the mid-2020s, when the country's urbanization rate is expected to reach equilibrium. The change has already contributed to an economic slowdown, where growth has declined from over 10 percent a year to under 7 percent a year. Over the next decade, China will need to manage this slowdown by continuing to integrate rural dwellers into the country's industrial economy, and reforming economic institutions to maximize efficiency rather than just maximizing employment.

There is no reason to think that China will necessarily navigate this transition successfully. The early reforms to China's economy that led to the Great Migration were pushed on the political leadership by a series of extreme circumstances—the inability to enforce collective farming after the Cultural Revolution, the return of the sent-down youth from the countryside, and the insolvency of the country's state-owned enterprises after decades of mismanagement. Even then, China struggled to reform the institutions that immiserated its population and pushed the government to the brink of bankruptcy. Completing the reforms that started the Great Migration will be difficult and require contending with entrenched political actors and status quo bias.

But there is a risk that the wrong lesson will be learned from China's slowdown. Even if China gets caught in a middle-income trap, the position of Chinese people today is exponentially better than it was thirty years ago. China achieved this success despite poor financial and fiscal management and a lukewarm commitment to the free market. Instead, the centerpiece of its development policy was aggressive labor market liberalization, a policy that is treated with suspicion even in the developed world. The results were remarkable.

The last chapter of this book will compare China's experience with the Great Migration with migration policy in other developed and developing countries. The only other country that has experienced migration on a level even remotely approaching the Great Migration is the United States. Not only is the United States home to 18 percent of the world's immigrant population, the country also has a long history of mass migrations in response to extreme economic and political events—the Irish potato famine in the 1840s, the mass migration to California during the Gold Rush, the Chinese immigrant rush following the Taiping Rebellion, the European migrations of the 1900s, the Dust Bowl migration from Oklahoma to California, the migration of African Americans to the North in the mid-twentieth century, Vietnamese refugees in the 1970s, the Mariel boatlift, and so on. These mass migrations spurred a number of different policy programs—some more successful than others—that reflected the unique political economy of the United States.

The differences between the political economy of China and the United States can mask the similarities between how their economies have developed. One of the unique accomplishments of the United States is the size and mobility of its single labor market, and the enormous success it has had integrating immigrant communities. However, like China, these achievements remain controversial, with local governments experimenting with a range of policy mechanisms to either discourage or encourage migrants, depending on the current political climate.

Comparing the migration policy experience of the United States with the various Chinese government initiatives implemented during the Great Migration can be illuminating. The hukou system during its heyday in the 1960s was almost uniquely horrible—part of a legal apparatus that killed 36 million people during the Great Leap Forward, Mao's disastrous attempt at Communist industrialization—and provided a model for Pol Pot's Cambodia. No other country in the world can replicate the economic gains from reforming the hukou system, because no other country has a hukou system to reform. Many countries, though, restrict urban construction, put soft restrictions on employment, and control the trade in rural land. Controls on migration are diverse and not always obvious to the casual observer, but they have real costs for both developed and developing countries. Both the United States and China have depended on migrants to drive economic growth, and they present unique lessons for other countries to learn from.

Development professionals are often hesitant to embrace migration as a tool in the fight against poverty, and often find the best course of action is to ignore or deny the incredible economic gains associated with the free movement of people. Despite the large role that migration has played in the development of the American and Chinese economies, it is not mentioned as a component of the "Washington Consensus" as described by John Williams in 1989, or any form of the "Beijing Consensus" as it has been written about by various foreign policy professionals and economists who have tried to pin down China's development policy.

Migration's tremendous potential should not be neglected. For the average Chinese, and for the average American, the most important thing they can do to increase their incomes is to move to the city. For many people in India, Africa, and even Latin America, that transition is much more difficult due to anti-migrant and anti-urbanization policies implemented by their governments. Reforming these policies would be life changing for millions of people. Migration policy not only deserves attention, it deserves urgency.

I

Leaving the Countryside

WHEN JIA LINGMIN tries to explain land rights in China, she likes to start with the story about the time that she was kidnapped.

In November 2009, residents of Qiliyan village, in the southern suburbs of Zhengzhou, a city in central China, found out that their homes were slated for redevelopment—or, in other words, destruction. It came as something of a surprise. No meetings were held and no one came to announce the government's plans. Residents woke up to find notices posted around the village giving them thirty days to vacate their homes. If they vacated within thirty days, they would receive RMB 20,000 (USD 3,250), which would go toward decorations and utilities at a new apartment that had already been set up for them. If they did not vacate within thirty days, then they would forgo compensation, and be forcibly made to vacate.

While the notice came as a surprise, the villagers knew what was happening. Much of Zhengzhou had been redeveloped over the previous few years, and the national news was filled with stories about people being cheated out of their land by corrupt officials. Each relocation was supposed to come with long negotiations over expected compensation. Some of these negotiations brought significant returns to the villagers, helping them buy better properties in urban areas and invest in businesses that could profit from regional development, while others had their homes stolen from them for a paltry sum and a ramshackle apartment. Violent standoffs between property developers and villagers were almost daily features in Chinese media, and by leading with an ultimatum, the government made it clear that they didn't expect to reach a compromise.

Ms. Jia, a schoolteacher from the village, was determined to resist to the best of her ability. She approached her fight as a legal problem. According to government law, before any land was sold, a public assembly was required, where villagers could vote on whether they wanted to sell and what compensation to request. The developers had to show judicial documents as well as plans for their new development. None of this had been done in Qiliyan, and Ms. Jia was determined to make sure that the law was followed before any of the villagers signed over their rights.

She delayed the project for eight months. Then on June 22, 2010 at 4 p.m., she was assaulted in the street, grabbed and thrown into the back of a van. She was driven to the mountains outside of town and thrown into a ditch. By the time she found her way back, her home had been destroyed, her pets killed, and her fields torn up.

Several others who had organized the resistance in the village were also kidnapped, and at least one was hospitalized because of his injuries. He identified the car's license plate, which the police traced to a local government office, but none of the victims were able to identify any of the perpetrators. Workers at the government office denied any knowledge of the event, and the police claimed there was nothing they could do. Eventually, most of the village signed over their land.

Ms. Jia did not. Instead, she built a shack on the ruins of her old house. Each time someone managed to tear down her shack, she would rebuild it. She refused to abandon her land until her fourth shack was destroyed in August 2012. Then, she finally took heed of the danger and abandoned her home. The crooks had won—at least for a while.

She tells this story both to explain the corruption that permeates many local governments and police stations in China's interior, and, in a strange way, to praise the laws that China has put in place to protect her. She was not arrested during the whole ordeal, nor was she ordered by a court to vacate her land. Her husband, who works as an engineer at a state-owned enterprise (SOE), kept his job. As long as Ms. Jia refused to sign over her land, there was nothing, legally, that the authorities could do to make her vacate her property. Her stubbornness forced them to act off the record and illegally in order to get what they wanted. "The law isn't the issue in land disputes," Ms. Jia says,

"The villagers don't know their rights, and police don't enforce their rights. But those rights exist."[1]

• • •

China's history with land rights in the decades following World War II is key to understanding the country's economic transformation and its story of migration.

At a politburo meeting in March 1979, Chen Yun, who was, along with Deng Xiaoping, one of the major architects of China's economic reforms, laid out what he saw as the problems facing China's development: "We have 900 million people, over 80 percent of whom are farmers. We are very poor. There are still people begging for food. We all want to modernize, but the question is what can we achieve? We need balanced development. In considering basic construction, we must first consider agriculture."[2]

Histories of China's first economic reforms tend to focus on China's turn from Marx, Lenin, and Mao and gradual embrace of Smith, Ricardo, Keynes, and Hayek. While this transformation would certainly happen during the thirty years following Chen Yun's speech, China's reform period started with leaders wrestling with the ideas of Thomas Malthus. In 1978, the average Chinese person ate only 66 percent of the number of calories taken in by the average person in a developed country, and 53 percent of the level of protein.[3] Despite substantial gains in agricultural output since World War II, China's largest problem continued to be how to feed its growing population. The government would soon introduce the one-child policy in an attempt to restrict population growth by force.

Managing agricultural productivity, and, by extension, agricultural land rights was not only important for the Chinese economy, but an issue of government legitimacy. Rural poverty and starvation had led to the collapse of countless other governments in China's long history, including the Republican government that the Communists had replaced. The Communists had already reformed rural land rights twice in the thirty years since they had taken over: the first time in order to redistribute the spoils of war and gain support among the population, and the second time as part of an ideologically driven plan to end rural poverty with communal land management. Both reforms rank among the worst human tragedies of the twentieth century.

The Problem of Land Tenancy

Farming is not only a labor-intensive activity; it's also a capital-intensive activity. Farmers must invest in fertilizer, seeds, machinery, irrigation, and other land improvements in order to increase yields and profits. Without strong land rights, farmers resist making these investments for fear of expropriation, and yields stagnate.

In a preindustrial society though, maintaining land rights over the long term can be extremely difficult. Land is a fixed resource, but the population that owns and works the land can be a growing resource. Unless those workers can be employed in other industries, new farmers enter the market with only partial property rights—a tenancy contract that gives them the right to invest in and cultivate the land, but which allows a secondary landholder to take rents and arbitrarily expel the tenant. This creates an adverse dynamic where farmers who wish to invest in land face the risk of losing their investment to either higher rents or expropriation.

This problem had been understood in China since at least the tenth century, and was the subject of a number of laws, particularly during the Ming and Qing dynasties (1368–1912). These governments introduced two separate categories of land rights—topsoil rights, implying the right to make use of and develop the land, and subsoil rights, implying the right to collect rents and the responsibility for tax payments. Over successive imperial administrations, topsoil, or land-use, rights were strengthened so landlords could not easily push tenants off their land, and rents were either fixed as a percentage of total output or as a set amount, allowing the tenant to benefit from any increase in production.[4]

The dual-ownership system was problematic, but it worked. The law was advantageous to land-use rights holders, who did not have to worry about changes in the tax rate and were at a legal advantage when negotiating rent. Though agricultural output figures from the period are unreliable, China saw its first period of sustained population growth under the Ming and Qing governments, implying significant improvements in food production. The country's population grew from 143 million in 1741 to 432 million by 1851.[5]

The system had a few significant loopholes that, when combined with rapid population growth, would undermine its success. In areas with a high population of landless peasants, individuals with land-use rights could further subcontract to secondary tenants, pushing investment and labor costs forward while the original landowner covered taxes. Secondary tenants could legally sublease as well, allowing the number of rent seekers to multiply as far as the productivity of the land would allow. These overlapping contracts, combined with weak enforcement of existing rights, could lead to the same problems that China's land tenancy laws were meant to avoid. At the end of the Qing dynasty, land disputes continued to be the largest reported cause of civil violence in the country, with rural dwellers continuing to complain about poor protection from rent-seeking landlords.[6]

The Communists introduced a program for dealing with these disputes even before declaring victory in the revolution. The first reform was gruesomely simple. Landlords—people with subsoil rights—would lose their land; most were beaten and shunned, many were murdered. While this reform has often been framed as a large-scale redistribution of private property, the reality is somewhat more complex. While people with subsoil rights were persecuted and often murdered, there was relatively little land redistribution among people with topsoil rights, because Mao worried such an attack would undermine support for the new government among wealthy peasants and disrupt the overall rural economy. This can be seen in income distribution statistics, which barely changed during the initial reform: in 1952, the top 10 percent of rural households still controlled 21.6 percent of total income, dropping only slightly from 24.4 percent in the 1930s.[7]

Despite the brutality, this reform proved to be surprisingly successful at increasing agricultural output. In the years that followed, agricultural output in China grew by approximately 3 to 4 percent a year, or roughly twice the rate of output growth during the Republican period.[8] The Communists claimed a win, and, despite the implications for the common conception of land rights, America would soon push Japan, South Korea, and Taiwan to implement similar reforms nonviolently—as much to fend off any Communist impulses as to increase agricultural output.

The strength of this reform is relatively straightforward. The role of a landlord had shrunk significantly by the time Mao took power, from someone who had the right to manage the land he owned to simply a well-paid tax collector, with most other rights going to people with land-use rights. For many of the richest landholders, the reform seemingly strengthened their own claim to the land by replacing a secondary claimant with the government. By removing the middleman between topsoil rights holders and the government, the reform gave farmers a larger share of their profit and more money to invest.

The reform, in other words, briefly strengthened land rights among people who already had legal rights to the land, with mild redistribution on the margins. But it did so with little regard for the long-term consequences. Besides the millions killed, millions more dispossessed moved to the cities as refugees. The reform made no plan concerning what to do once China's rural population once again outstripped land availability. This was, in part, intentional. The first land reform rewarded political allies and helped build enforcement infrastructure in the countryside, but it was never the reform that the Chinese government was aiming for.

The Return to Serfdom

Chinese cities grew rapidly in the late 1940s as refugees flocked to urban areas where they would find greater protection from the ravages of war and the land reform that followed in its wake. These refugees posed an immediate threat to the Communists' industrial plan, which called for consolidating what remained of China's existing industrial capacity after the war under state control. One of the promises of communism was that the government would take responsibility for providing full employment, but with limited financial means and a growing number of migrant workers, the government didn't have the resources to replace jobs lost in the nationalization of the private sector. Instead of admitting that there was nothing wrong with private employment or self-employment, the government demonized the migrants as "nonproductive" workers and suggested that there were far too many migrants for industry to ever be capable of employing them. An editorial published in August 1949 in *Dagongbao*, one of China's largest newspapers at the time, asserted that Shanghai could at most support 3 million of the 6 million people that were living in the city at the time. A later editorial called for "nonproductive" workers to be sent to the countryside to repopulate areas devastated by the war and grow their own food.[9]

In the early 1950s, a number of cities implemented mostly voluntary re-settlement programs. Individuals who agreed to return to the countryside were offered subsidies, often amounting to several months' living expenses, as well as free housing and occasionally free land. However, this did not stop the process of urbanization. China's urban population grew by 34.6 million between 1949 and 1956, pushed up by 19.8 million rural migrants. Shanghai, which sent more than 1 million people to rural areas between 1949 and 1957, received 1,820,000 migrants over the same period. The population of Beijing increased by 70 percent.[10]

China's land reform would very quickly turn against those who had re-mained in the countryside and benefited from the initial removal of landlords. In 1953, the Chinese government began the process of collectivization. The same year, the government established the state as the only legitimate purchas-ing and distribution agent for grain, meaning those who didn't initially lose their land were barred from profiting more than the government would allow. By the end of 1956, 97 percent of the rural population had given up their land.[11] As prospects declined for farmers, many headed for the cities, increasing the pressure on the government to create jobs and support the urban unemployed.

The central government would respond with a number of new policies aimed at monitoring and controlling population movements. In 1951, China introduced a household registration, or hukou, card: a basic identity card that listed a person's place of residency, with any changes having to be registered with the local police. At first, the card was relatively harmless, but within a few years, the hukou was being used to restrict migration and reduce urban employment opportunities for rural workers. In March of 1954, the Ministry of the Interior and the Ministry of Labor released a "Joint Directive to Control the Blind Influx of Peasants into the Cities," which prohibited companies from hiring rural workers without the permission of the labor department of the nearest prefectural-level city, and gave the police power, as well as funds, to send unemployed migrants back to their villages. The attitude of the gov-ernment was expressed in the term "blind migrant" (*mangliu*), which punned on a vulgar Chinese term meaning "hooligan" (*liumang*).[12]

Despite these new restrictions, the fundamentals of the labor market proved to be significantly stronger than the law. When demand for labor in the cities was high, factories widely ignored the hiring regulations, using direct contacts to hire workers.[13] In 1955, the government would tighten migration rules yet again. Migrants had to receive permission from officials in their place of residence prior to relocating, and those designated as "class enemies" required approval from the district- or country-level government. The government had also established a number of indirect controls on migration, which would prove to be more effective than direct restrictions. By 1955, the state had established a monopoly on urban housing, and required travel documents for those registered in hotels. The government had also taken control of the country's agricultural markets, and was mostly feeding its urban population through ration cards, which rural dwellers—who were expected to be self-sufficient—did not receive. The system was still fairly flexible, allowing some grain to be purchased, but it was an additional burden for travelers and created a further legal distinction between rural and urban dwellers.[14]

In 1958, at the start of the Great Leap Forward, China changed the household registration system yet again. The regulation extended household registration requirements to the entire population, and specified that rural-urban migrants would need to receive permission to relocate from the government in the place they intended to move to as well as from the authorities at their current residence. Checkpoints were put in place along major transit routes to arrest people without passes, and, in order to encourage deurbanization, the law specified that children would take on the hukou status of their mother—under the assumption that men would be more likely to marry lower status women than vice versa. This law remains the basis of China's current hukou system, even with substantial changes to the underlying systems supporting the law and how the law is enforced.[15]

Actual enforcement of the 1958 law did not begin until two years later. The start of the Great Leap Forward came with massive state investment in factories and industrial facilities, matched with loosened administrative controls on local governments. Suddenly, and very briefly, urban unemployment disappeared, and cities faced acute labor shortages. In autumn 1958, 38 million rural workers were recruited to work in urban factories, and by 1960, the permanent urban population of China had expanded from 15 to 20 percent of the total population.[16]

The economic forces underlying this period of urbanization were substantially different from earlier periods of labor migration. In previous years, labor demand was tied to economic cycles. People moved to the city during periods of strong industrial growth, and then, during bumper harvests, they returned to the countryside. At some point, labor demand would reach equilibrium, where rural workers would gain more by staying at home than by migrating. The mass migration that occurred between 1958 and 1960 was brought about by politics and state subsidies: on many farms, crops were left to rot, while factories found no market for their products.

Officials would respond to the decline in food production by taking from those in the country to feed those in the city. They would also increase grain exports—by more than 100 percent over three years—a policy that led to the mass starvation of the country's rural population. As the Great Leap Forward continued and the problem grew worse, officials cut costs in the cities. Between 1959 and 1962, 25 million workers were laid off and sent to the countryside where the government was not responsible for feeding them. Approximately 36 million people died of starvation.[17]

The hukou system was fully implemented in 1960 to prevent these starving people from leaving their homes in search of food.[18]

The End of the Communes

The Communist revolution that was fought in the name of China's rural poor completely destroyed the rural economy. By 1978, when Deng Xiaoping took control of the government, two-thirds of China's peasants had an income lower than in the 1950s, and one-third had an income even lower than in the 1930s.[19] Rural dwellers were not only poorer, but there were a lot more of them. Between the 1953 census and the 1982 census, the population of China grew by 73 percent, to just over 1 billion people.

By 1978, the government was also on the verge of collapse. The Cultural Revolution had weakened many of the institutions that had been used to control lower-level officials, with many poorer areas verging on anarchy. In the midst of this regulatory breakdown, many farmers began experimenting with markets as a matter of survival.

The first documented case of private farming was in 1976, when Nine Dragon Hill, a disastrously poor village in Pengxi County, Sichuan, allowed households in two production teams to use marginal plots of land for private cultivation. By the next year, these plots were producing output three times higher than the commune-managed land, and the rest of the village was turned over to private plots. The case that would eventually be cited in Chinese history books as prompting the government's rural reforms happened two years later. Eighteen peasants in Small Hill Village in Anhui signed a secret agreement to experiment with private farming. The results were strong enough that by the next year the surrounding villages had joined in the experiment.[20]

With few exceptions, the places that first experimented with private farming were the country's poorest and the hardest hit by the policies put in place by Mao. Much of this can be simply accounted to desperation. These villages were deeply impoverished, and many had to beg for food from surrounding villages in order to survive. There was little to lose, even if they were arrested.

But there was an additional structural reason why these areas were first to experiment with agricultural reform. Agricultural policy under Mao focused on grain production at the expense of all other crops, and since peasants were required to be self-sufficient, planting high-calorie crops like wheat and rice was considered a necessity for survival. Many of the places that experimented with reform early on were in mountainous regions, with less arable land per capita than the grain bases in the northeast and center of the country. They were poorly suited for the government's wheat-growing policy, but ideal places for growing vegetables, which were chronically undersupplied in the Chinese market. By privatizing production in marginal land, they were not only able to grow more crops, but also more valuable crops that brought in higher returns. This quirk of geography would have a long-term impact on how different regions of China developed. To this day, China has an official policy of maintaining self-sufficiency in grain, which, in effect, requires the government to closely manage how rural land is used in grain-producing areas, and how much agricultural land can be used for industrial purposes.

In 1982, the Chinese government officially approved an incentive scheme for farmers similar to the "household responsibility system" used in Small Hill Village, and by 1983, the program had been implemented over 95 percent of the country. The speed with which this program was implemented reflects both how far private farming had spread in the years since the end of the Cultural Revolution, and how difficult communal farming was to enforce. The government was putting its sparse resources into both helping the rural poor and preventing them from helping themselves. When those resources were exhausted, the countryside very quickly returned to some form of market-based exchange.[21]

That said, the household responsibility system was far from a private land-rights system or even a land-use rights system; workers were only given tenure for three years, and the state still specified what crops could be planted and how much would be paid for them. The only difference under this system was that workers were entitled to the returns in excess of an annual quota.

Despite weak land rights, private investment in agriculture during this period proved to be an unexpected success. Many critics of the household responsibility system expected investment to slow down and output growth to eventually hit a roadblock—after all, one of the few advantages of the commune system was that it made it easier for people to pool their resources for major projects like irrigation systems and road networks. While there was a decline in overall investment, particularly in irrigation, investment in roads, which was needed to get goods to newly developing marketplaces, saw especially strong growth both from all private sources or joint public-private investment schemes.[22]

Between 1978 and 1984, agricultural output expanded from 305 million tons to 407 million tons, while rural income grew by 11 percent each year, significantly faster than urban income growth during this period.[23] The household responsibility system was not the only factor contributing to rural growth during this period. The government increased grain procurement prices and the weather was generally accommodating, but given the scale of growth, it was hard to deny that the household responsibility system had been an overwhelming success.

But the reform had an unexpected consequence. Agricultural work by its nature produces a large pool of "excess labor," both because it is seasonal, which gives workers time to take temporary employment in other industries, and because land is a fixed resource while the working-age population is a growing resource. To some degree, extra labor input can increase the productivity of land, but at a certain point agriculture can only support more workers by reducing their productivity. As agricultural productivity increased more and more, Chinese were left looking for something to do.

Land-Use Rights and Village-Level Democracy

In late 1984, China lengthened the minimum legal tenure of households under the household responsibility system to fifteen years. Then, in early 1985, the government ended its monopoly on grain procurement. According to the new law, peasants would be required to supply a certain amount of grain to the state at lower prices, after which they were free to plant whatever they wished and sell their goods on the market. These laws reestablished the basic principles of land-use rights in China: peasants need security of tenancy in order to make investments, and the gains from investment should go to those who make the investment.[24]

There were obvious problems with this arrangement, the most notable being that fifteen years is still a fairly short tenancy given the time needed to develop certain crops and regain the fixed costs of major investments, particularly as the mandatory grain sales acted as a heavy tax. But this problem could, and would, be overturned by new laws. A larger and more immediate problem was posed by the hukou system.

To a certain extent, the hukou law actually strengthened land rights. Under the hukou system, it was the local government's responsibility to restrict migration, which prevented government officials from pushing workers off their land with the assumption that they could go elsewhere. The landlords were stuck with their tenants, and it was not particularly easy to rearrange land tenancies within the commune without upsetting everyone.

The flip side of this coin was that if a village's population expanded, land had to be redistributed in order to accommodate each new household. At best, this entailed transferring land that had already been developed by other people in the village; at worst, this gave unscrupulous officials the opportunity to rearrange landholdings in a way that would be beneficial to them or their families.

One of China's first responses to this problem was the introduction of village-level democracy in late 1987. This was widely misinterpreted in the foreign press at the time as the start of China's turn toward a Western system of government.[25] Seen in the light of the opening up of the USSR and particularly China's prodemocracy protests in 1989, this misunderstanding was reasonable, but it drew attention away from why the government was experimenting with democracy specifically at a village level and specifically at that time: namely, increasing tensions over land management.

Despite the various legal protections afforded rural landholders, in practice there was very little enforcement, with villages instead relying on informal cooperation between villagers and government officials to maintain the competing objectives of maintaining land-use rights and distributing plots among new households. Supporting new households was always the first priority. Landless peasants were more or less absent from China through the early part of the 2000s, a status quo that China could only maintain through regular and occasionally severe land redistribution.[26] Field research conducted in the late 1990s found that 65 percent of villages saw some form of land redistribution, though the severity varied widely.[27] Surveys conducted in 1999 and 2001 found that only 40 percent of households were confident in their land tenure.[28]

While village elections did not prove to be a harbinger of creeping democracy, they were moderately successful at improving cooperation between villagers and the government. A survey conducted in 1993 found that more than half of the villages in China were holding competitive elections. The amount of turnover in leadership varied by region and by survey, but the figures were uniformly high, ranging between 30 and 70 percent.[29] Villages that held competitive elections saw more agreement on policy issues between villagers and political leaders, and political leaders, emboldened by their electoral victories, were more successful at implementing government policy priorities. Property rights, of course, was the number one issue for rural dwellers, and the issue which most of these elections hinged upon.[30] A well-run local government could help make sure that major investment stayed in the hands of the investors and that no family received disproportionate benefits. Later reforms to village democracy were often explicitly focused on property issues, such as the 1997 law requiring the approval of two-thirds of the village assembly before any land redistribution—the law that Ms. Jia eagerly pointed out that her village head had ignored.

Several further efforts to strengthen land tenancy rights were enacted over the following years. In 1993, the government issued a policy directive to extend land-tenancy agreements for thirty years, a directive that was made into law in 1998. The 1998 law also required villages to issue documentation of land-use rights to help adjudicate disputes and improve farmers' perceptions of their rights. The program was effective when it was enforced. After an initial push, the program slowed down in the 2000s, with only 63 percent of rural households holding contracts by 2007, but those households that did enjoy well-documented property rights invested in their land at almost twice the rate of households without documentation.[31]

Lifting Barriers to Migration

By 1998, the situation in China's countryside had changed dramatically. The growing numbers of "excess workers" in the countryside were in increasing demand in urban areas, and willing to flaunt the restrictions of the hukou system to find work. Happily for them, China's restrictions on migration were beginning to break down.

The official law covering the hukou has changed little since 1958. What has changed instead is the network of laws, policy statements, and institutional arrangements that specified what privileges urban dwellers held over rural dwellers and how those privileges are enforced. Starting in the early 1990s, these changes transformed the hukou system from a hard restraint on migration to a soft restraint meant mostly to reduce social services costs. Even without social services, the advantages of living in the city were obvious, just as the risk was minimal. Earnings in the city continue to be, on average, three times higher than those in the countryside, while rural workers who failed to make it in the city still had guaranteed access to land back home.

A Chinese person's hukou status has two separate designations: the hukou type and the hukou location. In the first case, each individual holds either a nonagricultural or an agricultural hukou (often referred to as an urban or rural hukou). During the Maoist period, this specified whether you belonged to an urban work group or a rural commune. After the communes and work groups were broadly dismantled, this designation continued to affect how people were supplied with state-provided social services. People with a non-agricultural hukou (who mostly, but not entirely, lived in urban areas) were entitled to a grain stipend and state housing, while individuals with an agricultural hukou were provided with a plot of land and were mostly expected to be self-sufficient.

The second designation was the location of residency, which specified what region was expected to provide you with social services such as education, pensions, and healthcare. Each location had a mix of nonagricultural hukou holders in the urban core and agricultural hukou holders in the suburbs and exurbs of the city. Ms. Jia, for example, held an agricultural hukou from Zhengzhou, even though the urban area was rapidly encroaching on her land.[32]

Through the 1980s and 1990s, the central government attempted to improve its fiscal situation by transferring responsibility for social services down to local governments. In 1992, China completely ended urban grain subsidies, one of the main benefits enjoyed by urban residents. This also brought down the cost of food on the secondary market, which was, until then, primarily used by rural migrants. Housing was privatized in 1994, which made it easier for migrants to find places to live without going through government.[33] Meanwhile, local governments began providing pension payments and (occasionally) healthcare payments, which were previously covered by state-owned enterprises. In terms of social services, the importance of hukou type was shrinking, while the importance of hukou location was growing. The central government formalized this change with directives in 1992 and 1998 allowing local governments to issue local hukou without central government permission. In 1995, the Ministry of Public Security was no longer registering hukou type, though it was still part of the statistical system, as it continues to be today.[34]

Even after hukou transfers were devolved to local governments, for most migrants a hukou from their place of residence was well out of reach. In larger cities, local hukou cards were mostly given to investors, government workers, and family members of people with local hukou cards. The more practical consequence for migrants was that the central government had removed itself from the enforcement of hukou regulations. Local governments were now able to manage enforcement of migration restrictions based on local labor market conditions—for example, by emptying out slums, but ignoring factory workers. Migrant workers remained in the shadows of the legal system, but the actual process of migration had been made considerably easier. China's poor and hungry were quick to notice.

The Changed Countryside

Between 1995 and 2000 China's urban population grew by over 100 million people—twice the rate of growth seen in the first half of the decade—while interprovincial migration tripled to 32 million people. China's rural population would peak in 1991 at 836 million, declining by more than 230 million people by 2015. Mass urbanization was no longer a threat; it was a fact.

This change was as significant for the countryside as it was for the city. The impact of this demographic shift can clearly be seen in the 2002 Rural Land Contracting Law, which allowed villages to contract out land to other villages and formally banned the practice of land readjustments "except in special circumstances such as natural disaster." While earlier reforms to land laws were trying to improve the system for readjusting land distributions as villages expanded, this law was the first to assume that demand for rural land was, and would continue to be, shrinking.[35]

Taken from a broader perspective, China had made the transition from an agricultural economy to an industrial economy. Many of the problems involved with land tenancy disappear after this transition. Farmers who lose tenancy on their land can find jobs in factories. The people left in the countryside are those who can make money farming and who need to have ownership of their land in order to do so.

In 2007, China introduced a land law that, for the first time, acknowledged land-use rights as property rights rather than contractual rights. It also specified that tenancy contracts should be renewed at the end of thirty years, effectively making land-use rights indefinite. On paper, the only major divergence between China's land-use rights system and a functioning land-rights system is that land sales are still determined on a village basis rather than on an individual basis. This was addressed in the 2007 law as a goal of further reform, but so far there has not been much progress on this front.[36]

One simple reason for the failure to reform land ownership is that most Chinese cities are facing incredibly bad financial situations. One of the basic features of the hukou system is that while urban dwellers get access to better education, larger pensions, and better healthcare subsidies, rural workers have access to the basic income provided by their land. While this guarantee is valuable to some, in most cases this acts as a way to deny agricultural hukou holders access to social services that cities can't afford to provide. This is becoming a more serious problem due to the increase in the number of landless peasants over the past decade.[37] These individuals are caught between the rural and urban social safety net, with few incentives for any local government to take responsibility for them. A reform to the land-ownership system would in theory make this problem worse, unless it is accompanied by a reform to the hukou system and how social services are provided.

The current land-rights system also gives local governments a very easy opportunity to make money. According to the current law, the Chinese government must act as a middleman in any land transaction that involves a change in legal status from agricultural to nonagricultural land: first purchasing the land from villagers, then changing the legal status, and then selling it to a developer. According to the current land-contracting law, in order to purchase rural land, the government has to pay no more than thirty times the annual agricultural output of a plot of land, while it can sell the land to developers for market cost, which can be as much as four times the price they paid.[38] This scheme currently accounts for upward of 30 percent of the annual budgets of most local governments.[39] Under a normal land-rights system, these gains would be enjoyed by the people who worked and sold the land.

Besides the obvious moral problems with this system, local government dependence on land expropriation created problematic economic incentives. Instead of building up, Chinese cities started building out, creating large suburbs that would allow them to expropriate larger tracts of land. Urban development was also progressively less associated with migration, with many regions that were seeing net outflows of migrants building larger urban areas in order to access land sale revenues. Government-owned banks were generally cooperative in this scheme, which, as we will see in later chapters, contributed to the development of a property bubble in many of China's third-tier cities, and rising indebtedness at Chinese banks as property sales slowed down.

Local government's dependence on land expropriation for income is also, without question, the largest cause of political unrest in China today. Over the last thirty years, Chinese people have been given a rudimentary form of land rights, and they treat those who would take it away as criminals. As we saw in the case of Ms. Jia, many of the bureaucrats who took part in land expropriations were in fact criminals who did not hesitate to break the law during a land-sale transaction, and were often caught embezzling a portion of the income for themselves.

Living in the Shadows

In March 2003, Sun Zhigang, a 27-year-old college student from Wuhan was arrested by Guangzhou police for failure to carry his temporary residence card. He would die in custody, with an autopsy revealing substantial internal damage from a brutal beating by his jailers. A month later, Sun's family reported the case to *Southern Metropolitan Daily*, a Guangdong newspaper, setting off a flurry of media and Internet coverage.[40]

This wasn't the first time these detention centers had come to public attention. Police treatment of migrants was often abysmal, with prolonged detention without trial, extortion of the detained or their families, as well as beatings and deprivations of those held in custody. Sun's case was different, though. Sun was educated and came from an urban area. He was part of China's growing middle class. While rural-urban migrants were still by far the most victimized group by China's hukou system, the growth of interprovincial migration after 1995 meant that most people knew someone who was vulnerable to being arrested, abused, extorted, and even murdered by the police with few consequences.

Sun's murder did have consequences, though. A total of nineteen people were put in prison, two of whom received death sentences (one suspended). Then, in August 2003, Premier Wen Jiabao surprised everyone by abolishing the law that allowed the police to detain and repatriate migrant workers. With one announcement, Chinese people were now free to move around their country without needing government permission.[41]

In the same year, Wen Jiabao accidentally initiated another campaign to help migrant workers when he helped a migrant family recover back pay owed to the breadwinner by his urban employer. This drew attention to one of the largest ongoing problems faced by migrant workers—wage theft by employers. The problem is far from resolved, but since Premier Wen's involvement, several cities have passed schemes to punish employers who fail to pay their workers. In Henan Province, for example, the government required construction companies to make a deposit equivalent to a portion of each worker's wages that would be held as security until a project was completed, while Shanghai announced that employers who failed to pay their workers would be fined an additional 25 percent of the wages due. Other cities pushed employers to make sure that all employees had contracts, and expanded access to legal aid for migrant workers so they could sue their employers for back wages.[42]

By the 2000s, China was no longer trying to hold back migration, but it was unwilling to fix the underlying fiscal problems that prevented local governments from treating migrants on equal footing with locals. For example, in 2001, the central government issued a policy directive requiring cities to provide nine years of schooling for the children of migrants. Over the next decade, this directive would be almost entirely unenforced, with many schools either turning away migrants or charging them higher school fees. As late as 2009, only 36 percent of migrant children in Shanghai were attending public schools. In 2011, Beijing shut down twenty-three illegal migrant worker schools affecting 14,000 children who had found the public school system inaccessible or unaffordable.[43]

There have also been efforts on a city-by-city basis to enroll migrants in local pension programs, with 31 percent of migrants reporting participation in 2012, compared to 18 percent four years earlier.[44] Fiscal problems have actually been helpful in addressing this issue, as migrant communities are generally young and still paying into a social security system rather than taking out of it. Whether migrants will eventually see this money on retirement is uncertain, as pensions are still managed on a city-by-city basis, and so far there is no system in place to ensure that those who change cities will see their pensions transfer with them.

The Consequence of Reforms

Since at least 1949, China has been struggling to manage the flood of people trying to escape poverty in the countryside in order to move to the comparative wealth of the cities. This migration has come with a predictable list of problems—high costs to social services, hunger for land, and a demand for employment. China didn't have the resources to satisfy these demands, and the government was uncomfortable letting its citizens work for themselves.

China's first attempt to solve its migration problem was barbaric, involving the murder of tens of millions of people, and strict controls over hundreds of millions more. Its second attempt has been problematic, but broadly successful. As rural dwellers pressed for reforms of rural land rights, the Chinese government responded by liberalizing the hukou and allowing urban development to act as a pressure valve employing underutilized rural labor.

By the middle of the 1990s, the Great Migration of China's rural poor to the country's growing urban industrial centers had become unstoppable, and Chinese politicians would have to find some way to live with the consequences.

Deng Xiaoping described China's adaptation to the influx of migrants and the changes in the Chinese economy as "crossing the river by feeling the stones." This has usually been depicted as openness to experimentation with different policies in order to determine what works to resolve a particular problem, a commitment that was particularly admirable in the light of the dogmatic failures of the Maoist era. But a second, less recognized, consequence of this policy-making process is that China has devolved a considerable amount of policy making to local governments, and often gives local governments significant leeway to determine the pace at which they implement government directives, as well as granting a degree of discretion as to whether they implement government directives at all.[45] Similarly, local governments have traditionally given village governments a degree of discretion, particularly in poorer regions where the consequence of failure was not as large as in more wealthy regions. This devolution of responsibility trickled down to the individual and firm level, opening up opportunities along the way for the development of markets for land, goods, and labor. This decentralization has allowed local governments to experiment with policy priorities in a way that is more responsive to local market forces than the top-down actions of the central government.

On the other hand, administrative decentralization is a problem for Chinese people looking to guarantee their economic rights. Local governments, which lack the funds to pay for social services and new infrastructure, have incentives to rob those with the least power, either actively, through land expropriation, or passively, by denying them services enjoyed by their fellow citizens. These are problems that are far from being resolved.

• • •

After Ms. Jia abandoned her home, she started developing educational videos teaching rural dwellers their rights under the Chinese legal system. The videos detail the procedures that the developer has to go through before the expropriation process begins, what legal documents developers need, what a land contract should look like, how to respond to violence, and how to conduct yourself in a police interrogation. She also details some of the popular scams run by local governments. One government, she says, built a wall around a villager's farmland and then arrested him for destroying government property when he took it down. In another, more Kafkaesque scam, a local government will form a new government agency to manage the destruction of a single village. The agency will be staffed with people approaching retirement, then dismantled so villagers have nowhere to go with their complaints.

From this work followed a pro bono career as a legal representative in land dispute cases. Though not a lawyer, Ms. Jia helped rural dwellers navigate the legal system and spoke for them in court. She used the online following she gained during her ordeal to bring media coverage to cases that would otherwise be ignored. She said she was seeing progress—a case she managed in Jiangsu Province, on China's coast, ended with a criminal court finding the government at fault and demanding compensation, though just as often the courts throw her out without hearing her complaint. Still, it was enough that when I spoke to her in 2013, she was cautiously optimistic that China was progressing toward full, enforceable land rights.

In May 2014, she was arrested while protesting a forced demolition. The usual swift speed of the Chinese legal system had to slow down for her. She was initially registered under a different name, to prevent her lawyers from reaching her. Her case was returned twice to the police due to lack of evidence of any criminal offense, then the trial was adjourned due to procedural violations. Eighteen months after she was arrested she was finally sentenced to four and a half years in prison for publishing false information online.

Ms. Jia, who had committed her life to teaching Chinese about their rights under the law, called the decision one of the "darkest days in Chinese legal history." Of course, there were many before that.[46]

Coming to the City

ON FEBRUARY 1, 2012, the Hong Kong newspaper *Apple Daily* released an ad paid for by funds crowd-sourced from two seemingly unrelated websites, hkgolden.com, a website for people to discuss computer products, and baby-kingdom.com, a parenting website. The ad showed a picture of a locust overlooking Victoria Harbor, and warned against a plague of pregnant women swarming across Hong Kong's northern border:

> Do you want Hong Kong to pay 1 million HKD every 18 minutes raising illegitimate mainland children? Hong Kong people have had enough of it! We understand that you suffer from contaminated milk powder, so we tolerate your raid upon our milk powder; we understand that you don't have freedom, so we allow you visa-free access; we understand that your education is poor, so we share our educational resources; we understand that you can't read traditional Chinese, so we will use "crippled" Chinese to say: "Please respect our local culture when you are here, without Hong Kong you are all doomed." The government must reform the law to stop the invasion of pregnant women from the mainland![1]

The ad caught the attention of the Chinese Internet, and within a day, web forums in all the major cities had photoshopped the original ad to communicate their own thoughts about mainland Chinese migrants. These thoughts ended up being overwhelmingly negative, with Internet communities in Beijing, Shanghai, and Guangzhou ignoring the fact that the original ad was targeting middle-class Chinese with money to travel to Hong Kong—people like them—and instead making their ads about rural migrants.

Do you want the migrant population of Beijing to continue to grow? Beijing people have had enough of it! Beijing already has a migrant population of 20 million, with 478,000 migrant children. You damage Beijing culture, harm public order, push up housing prices, and bring your children born in defiance of the one-child policy here in order to make the college entrance examination worse for the rest of us; you benefit from Beijing but still complain about it; please do us a favor and go back home. We demand the government amend the law to stop the massive growth of the migrant population in Beijing.[2]

In Shanghai, the ad complained about the effect on public pensions, and in Guangzhou the ad complained about public transportation. All three ads used inaccurate numbers to inflate the problem, and complained about the behavior of the migrants.

One city, though, took a different tack. In Shenzhen, where around 95 percent of the population were migrants, instead of a locust the ad featured a photoshopped statue of Deng Xiaoping overlooking the city. The ad read:

You are one of us if you come to Shenzhen. Shenzhen welcomes you! We welcome you, because we are all away from home; we welcome you, because Grandpa Deng made this city for all of us; we welcome you because you are part of the momentum that keeps Shenzhen going; we welcome you because you are the reason behind our thirty years of prosperity; we want the whole world to know this, so we will say it in English: Welcome to "hometown Shenzhen." We welcome all hard workers to Shenzhen. We wish Shenzhen people a happy new year, and may all your wishes come true.[3]

The Urban Experience

While China's Great Migration has been singular in its size and its speed, the experience of sudden urban migration is a consistent feature of industrializing countries. Between 1800 and 1900, the population of London expanded from 1 million to 4.5 million, while between 1890 and 1930, immigrants and rural migrants pushed New York's population up from 2.5 million to 6.9 million. The scale, if not the size, is similar to many Chinese cities—between 1980 and 2010, the population of Beijing expanded from 9 million to 21 million people, while the population of Shanghai grew from 11 million to 20 million. Shenzhen, which grew from a town of 300,000 people to a city of over 10 million people, is in a league of its own.

Periods of rapid urbanization produce some predictable effects. The most obvious is the effect on infrastructure. Industrial London faced constant problems maintaining its sewage system to meet the demands of new residents, leading to several cholera outbreaks, and the "Great Stink of 1858" when the River Thames took on the smell of a toilet. The city's first major zoning law was introduced in 1844, with new restrictions introduced over the century as problems got worse.[4]

Rather than a shortage of sewer pipes, New York saw a shortage of housing. Rents surged in the first part of the century, spawning regular protests by tenants, many of whom were forced to move several times a year. In December 1907, thousands of tenants in Manhattan and Brooklyn collectively organized a rent boycott, withholding payments to their landlords to protest rent hikes while the country was experiencing a depression.[5] By 1919, the city's vacancy rate had dropped to 1 percent. The courts were clogged with eviction proceedings—an average of 265 a day—prompting the introduction of emergency rent control laws the following year.[6]

The impact of migration on wages is more complicated than its impact on infrastructure. Migrants and immigrants come to urban areas seeking higher wages, and nearly all prospective immigrants experience better outcomes if they are allowed to migrate. Over the long term, local wages increase as well, as the influx of low-skilled workers creates more opportunities for specialization. Over the short term, competition for low-skilled jobs increases, repressing wages as the economy adjusts to the larger population. This problem is particularly pronounced during periods of mass urbanization, when labor supply is expanding faster than the corresponding expansion in industry. In New York, wages actually declined between 1890 and 1914, further accentuating the tensions from increased rents.[7] Less data are available from industrial England, but what data we do have indicates that, until the second half of the nineteenth century, wage hikes were offset by higher costs of living and worse health standards.[8]

Mass migration also leads to social disruption and prompts sometimes hysterical concerns about integration. American politicians were particularly concerned that migrants should be literate in English, both to increase the overall quality of the workforce and to maintain the country's "Anglo-Saxon heritage."[9] London papers were awash with stories of a migrant crime wave that statistically didn't exist.[10]

In each case, policymakers mixed constructive policies, including support for job-creating enterprises and public and private investment in infrastructure construction, with direct and indirect controls on the number of migrants. In the early phase of the Industrial Revolution, the UK attempted to control migration through a system strikingly similar to the hukou system in China. The Laws of Settlement, passed in the seventeenth century, allowed a parish to remove any migrant who might become a burden on local government. The law was effective enough that, in 1776, Adam Smith complained that "it is often more difficult for a poor man to pass the artificial boundary of a parish than an arm of the sea or a ridge of high mountains."[11] The law was reformed several times during the Industrial Revolution to give authorities less discretion over whom they removed, but as late as 1907 around 12,000 people were still being removed annually from British cities and being sent back to the countryside.[12] Similarly, in 1921, America implemented a quota system for new immigrants that aimed both to slow down population growth and maintain the country's ethnic composition as predominantly Anglo-Saxon.[13]

China would face the same problems when dealing with the Great Migration, but it did so from a substantially different starting point. While England and the US were broadly liberal countries with thriving private markets, at the start of China's reform period, all companies were owned by the state and all workers worked for the state, with their jobs and their income guaranteed for life. Changing this system would not only require a break from the country's communist ideology, but also an overhauling of China's entire fiscal system, which prior to reform was based on profit remittances from state-owned enterprises (SOEs). With hundreds of millions underemployed in China's countryside, the government didn't have much of a choice.

Willing to Work

China's first industrial reforms at the end of the Cultural Revolution (1966–1976) were prompted by a migration crisis that was substantially smaller than the one that would hit the country a decade and a half later. During the ten years of the Cultural Revolution, China sent roughly 17 million youths "down to the countryside" for class education. Most of these sent-down youth had not volunteered to go, and many began making efforts to return within months after arriving in their destination village.[14]

The sent-down youth program was disbanded in 1978, opening the door for all 17 million young people to return to their urban homes. But there was a problem. Under Chinese Communism, unemployment was not permitted nor was private employment. The sent-down youth program, like the hukou system, had conveniently squared the circle between this requirement for full employment and China's dismal industrial performance. The sudden return of millions of workers turned an employment problem into a severe political challenge for an already unstable government. In 1979, returning youth made up 8.6 percent of the population of Beijing, and 11.7 percent of the population of Tianjin. Decades of state ownership had left the urban economy utterly unprepared for the sudden shock of these returning migrants. In September 1979, following several major protests, the head of state, Ye Jianying, announced that the country would legalize self-employment in order to accommodate the returning youth. The country's first private business officially registered on November 30 in Wenzhou, Zhejiang Province. Two years later, this short-term policy directive was formalized into law, officially ending the government's monopoly on labor.[15]

Private businesses would continue to face substantial restrictions. According to Chinese law at the time, private enterprises were restricted from employing more than seven people—a number picked from a passage in Marx's *Das Kapital*. Private companies were also at a disadvantage compared to SOEs in obtaining resources, and because their success was subject to market discipline rather than government regulations, private-sector jobs lacked the security that most Chinese had come to expect.[16]

While private employment was initially legalized in response to the return of sent-down youth, the largest factor affecting the development of private enterprises was the availability of surplus rural labor. Regions that saw an early turn to private enterprises were not the most populous, but rather those with denser allocations of farmland and little central government support. These areas were enthusiastic about the ability to reemploy these excess workers in industry, and developed some of the first large-scale private enterprises.[17] From the start, the seven-employee rule proved impossible to enforce. In 1985, private companies employed thirty people on average, with the largest companies employing between fifty and one hundred people. Though these numbers are significantly smaller than the many thousands that would be employed by factories in the coming decade, they indicate that there was a degree of pragmatism shown toward private business that allowed for experimentation.[18]

The development of private enterprises in these regions was also helped by the relative decentralization of the Chinese government. While the central government and many local governments resisted the development of private enterprises because they weakened fiscal returns from SOEs and the government's control over industrial inputs, areas without a substantial SOE presence saw no downside to encouraging the private economy.

Rural dwellers were among the most active entrepreneurs during this period, again reflecting the strength of rural labor markets, lack of government involvement, and general desperation. Besides the large number of "household firms" in the countryside, the early part of the 1980s saw the rise of township and village enterprises (TVEs), a title that was coined in 1984 to reflect how former commune and brigade enterprises had transitioned from SOEs to private or mixed-ownership firms in response to expanded economic freedoms. TVEs included state-owned companies managed by private individuals and subject to market discipline (due to budget constraints), "red-hat" firms that gave the state partial ownership in order to improve access to financing and resources, as well as fully private firms with little or no state involvement. By 1994, the Chinese government admitted that 83 percent of TVEs were private in all but name.[19]

The boom in TVEs and household businesses was, by all accounts, an economic miracle in its own right. By 1990, 39 million rural dwellers were employed in household businesses, while another 55 million were employed through public or private TVEs. The TVE phenomenon would peak in 1995, employing 135 million people, over 10 percent of the population. From 1978 to 1996, the share of output from TVEs grew from 6 percent to 26 percent of GDP during a period when GDP growth averaged over 10 percent a year.[20]

The success of TVEs would surprise even their supporters. In the early stage of the reform period, Chinese leaders still saw the problems facing the economy in terms of capital efficiency and economies of scale, while China's enormous labor pool was seen more as a liability than an asset. Without recognizing the waste that was involved in China's chronic underutilization of labor, the success of TVEs would have truly been baffling. According to one estimate, the ratio of labor to fixed capital was eight times higher in TVEs than in state-owned enterprises.[21] These labor-intensive businesses would quickly run their capital-intensive competitors into the ground.

China's Great Decentralization

The growth of private enterprise would force the Chinese government to substantially change how it raised revenue. Between 1978 and 1995, government revenue as a share of GDP would drop from 47 percent to 10.7 percent. The central government saw the brunt of this, with its share of total government revenue falling from 43.9 percent to 22.9 percent in 1993.[22] This decline would have a long-lasting impact on China's industrial policy, its treatment of migrants, and how Chinese cities developed.

China's fiscal system at the end of the Cultural Revolution was both simple to maintain and incredibly inefficient. Enterprises and communes would produce according to a plan and prices were fixed, which meant profits were fixed. Local governments would expect revenues according to the profits specified in the plan, and with few taxpayers, most of which were SOEs, tax collection was simple. Local governments had no discretionary spending power, with all money left over after fixed-expenses going to the central government. If a local government could not cover its expenses, it would receive payments from the central government.

This tax system was both highly centralized and highly redistributive. Wealthy regions, like Shanghai, often gave up as much as 80 to 90 percent of their tax revenues to the central government, while poor inland provinces could receive up to two-thirds of the money needed for their social services programs from the central government. The government maintained cripplingly high levels of taxation that could only be supported with price fixing and that limited the room available for reinvesting profits.[23]

This system would break down fairly quickly after the introduction of private employment and market pricing. Remittances from SOEs—which in 1978 accounted for one-third of total revenue, and more than half of all central government revenue—declined steadily through the early part of the 1980s, until they all but disappeared by the end of the decade. Through the 1980s, the central government tried to encourage local governments to raise revenues more aggressively from private companies with a number of incentive schemes that allowed provinces to keep a portion of the revenue they collected. These programs along with the introduction of the enterprise income tax in 1984 managed to stop a five-year-long absolute decline in tax revenues, but they came with their own set of problems.[24]

Each revenue-sharing agreement was individually negotiated by the local government, with economically or politically important governments often able to negotiate better terms with the central government. Guangdong, China's fastest-growing province in the 1980s, managed to negotiate a revenue-sharing agreement that allowed the region to keep all revenue over RMB 1.4 billion—indefinitely. Even after the central government renegotiated the contract to increase the amount Guangdong was sending to it every year, Guangdong still held on to all but 7 percent of its revenue as of 1993. Shandong managed to keep remittances to 3 percent of revenue as of 1993.[25]

The central government's regular efforts to renegotiate contracts in order to get more favorable terms encouraged local governments to push revenue off budget, and particularly into the coffers of SOEs, TVEs, or favored private investors. Extrabudgetary funds accounted for 41 percent of local expenditure in 1992, money that was mostly raised by cutting taxes and getting money back in the form of retained earnings and infrastructure-related fees. These funds were primarily controlled by SOEs and set aside for technical transformation, maintenance, or working capital.[26] The extra-budget money could also be plowed back into infrastructure and other local priorities, with projects sponsored by companies receiving a tax write-off. This allowed local governments to circumvent the central government tax-sharing rules and keep tax revenues within the province.

Between 1985 and 1989, central government revenues grew by a meager 6.5 percent, compared to a nearly 89 percent increase in nominal GDP.[27] Besides renegotiating the terms of revenue-sharing agreements, the central government responded to the decline in revenues by cutting subsidies to poor provinces and pushing a number of expenses to local governments, particularly social services that had previously been covered by SOEs such as pensions and healthcare. Between 1981 and 1993, the local-government share of expenditures grew from 45 percent to 72 percent of the total. This pushed some social services to the point of collapse.[28] Lower levels of government were significantly worse suited to cover expenses like healthcare and social security, due to smaller and less diversified risk pools. By 1993, less than 10 percent of the rural population was covered by state-provided health insurance, and less than 20 percent had any kind of health insurance whatsoever. This problem would move to the cities as migration picked up over the next decade, with state-coverage rates in urban areas falling from 65 percent to under 40 percent between 1993 and 2003.[29]

Declines in fiscal transfers also increased regional disparities, allowing more successful regions to invest heavily in infrastructure while poor regions struggled to support SOEs and cover social services. The ability to retain increasing revenues substantially improved the prospects of regions whose poor agricultural output had encouraged an early transition toward the private sector to employ excess rural labor, leading to a wealth disparity that would further fuel migration over the next decade.

The Collapse of SOEs

For a brief moment following the Tiananmen Square massacre in June 1989, it looked like China's reform and opening program could come to an end. Much of the immediate political backlash fell on private enterprises, whose numbers dropped to 90,000 by the end of the year, from 200,000 the year before.[30] In December 1989, Premier Li Peng announced a plan to restructure and consolidate TVEs in order to ensure that they carried out the state's industrial priorities, undermining China's fastest growing industrial sector. TVEs would never recover. Starting in 1991, the government gradually moved most budgeting and management decisions out of elected village governments, giving responsibility for rural budget decisions to Communist-appointed township governments. With an average of only one township for every thirty-four villages, this effectively ended independent policy experimentation and activism on behalf of rural dwellers.[31]

While the proximate causes of the "Tiananmen intermission" were the protests and violent crackdown, the crisis that the government faced was as much economic as it was political. By 1987, subsidies to SOEs made up one-third of total government expenditures.[32] In 1988, an ill-fated attempt to end dual-track pricing—where state-owned enterprises purchased and sold at government-set prices while private enterprises purchased and sold on the market—would see inflation shoot up to 38.6 percent, leading to widespread panic buying.[33] The government quickly backpedaled, introducing an austerity program in 1988 that would be the basis of the Tiananmen protests.

Market reform had outrun the government's management capacity, and the reflex for many in the government was to retreat to a system that allowed them to maintain the existing mechanisms of government control by removing competitors to state-owned enterprise, reestablishing price controls, and destroying rural industrial activity that allowed people to leave the farms— a system that had been a moderately stable basis for Communist power under Mao, no matter how much it impoverished China's citizens.

The Tiananmen intermission would not last very long. In 1992, Deng Xiaoping, then 87 years old and holding no formal position within the Communist Party, took a trip to Shenzhen and Zhuhai, two cities in southern China that had benefited most from reform and opening. In both cities and various stops along the way, Deng exhorted local governments to continue experimenting with market reforms. The "southern tour" ended in Shanghai, where Deng expressed regret that the city hadn't had the same opportunities as its southern, more liberal, counterparts.

The trip was a clear statement of support for the reformers, who, by the end of the year, had managed to take the initiative again. In October 1992, during the fourteenth congress of the Chinese Communist Party, China's leadership declared that markets and private enterprise were an integral part of socialism and deserved equal protection under the law. Private enterprise, which had been introduced in 1980 to deal with a labor crisis, was now officially the basis of the Chinese economy.[34]

The number of private enterprises would increase substantially in the following years, but the more significant policy changes had to do with SOEs. The state's share of industrial production had plummeted from 77.6 percent in 1978 to 34 percent in 1995. In 1988, it was reported that almost 11 percent of state-owned enterprises were insolvent, a figure that would rise to 30 percent in 1993.[35] In the last months of 1992, China finally succeeded at ending the dual-track pricing system, forcing SOEs to purchase inputs at market prices.[36] This dual-track system had been a substantial subsidy to SOEs, given at the expense of the private sector, which had to pay higher prices for goods because a portion of supply was being rerouted to the state at a cheaper price. Full market-based pricing would push more SOEs into insolvency.

Local governments responded, rationally, by trying to privatize their insolvent SOEs. The most famous case was Zhucheng in Shandong Province, which between 1992 and 1994 quietly sold off its share in 90 percent of the city's state-owned and collective enterprises, mostly by selling shares to company employees. This practice was wholly illegal at first, as it constituted selling state assets. Though legalized in 1993, privatization of SOEs remained problematic to implement across much of China.[37]

The problem, again, boiled down to the labor market. At that time, SOEs still accounted for well over half of total urban employment.[38] State employment was guaranteed for life and SOEs were responsible for providing social insurance, including medical care and pension payments. Employees belonged to their work units, and their work units were responsible for them.

Starting in 1993, the Chinese government introduced a number of reforms aimed at liberalizing the labor market. That year, the government debuted an unemployment insurance system, though unemployment was only legally recognized the following year. In 1994, state-owned housing units were sold to residents for below-market value, which allowed employees to change jobs without losing their homes. Between 1994 and 1998, the pension system and responsibility for healthcare coverage was moved over to local governments and made part of the hukou system.[39] Several local governments offered a portion of the proceeds from privatization to employees giving up their "iron rice bowl" (guaranteed lifetime employment). These reforms would help minimize social disruptions from the mass layoffs that were ahead.[40]

The 1994 Fiscal Reform

The fiscal law introduced on January 1, 1994, was the largest change to China's institutional infrastructure since 1949. The core of the law was a radical simplification of the tax system, along with the introduction of a national unified tax-sharing system specifying what percentage of tax revenues would go to the central government. This reform would make it so all provincial governments were at least playing by the same rules, and it would significantly improve the central government's fiscal position, which would see its share of total revenues expand from 22 percent in 1993 to more than 50 percent by 1996. The reform would not, however, centralize expenditures, almost three-quarters of which were controlled by local governments.[41] This tension between a fiscally conservative central government with a growing revenue base and fiscally burdened local governments facing increasingly severe tax shortfalls set the scene for the Great Migration, and it continues to define government spending and government industrial policy in China today.

Under the new tax system, corporate and personal income taxes as well as value-added tax (VAT) revenues, which had previously been primarily controlled by local governments, were shared at a fixed rate with the central government. After several adjustments, the central government share of revenues was finalized in 2002 at 60 percent of income taxes and 75 percent of the VAT. SOE remittances, which had already fallen to only a fraction of the total budget, were mostly eliminated. There was a substantial simplification of tax rates, with a variety of product taxes unified into a single VAT, and the top corporate income tax rate reduced from 55 to 33 percent.[42]

VAT and income taxes continued to be a major source of revenue for local governments after the reform, but the largest contributor to local-government income was now a 3 to 5 percent tax on corporate revenue, with the higher rate primarily levied on construction, real estate, and services companies. Local governments also got all of the money from urban maintenance fees charged to corporations for maintaining local infrastructure, business registration fees, and land-use taxes, as well as one-off revenue from transferring agricultural land to urban land (described in the previous chapter).[43] As a consequence of this reform, urban development went from a costly necessity for raising business revenues to a primary source of income for local governments. Despite the aggressive centralization of taxation power during this period, expenditures remained the province of local government. The subnational share of total expenditure continues to account for around three-fourths of total spending, compared to an average of 32 percent in Organisation for Economic Co-operation and Development (OECD) countries and under 20 percent in developing countries.[44] The budget reform did not centralize management of the economy; rather, it forced China's main government actors to operate with a lot less money. This helped shrink systemic risks at the central level, but at the local level, governments were often forced to resort to indirect fundraising in order to meet their development targets.

Decentralized responsibility for expenditures decisively shifted China's development in favor of urban areas, where local governments could raise money through land sales and administrative fees associated with real estate and infrastructure construction. The new turnover tax meant that local government revenues were now dependent on the quantity of business activity rather than the type of business activity. This made the government less picky about which investments to encourage and which to discourage—a privately owned factory with bare-bones margins paid the same percentage of its income to the local government as a government-supported "state champion."

Following the 1994 reforms, funds for social services would dramatically decline, which further weakened the importance of the hukou. Local governments were often unable to pay for pensions, and many local governments began demanding arbitrary fees for access to education and health coverage. Dropout rates in rural schools skyrocketed, with adult illiteracy rates increasing from 6.7 percent to 11 percent between 2000 and 2005.[45]

The 1994 reform also formally banned local governments from taking on debt, though there were significant loopholes in this ban. The most obvious was that local-government projects could be funneled through SOEs, which didn't face any similar restrictions. This would help undermine the already struggling SOE sector, which picked up more and more infrastructure and real estate projects with long-term profit horizons.[46]

The breaking point would come in 1998, with the collapse of the Guangdong International Trust and Investment Corporation (GITIC), the investment arm of the Guangdong provincial government, which in late 1998 defaulted on a USD 120 million loan to foreign lenders. China surprised many foreign investors at the time by refusing to bail out GITIC, instead entering it into bankruptcy proceedings in January 1999. The Chinese premier at the time, Zhu Rongji, unequivocally stated that the GITIC bankruptcy was not a matter of the government's capacity to pay for the debt of its SOEs, but rather its willingness:

> I think that those [international] banks and a few financial institutions are too pessimistic in their estimates of this problem; that is, they believe that China is already in the midst of a financial crisis and does not have the capacity to support its payments and is not creditworthy. China's economy is rapidly growing; we have USD 147 billion in reserves and balanced international payments. We are completely able to repay our debt. The issue is whether or not the government should repay this kind of debt.[47]

The audit of the company that followed found that more than 80 percent of the company's equity investments had failed and were without value. Most of them were real estate and infrastructure projects that would eventually be taken over by other arms of the government.[48]

While Zhu Rongji was correct that China would be able to cover its debts, he was wrong to say that China wasn't in the middle of a financial crisis. At the same time as the GITIC collapse, thousands of other SOEs were being shuttered or privatized. These companies were in a very different situation from GITIC, though. In GITIC's case, over 80 percent of the company's creditors were foreigners, which meant that running the company through bankruptcy was an easy way to stick someone else with the bill for the government's expensive and underutilized investments. This option was unavailable to most SOEs, which were indebted to the country's state-owned banks. By the end of the decade, China's banks were reporting nonperforming loan ratios in the realm of 40 percent of total book value. During the early part of the new millennium, the central government would restructure all four of the country's largest banks—either by writing down the loans or moving liability for the loans over to the taxation authority. The banks were then recapitalized through government injections and partial public listings.[49]

China's banking system only survived this crisis because of the central leadership's aggressive restructuring of loss-making SOEs. Between 2001 and 2004, the number of state-owned enterprises in China fell by half, and the SOE share of employment fell to under 30 percent; it would reach 18 percent by 2012.[50] This by no means ended the state's involvement in the Chinese economy, but it pushed the country further in the direction of private markets.

Even after the restructuring, though, approximately 80 percent of bank capital was still being lent to SOEs, companies that were still required to pursue long-term or unprofitable investments in order to meet state industrial goals instead of responding to market incentives.[51] China set caps on interest rates, reducing competition for deposits, ensuring that banks would maintain a healthy profit margin whoever the borrowers were, and helping banks swallow whatever new bad loans that were created by the remaining SOEs. The government also formalized a series of existing restrictions to moving capital in and out of the country in order to prevent a run on the system, culminating in the country fixing the exchange rate against the dollar in 1997.[52]

The 1994 tax reform and the ensuing reforms to SOEs and the financial system were not the brilliant work of a central planner; they were desperate efforts to forestall a fiscal crisis. The return of the sent-down youth from the countryside and the collapse of rural communes created a political environment where maintaining controls on private employment was increasingly difficult. Once China ended the outright ban on private enterprise, the position of SOEs became increasingly precarious. Private enterprises were able to use China's vast labor force and market discipline to overcome the advantages that SOEs had in terms of access to capital and subsidized inputs. By the end of the 1980s, the contributions of SOEs to the tax base had turned into an expense, and over the next decade, the government was forced to cut costs, shuttering thousands of SOEs, selling off assets, and substantially reducing the delivery of social services. Despite these problems, China has remained committed to maintaining a state-owned sector—a commitment that requires substantial subsidies from the state-controlled financial sector.

After the 1994 fiscal reform, there were very few reasons for working-aged people to stay in rural areas. The Tiananmen intermission had put an end to most of the TVEs that had been supporting rural workers in the 1980s. The collapse of social service provisions in rural areas meant that hukou restrictions had less bite. At the same time, cities started aggressively building housing and industrial areas in order to take advantage of the new turnover tax and urban land sales revenues. Whatever problems there were with the 1994 reform would be quickly overwhelmed by millions of migrants who were willing to work.

The Returns to Labor

Between 1993 and 1998, while access to capital was being undercut by China's ongoing fiscal problems, private sector employment grew by an average of 41 percent a year.[53] Unsurprisingly, these new workers were entering labor-heavy industries with low capital barriers to entry. In 1997 and 1998, there was a 70 percent correlation between employment gains and output gains in the private sector. By comparison, the South Korean economy during its initial take off in the 1970s saw a 50 percent correlation between employment gains and GDP growth, dropping to 31 percent by the 1990s.[54] In China, most of these new employees were migrants—in some cases an overwhelming number. In 2000, more than 80 percent of the employees in Guangzhou's rapidly growing textile industry came from the countryside.[55]

The importance of rural migration to increasing tax revenues allowed workers to "vote with their feet," and encouraged policy experimentation. Several cities tried—and mostly failed—to reform their hukou approval process to accept more migrants. Most notably, in 2001 Zhengzhou, the capital of the populous Henan Province, announced a major simplification of the hukou approval system that was meant to encourage migrant workers to get local residency. The program was shut down in 2004 due to rising expenditures on education and infrastructure and reports of rising crime. For most cities, the changes were felt through declining enforcement of hukou regulations rather than changes to the law, which allowed cities to enjoy the economic benefits of migration without paying for social services for the migrants.[56]

By 2000, it was Chinese government policy that rural households should have at least one person working off-farm.[57] There were clear financial advantages to this for poorer provinces. In 2000, Sichuan Province received RMB

202 billion in remittances from migrant workers, roughly equivalent to the province's fiscal revenue for the year. That same year Anhui Province received RMB 174.3 billion in remittances, 33 percent more than fiscal revenue.[58] Migration left fewer people eligible for social services, allowing poorer provinces to use tax income for other purposes. It also helped educate a province's workforce in industry and provided business connections that could be used to develop companies back home.

These new private sector workers would rapidly gain the skills and market knowledge needed to compete in industries with very low barriers to entry. Within a few years, new company formation would skyrocket, as experienced workers would try to capture some of the revenues created by the rapid influx of workers coming from the countryside. Between 1993 and 1998, the number of private sector enterprises in China increased from 238,000 to 1.2 million, reaching 19 million by 2015.[59]

Competition between factory owners was becoming as intense as competition between job seekers, and, without access to capital to invest in marketing and R&D, companies would be forced to look for any and all means to cut costs and capture volume. This was the origin of China's traditionally weak intellectual property regime. The purpose of intellectual property protection is to increase the efficiency of R&D investment by restricting the dispersion of knowledge within the labor force. Weak intellectual property protection, on the other hand, encourages rapid knowledge transmission, improving labor productivity at the expense of capital efficiency. For a country like China that has a high cost of capital and a low cost of labor, economic incentives make intellectual property laws very difficult to enforce.[60] Chinese companies did not have the capital to invest in R&D, so they would use the research of companies that did have the capital. They did not have the capital to invest in marketing, so they would use the brand logos of companies who could invest in marketing.

As a consequence, innovation in the Chinese economy would look very different from innovation in the developed world. Capital-poor and labor-rich Chinese companies would be defined by flexible business practices and low fixed costs. Chinese factories could scale up output in a matter of weeks— it was just a matter of hiring more workers and firing them when a contract was done. They could adjust product specifications in a matter of hours—

there was no machine to be reprogramed, only people to be told what to do. Between 1990 and 2011, a period when China's share of global clothing exports grew from 9 percent to 37 percent, the average product development cycle in clothing markets dropped from 6 to 9 months to 4 to 6 *weeks*.[61]

This proved to be an irresistible draw to foreign investors. Between 1991 and 1995, realized foreign direct investment (FDI) grew from USD 4.37 billion to USD 37.5 billion, or from roughly 2 percent to 11 percent of global FDI flows, and 19 percent of China's total fixed asset investment.[62] Foreign-invested enterprises would never account for a major share of China's employment levels, but they would encourage the dispersal of modern production techniques, foreign technology, and, most importantly, business connections. This helped China's private companies rapidly integrate into the larger Asian supply chain and access logistics infrastructure connecting to Europe and America.

The collapse of China's state sector in the 1990s had the effect of pushing China's overall economy into a very specific part of the supply chain. Capital-intensive growth was taken off the table, so China had to rely on its largest untapped asset—its people. China could not design a product that brought in the high margins of the iPhone, because it didn't have the capital or the legal environment to invest in R&D, but no other country could compete with the efficiency of China's manufacturing process, because no other country had a similarly flexible labor force.[63]

• • •

The commanding heights of China's economy consistently failed to produce growth at anywhere near the levels China needed to escape poverty and came very close to sending the country into bankruptcy. While the 1994 fiscal reforms would stave off an immediate crisis, China's fiscal system and its financial system continue to be a drag on the overall economy. Overspending by local governments, misallocation of capital, and weak financial markets continue to be prominent features of China's development story.

Without a functioning financial system, China has depended on its migrant workforce as the main driver of growth. This had a number of consequences for China's long-term development: the concentration of industry in areas that were agriculturally poor; a focus on industries with low-capital costs of entry, low margins, and high volume; poor intellectual property rights enforcement; and weak investment in social services relative to other developing countries (including education) with relatively strong investment in hard infrastructure, like housing, road construction, and industrial parks, which contributed to the local government tax base. By increasing competition for wages and providing resources for labor-intensive production, the Great Migration helped financially strapped investors make the most out of what little capital they had, and encouraged the development of a burgeoning private sector.

This economic system has a limited lifespan. More people have migrated during the Great Migration than ever before in history, but rural migrants are still a limited resource. China has yet to make the transition from an economy based on mobilizing labor to an economy based on capital efficiency. If it fails to make this transition in the next decade, it may run out of room to grow.

3

Wenzhou

THE GREAT MIGRATION affected different parts of China at different times. Perhaps the first city to embrace China's unique development strategy was Wenzhou, a small city in Southeastern China that, very early in China's reform process, identified underemployed rural workers as an untapped asset. While there were some unique features of Wenzhou's development story, a closer look at its history provides insight into both why the Great Migration developed as it did, and how important the Great Migration has been to China's transformation.

• • •

There was a time when Wenzhou was the most isolated place in China. Sitting at the mouth of the Ou River, surrounded by sudden and occasionally dramatic mountains, there were no railways and few roads connecting the city to the outside world. The people of Wenzhou were dependent on the sea, trading up and down the coast and eating what they could catch from the river. This isolation is attested to in the city's language, a dialect of Chinese known for being nearly impossible to learn and difficult enough to decode that it was used for military transmissions during World War II.

For this isolated plot of land, sitting a mere 300 miles from Taiwan, life under Mao was an unmitigated disaster. Between 1949 and 1978, Wenzhou was transformed from a major trading center on the route between Hong Kong, Shanghai, and Taipei, to one of the poorest cities in the country. Mao stripped the city of industrial capacity, fearing that any factories might fall into the hands of the Taiwanese. Ninety percent of the population was forced into agricultural work, despite the fact that there was very little agricultural land to work, and most of it was rocky and hard to farm. Many people went hungry.[1]

The city's disadvantages under Mao would become its biggest strengths after Mao's death. Rural farmers in Wenzhou had less land and worse yields than farmers in other regions, giving them more incentives to move to the cities. The local government had no incentives to either enforce migration restrictions or prevent the development of private enterprises—the absence of state-owned enterprises (SOEs) in the economy meant that Wenzhou attracted very little attention from the central government and had few economic incentives to restrict self-employment. In the decades following the death of Mao, Wenzhou would become ground zero for the development of China's labor-heavy development model, and one of the richest cities in the country.

Wenzhou's government had few resources at its disposal and was happy to let private citizens take on some of the burden of development. In 1979, Wenzhou registered China's first private company.[2] Over the next fifteen years, per-capita output in Wenzhou increased by an average of 19 percent a year.[3] China's most libertarian city would rapidly grow into one of the largest producers of textiles in the world, and a leading producer of other light manufactures. By the end of the century, Wenzhou boasted an independent banking system, a trading network that stretched to Europe, and GDP per capita twice the Chinese average. In China, the city's name would become proverbial for business acumen and an almost complete absence of the government. Wenzhou was the city where "the mountains are high and the emperor far away"—the place where all the rules could be broken.[4]

The Wenzhou miracle is one of the great stories of China's economic rise. It is also the first example of how the Great Migration transformed China. Wenzhou developed without an industrial policy, with little access to capital, and with no government support. Even the most obvious example of China's state-led development policy—the government's heavy investment in infrastructure—was largely absent from Wenzhou. The first railroad connecting the city to the rest of China was only built in 1998 and funded by foreign and private capital, and even today Wenzhou's road network is largely funded by the private sector.[5] "Wenzhou developed because of its entrepreneurs," one government official told me over dinner. "We didn't do anything."[6]

The development of Wenzhou followed the same path as many other Chinese cities, only faster and with less regard for the consequences. Entrepreneurs matched excess labor from agriculture with industries with low barriers to entry. The government stayed out of the way, leading to pollution, poor social services delivery, and rapid poverty alleviation. Though Wenzhou was extreme in the extent that it pursued economic development through labor mobilization, the economic forces that shaped the city are entirely typical of the Chinese economic miracle as a whole.

Creative Geography

From the moment you drive into Wenzhou, it's clear there is something different about the city. Wenzhou is an unplanned city. The roads were constructed piece by piece by businesspeople trying to connect their factories to the main thoroughfare leading to the city's port. There's no eminent domain letting entrepreneurs tear down buildings that get in their way; instead, roads twist and turn to make way for factories, dormitories, and apartments. Construction is everywhere. Roads remain half completed in places, with new buildings rapidly changing the surrounding landscape.

It is also clear that Wenzhou is a city where a lot of business is conducted. Commerce is everywhere, ranging from low-end consumer goods to specialty business equipment and industrial inputs. Outside of downtown, the city is a network of loosely connected factories, making everything from house paint to auto parts to designer clothing. This network spreads well into the countryside and surrounding factory towns, with only 30 percent of Wenzhou's population living in the city proper. Many factory towns would, in any other country, be major cities in their own right. Rui'an, which boasts to being "China's car and motorcycle spare parts capital," is home to 1.4 million people, as is Yueqing, which hosts large power equipment and precision molding industries.[7] Qiaotou Township in northwestern Wenzhou, which rose to fame as the largest producers of buttons and zippers in the world, has a population of 800,000.[8] Besides Rui'an, Yueqing, and

Qiaotou, a number of smaller townships specialize in plastic bags, cigarette lighters, clothing, and low-voltage electrical appliances.[9]

This dispersed production system is an inheritance from the township and village enterprise (TVE) period, when Wenzhou first took off. Unlike Shenzhen, which was a town built by and for migrants, Wenzhou's early development occurred while hukou regulations were still in effect. Wenzhou had a large population that was eager to move from the farm to the factory, but various controls on urban building and urban migration meant that factories had to come to farmers. This situation would not last forever. After the start of the Great Migration, Wenzhou became a major draw for migrant workers, to the extent that it is now uncommon to meet a cab driver, a factory worker, or a waiter in Wenzhou who was actually born in the prefecture. Between 2000 and 2010, the population of Wenzhou's central city grew by 59 percent, making it the fifth fastest growing city in China during this period.[10]

The government's lack of involvement in the economy is visible at a glance. The city is badly polluted, with trash clogging up the streams that lead to the Ou River. Wenzhou is also one of the only cities in China that turns a blind eye to urban slums. Makeshift housing made out of concrete blocks and corrugated iron is thrown up in the middle of abandoned lots, occasionally only a few blocks from downtown. In the rundown parts of town, where people live in crumbling buildings from the 1930s, people collect scraps of paper and metal for sale to the factories, or repair televisions and air conditioning units to sell to secondhand goods shops. This is the sort of poverty that is regularly hidden from view in other cities, pushed into dormitories or back to the countryside to clean up the city for visitors. Needless to say, migrants receive little in the way of social services. What they do receive is one of the highest wages for unskilled laborers anywhere in China.[11] For many migrants, the money is worth the tradeoff.

How to Deal with a Lack of Capital

Prior to the banking reform in the late 1990s, there was little difference between China's formal banking system and the state treasury, meaning that a lack of government support translated to poor access to financial services and poor access to capital in general. In order to get around this restraint,

Wenzhou very quickly developed an informal financial system that allowed entrepreneurs to access investment capital and bridge loans as well as pool resources for infrastructure development. By setting up mechanisms to reinvest earnings from one successful venture into an unrelated second venture, Wenzhou was able to build an independent capital base to fund increasingly complicated projects without having to worry about the changing political fates of local authorities.

While similar unofficial financial systems would develop in other parts of the country, the government's hands-off attitude in Wenzhou allowed the banks to develop a scale and a legitimacy unseen elsewhere.[12] According to the People's Bank of China (China's central bank), which follows both the scale and interest rates in underground financial markets, in 2010, informal banks were used by 89 percent of the local population as savings vehicles, while 54 percent of companies used the underground financial system as a source of working capital or investment funding.[13]

The informal financial system usually works in one of two ways. Smaller depositors can entrust their money to pawnshops, loan sharks, and credit-guarantee institutions that provide short-term working capital loans. The loans provided by these institutions can often be for fairly large sums if enough collateral is provided. Pawnshops in Wenzhou, for example, have been known to provide loans in the millions of dollars, backed by home equity and company shares. This has the secondary consequence of supporting property investment in the city, as businesspeople often own five or more apartments for collateral.

A more practical form of long-term borrowing involves bringing in wealthy investors either by offering shares in the company or a guaranteed return on investment (i.e., interest). This is a less liquid pool of capital, but investors are usually working with their own money and are aware of the risks they are running, meaning they are in a better position to take losses. In the market for short-term loans, repayment can be enforced either through claims on collateral or physical threats. In the market for long-term loans, a borrower who fails to repay would be blackballed from receiving any further credit within the tight-knit Wenzhounese business community.[14]

This informal financial network allowed Wenzhou to develop an alternative source of capital from the state banking monopoly and foreign investment, but it was a poor substitute for a functioning financial sector. Wenzhou's informal banking sector has a smaller depositor base than the formal sector and no mechanism for interbank lending, which makes it more difficult to diversify risk. As a consequence, interest rates, both for depositors and borrowers, can be extremely high, meaning that lending over longer time horizons without collateral is, if not impossible, at least irresponsible. Less diversification in lending portfolios makes the system more volatile than a formal financial system. It also makes it prone to financial fraud.

An example of the problems this causes was brought to national attention in 2009 when a 29-year-old Wenzhounese woman, Wu Ying, was sentenced to death for running a large-scale Ponzi scheme. During the trial, it came out that Ms. Wu, who at one time was ranked the sixth-richest person in China, raised RMB 770 million (USD 126.6 million) from investors, promising returns of upward of 80 percent on projects around Wenzhou. Despite the ample evidence that she was running a large-scale fraud, Ms. Wu received significant public support from Chinese media in the aftermath of the trial, with several newspapers publishing op-eds laying the blame for Ms. Wu's crime on the failures of the government financial system.[15] After the intervention of the former Chinese premier Wen Jiabao, Ms. Wu was given a reprieve in 2012, which was commuted to a life sentence in 2014.[16]

More broadly though, Wenzhou's informal sector was good at providing short-term working capital, but it was very bad at providing the sort of capital that would be necessary to invest in technical upgrades, marketing, or R&D. As a consequence, local entrepreneurs have had to specialize in industries with low barriers to entry, high volume demand, and extremely low margins. The scale of a business was more or less determined by how many people the factory could employ, which created a high demand for labor, and translated into strong wages for unskilled workers.

Following the banking reform in the late 1990s, it became somewhat easier for large Wenzhou companies to tap the formal financial system. State-owned banks were increasingly willing to lend to larger private enterprises, or private enterprises that could back their borrowing with collateral. The local business community took advantage of this by building capital through revolving loans in the informal sector, then paying off the informal loans with a low-interest formal bank loan. The city's history of building its own infrastructure has also been exploited to help bring in money from state-owned banks, with entrepreneurs bidding for government infrastructure contracts, then redirecting a portion of the bank loans for the project to unrelated businesses.[17]

Since China's 2009–2010 stimulus program, the process of capital formation has struggled to keep up with rising wages. The development of new manufacturing clusters in inland China has increased competition for migrant workers and undercut the sustainability of Wenzhou's low-cost, low-margin production chain. In 2009, local entrepreneurs were reporting that workers were demanding 50 percent salary hikes. Though wage growth has slowed since then, average salaries in Wenzhou come in at RMB 5,360 a month (USD 807) according to one headhunting firm, lagging behind only Shanghai, Beijing, and Shenzhen. Wenzhou companies are already outsourcing a lot of their labor to regions further inland—particularly Jiangxi and Anhui—while keeping a presence in the city either for fundraising or networking.

The central government has been dabbling with the idea of legalizing the local financial system in order to improve access to capital and manage some of the underlying risk. In 2012, the city was named a pilot area for private banking reform, which essentially gave the local government permission to experiment with a variety of different private financial institutions, ranging from rural credit cooperatives and insurance companies, to full-blown private banks. The citizens of Wenzhou were also given permission to invest up to USD 3 million abroad without receiving central government approval, a nod to the large Wenzhou diaspora, which owns businesses and trading companies across Europe and the Middle East.[18]

These reforms are more an effort to regulate what is already happening than a substantial attempt at financial reform. In February 2014, the government announced that it would allow private banks to make loans up to RMB 3 million (USD 500,000), and borrowers to take on loans up to RMB 10 million, both fractions of the amounts regularly handled by Wenzhou's underground financial system, and fractions of the amounts that Wenzhou will need if it wants to upgrade its manufacturing sector. The city's first legal private bank, Wenzhou Minsheng Bank, launched in March 2015, with its first loan valued at RMB 300,000 (USD 48,000). Commentators noted that without a deposit insurance system, the bank would likely struggle to hold onto depositors when competing against state-owned banks with a government guarantee.[19]

Any financial sector reform will have to challenge the state's monopoly on finance, a monopoly China depends on to subsidize loss-making SOEs and profligate local governments. Reforms to Wenzhou's financial sector can help stabilize local financial institutions and could even bring more money into the sector, but legal private finance is unlikely to replace underground finance any time soon.

The Social Network

The first thing many Wenzhounese did after the Cultural Revolution was to try to leave Wenzhou. The Wenzhounese had a long history of migration, dating back to the nineteenth-century porcelain traders who had settled in France. When migration controls weakened, many Wenzhounese took the opportunity to find family members abroad, or in richer parts of China. Today Wenzhounese is the primary language of Chinese immigrants in Italy, France, Spain, and the Netherlands, and marketplaces run by the Wenzhou Chamber of Commerce are operating in cities across China.[20]

Outward migration from Wenzhou would end up being a major contributor to the city's long-term development. The Wenzhounese population in France and Italy would help integrate the city with Europe's clothing industry by helping establish export markets for Wenzhounese textiles and transmitting information about production techniques and local styles to businesses back home. Migration within China played a similar role, creating a social network that allowed businesses to become better integrated into national supply chains. It also allowed Wenzhou's slowly growing pool of capital to diversify into other regions, including Guangdong's electronics firms, Beijing real estate, and coal mining in Inner Mongolia.[21]

Relationships between local and foreign Wenzhounese communities can often only be maintained through semi-legal means. For example, the city has developed a specialized industry in providing group tours for business travelers as a way to expedite visas. Fashion designers in Wenzhou report taking trips to Italy two to five times a year, in order to see the latest fashions, meet with business partners, or illegally move some of their money offshore. They usually travel with tour groups.[22]

Much of this international community is maintained through the Wenzhou Chamber of Commerce, which acts as both an advocate for the Wenzhou business community and as a sort of social club where Wenzhounese businesspeople can meet and discuss business opportunities. The chamber of commerce has been known both to negotiate investment deals and challenge trade sanctions on the behalf of the Wenzhou community, as well as invest in showrooms across China for Wenzhounese businesspeople to advertise or sell their wares.[23]

While inward migration fueled Wenzhou's transition from an agricultural economy to an industrial economy, outward migration moved Wenzhou from the periphery to the center of global supply chains. Within a few decades, Wenzhou was one of the largest clothing producers in the world, and a major producer of plastics and electrical equipment. Outward migration also helped fuel the development of civil society institutions that allowed Wenzhounese businesspeople to organize campaigns advocating their city's interests and to exchange information about global investment opportunities and ways to spread risk outside of the volatile environment of their hometown.

The Transition from Labor to Capital

Wenzhou's low-cost, low-margin production system is notorious for producing low-quality goods. For a long time, the city was known for producing exploding lighters—a consequence of the fact it produces the vast majority of the world's lighters.[24] The city lacks the upmarket charm and associated brand cache of Hangzhou and Shanghai, instead being known (accurately) for trash-clogged rivers, gray skies, high crime, and industrial architecture.

Wenzhou companies have traditionally accommodated this prejudice by latching onto other brands—providing finishing work or full manufacturing lines for brands designed, or just headquartered, elsewhere. But, as migration has slowed and labor costs have risen, Wenzhou businesspeople have tried to transition to a more capital-intensive growth model that includes investment in R&D and product development.

This change in business focus has become more urgent in recent years, as migrants have dried up and businesspeople are looking for ways to compete on margins instead of volume. Weng Wenbiao runs New Product Design, a

A BAR IN WENZHOU

When I met Cai Shuxian, he was the 30-year-old CEO of a clothing factory.[25] Cai is a small and lightly built man. He dresses well, but not formally, in Italian clothes and tries to put on the poise of a business executive. It doesn't suit him very well. He seemed excited and moderately uncomfortable about being interviewed. His desk was three times his size, and when the interview was over, he made a point of having someone borrow his BMW (as opposed to their own BMW) to drive me back to my hotel. He was extremely likable, but also unsure of himself. He had done well in life and wasn't sure how to show it.

Anywhere else in the world Cai's story would have sounded unbelievable. Cai is a high school dropout who took his first job at 16 working on a production line. He earned roughly RMB 600 a month (approximately USD 100), which even by the standard of the day was fairly little. But what Cai didn't have in education, he had in ambition. Within six years of starting his first job, he opened his own company, which by the time I met him was employing over one hundred people and earning in the realm of a million dollars a year. He wasn't forthcoming about where he got his startup capital from, but it was clear that Cai knew how to build connections, with an investment portfolio covering five cities and business partners in another three.

After our interview, I invited Cai to a bar, hoping that with a few drinks the stories about China's "city with no laws" and his personal business history might become more colorful. Things didn't work out that way.

The "bar" that I was directed to was a thumping club, with a dance show in the middle of the room and people standing awkwardly at scattered tables. Cai had a large table in the back, where he sat with a group of friends. Pairs of his friends were split up, playing a popular Chinese drinking game called "liar's dice," and drinking Hennessey mixed with sweet tea. Cai was sitting alone on one side with a large wad of money in his hand paying for drinks when the waitress came by.

I was introduced quickly to Cai's wife, and then Cai and I sat together and I tried as best as I could to engage him in conversation. The music was too loud to talk, but Cai was friendly. We discussed alcohol for a little while—and work. Eventually, the conversation was drowned out by the music and we went back to silence. Cai stared ahead, like he was thinking about something, only looking up when he had the chance to buy everyone new drinks.

One of his business partners took me back to my hotel. He explained on the way that everyone else there was a friend of Cai's wife from university. Despite making more money than any of them, Cai, the high school dropout, never felt respected.

"These days everyone would prefer their children to go to school and get a government job," he said. "Being a businessman is just too hard."

company that mostly designs and sells women's jackets for the over-40 crowd. Weng has cut labor costs at his company by outsourcing production to thirty factories in Zhejiang, Anhui, and Jiangxi Provinces, the traditional sources of migrant workers to Wenzhou. These companies often outsource production yet further if they think secondary factories can produce at the same quality for lower costs. The company runs two brands, 久川 and 埃文 (A-Won), which it markets in China through a franchise model. The company's main assets are its designers, who are paid between RMB 10,000 and RMB 30,000 (USD 5,000) a month—the latter figure an almost unheard of rate in China. Besides paying his designers more, Weng has invested heavily in marketing, increasing oversight of the company's franchises, and putting whatever money he can spare into overhauling retail spaces to make them more appealing to young people.

As his inspiration, he cites JNBY, another Hangzhou company, which produces midprice designer fashion and has successfully expanded abroad. JNBY adapted the early model of labor-heavy, capital-light production to changes in the composition of China's workforce. The company has close relationships with local design schools, which it uses to bring in a large number of low-priced designers that can rapidly put out new styles. These designs are then transmitted to inland factories, where labor costs remain low. This model allows JNBY to produce unusual new fashions quickly and for little money. A JNBY store rarely has more than one piece of a particular design on its racks, and is continually rotating new designs in and out as fast as the company's designers are able to produce them. For a long time, one of the company's advertisements was a poster of a Caucasian woman proudly holding up a picture saying "Made in China."

For those with more money than patience, Wenzhou companies have developed fake foreign brands in order to provide a sheen of European luxury to local products. Lawyers at Chiomenti Studio Legale have gotten requests from clothing companies to look into respected 100-year-old Italian clothing companies that they planned on buying through a local Wenzhounese intermediary, only to find out that one of these Italian companies was registered only a month earlier, and never existed in any form except for a company registration.[26] Wenzhounese insist that investors know that the companies they buy are fake. The customers, though, may not.

Migrants

The Wenzhou miracle started with migrants—migrants from Wenzhou's own countryside moved to urban areas where they could work together to develop businesses that could make a profit. Many of today's Wenzhounese millionaires were born in the countryside and moved to the city to find jobs as production line workers, earning little more than USD 100 a month. Education levels in Wenzhou continue to lag behind other rich areas of the country, which has had little effect on the city's overall success.[27]

As the city became richer, it attracted more migrants from nearby provinces. Since 1995, Wenzhou has been one of the largest recipients of migrants in the country, a testament to the city's high wages and continuing appeal as a place to make money. Today the taxi drivers and manual workers in Wenzhou are mostly from Jiangxi and Anhui, two neighboring provinces that were slow to join China's free markets.

But recently, the patterns of migration to Wenzhou have changed. As opportunities grew in the rest of China, Wenzhou's draw has diminished.

Wenzhounese business owners are now outsourcing to Anhui instead of using migrants from Anhui. The city's competitive advantage, a relatively formalized private financial system, is not quite formal enough to develop capital-intensive companies. The city's polluted waterways and bad education system are not the sort of thing educated workers are looking for when deciding where to move, making it difficult for the city to move up the supply chain.

In order to succeed in the next decades, Wenzhou needs to reinvent itself as a place to meet experienced business managers, discuss financing options, and hire experienced professionals. In order to accomplish this, it needs a financial system that works, access to competitive markets, and better educational resources both for migrants and for locals.

For years, Wenzhou was isolated from the rest of China. Today it takes a little more than four hours to get there by high-speed train from Hangzhou. Because of its migrants, the city is more connected to China than ever before.

4

The Returns on the Great Migration

NEARLY EVERYONE EXPERIENCES the economic gains from migration at some point in their life. For Candy Nichols that moment came when she decided to move from Idaho, where she went to nursing school, back to California where she had grown up. She had lived in Idaho for several years after graduating, had married and started a family, but she wanted to go home, and someone was willing to pay her a lot of money to do so. The job Ms. Nichols found in Santa Clara, California, paid 72 dollars an hour, compared to 27 dollars an hour in her previous job in Idaho—roughly an additional 90,000 dollars a year.

This impressive pay raise does not only measure her personal gains from the move, but also measures the wealth that she has created that she can then share with others in the economy—helping to pay the higher wages of the plumber who repairs her sink, the nurse who takes care of her when she's sick, or the people who gain from Silicon Valley's out-of-control housing prices. Moving to Silicon Valley increased Ms. Nichols's productivity, not because she worked harder, but because she was contributing to an economy that creates more value per worker than the economy of Idaho, Arkansas, or Texas.

At the most basic level, the potential gains from migration can be measured by looking at the net wage gains involved in workers moving from one location within an economy to another. Direct comparisons, however, are often more difficult than they sound. If Ms. Nichols weren't a nurse educated in Idaho but rather a doctor educated in India, she would likely have faced more difficulties getting local certification in California, both due to legitimate concerns about educational equivalence and illegitimate efforts to increase local wages by restricting the supply of new doctors. If she were a computer programmer, she wouldn't have the same access to local business networks as a long-time resident would, or the skills gained from experience with local Silicon Valley companies.

While migrants are usually not paid as much as local workers, they can contribute to local workers' wage growth by creating more opportunities to specialize. A computer programmer educated in Wuxi, China, may work on basic coding, while the one educated at Stanford does higher level design. A nurse educated in Idaho may do primary care, while a nurse educated in the Philippines may do routine work. Without the lower cost labor, the better-educated programmer from Stanford or the better-educated nurse from Idaho would be stuck doing work with less value added.

Migrants also come with their own network effects. Their connections to their home country open up new trade and business opportunities. Migrant communities, like school alumni communities, help people find jobs and build connections between firms. Academic research has regularly found migrants to be more entrepreneurial and more active job creators than locals, in part due to this network effect.[1]

Large-scale migration has also pushed governments to reform legal barriers to employment both in positive and negative directions, depending on whether the government and local interest groups see more danger in declining productivity or rising social services costs and weakened local wages. For example, Michigan, on the border with Canada, has rules in place to quickly certify foreign doctors; Arizona, home to some of the country's most aggressive anti-immigration activists, does not certify doctors from other states in the US.[2]

The full answer to the seemingly simple question "To what degree has the Great Migration been responsible for China's growth?" would account for all of these factors: How many people migrated? How do migrant wages compare with locals? Did the migrants create jobs or take jobs? How much do migrants suppress wages? How much do government regulations suppress migrant wages? Have those regulations changed?

The answers to some of these questions are considerably more difficult to estimate than for others, which hasn't stopped a number of brave econometricians from trying. Studies have repeatedly found that labor reallocation from agriculture to industry is directly responsible for between 20 and 33 percent of China's economic growth, with additional indirect benefits that are more difficult to quantify.[3] According to these studies, China has a bit over a decade left of migration-driven growth, as hukou restrictions are gradually lifted and wages equalize between the countryside and the cities. By 2030, the Great Migration will transition into demographic decline, as China reaches natural levels of urbanization and the population starts to decline due to the one-child policy.[4]

To understand the relationship between migration and China's growth, it helps to look at the main sources of Chinese growth over this period: labor reallocation; sectorial productivity increases from industrial productivity, human capital gains, and capital investment; controlled inflation; and the growth of China's working-age population.

Migration is strongly linked with each of these sources, especially in three areas where it majorly contributed to growth: the most obvious is the transition of workers from agriculture to industry as rural hukou holders have been allowed to leave the countryside to find jobs in the city. Productivity levels in the countryside, measured by wages, have remained roughly three times lower than in urban areas, providing a straightforward gain both to the wealth of migrants and to the community that they are working in. Second, the gradual de-linking of social services and state employment has contributed to labor reallocation within and between urban areas, which has allowed companies to more efficiently utilize workers. Third, the increase in industrial employment has led to human capital gains in work experience and business knowledge, that has allowed workers to transition into higher-value-added industries as capital inputs became available.

Labor Reallocation

The broad consensus among economists is that labor reallocation was responsible for more than 20 percent of GDP growth during the first two decades of the Great Migration. How much more than 20 percent depends on how we account for agricultural productivity growth during this period.

Under the most basic model of rural-urban reallocation, you could measure the gains from reemployment by comparing the salaries of agricultural workers and industrial workers and calculating how much more productive workers are after transitioning to industrial work. Without question these gains have been substantial, but they have been tempered by increases in labor productivity in agriculture, which grew 6.5 percent annually between 1991 and 2009.[5]

The question is whether agricultural productivity would have increased at nearly the rate it did without improvements to labor mobility. Land is a fixed resource while labor is not, so adding labor to an already saturated agriculture sector will lead to declining labor efficiency. China continues to have significant pools of underemployed "excess labor" living in the countryside, which reduces per-capita agricultural productivity. This can be seen clearly both in the slow growth of industrial wages relative to productivity, which implies that there is substantial competition for the best jobs, and the continued large rural share of the workforce despite the substantially higher wages in urban areas.[6] Moving these workers to factory jobs should both increase their productivity and the productivity of the workers who remain in agricultural work.

Besides the direct impact on productivity, excess workers have had a negative impact on land rights. In order to implement the household responsibility system while restricting urbanization, China needed to ensure that new rural households would have access to land, entailing fairly regular land redistribution within villages. It was only when China's rural population started shrinking due to migration that China introduced reforms that significantly restricted redistribution.

Reports that have made the more conservative assumption that agricultural productivity growth and labor reallocation are separate phenomena put the impact of labor reallocation at around 20 percent of GDP growth. Reports that link agricultural productivity growth and labor reallocation have put the contribution at closer to 33 percent of output growth. Either way, the contribution has certainly been substantial, particularly considering the country's average rate of growth was almost 10 percent during the first three decades of reforms.

Sectorial Reform

The other 66 to 80 percent of GDP growth is accounted for by growth of the working-age population and within-sector productivity growth. While sectorial productivity growth can come from a range of factors, the three that stand out during the period are industrial reform, human capital development, and capital investment. While these issues are less directly connected to the Great Migration than rural-urban labor reallocation, urbanization and labor market reforms that were heavily influenced by migration have contributed to growth in all three areas.

Industrial Productivity

In the late 1990s, China experienced the fastest sustained growth in industrial productivity in the country's history. For several years, industrial productivity expanded more than 10 percent a year, as industrial restructuring pushed workers from the bloated and inefficient state sector to the country's booming private sector manufacturers.[7]

While much of this shift was due to a top-down effort to clean up government finances and close bankrupt state-owned enterprises (SOEs), a closer look at the data has found that industrial restructuring was highly dependent on larger labor market reforms. One study by Haiyan Deng et al. looking at hiring activities of 22,500 medium- and large-size firms annually between 1995 and 2003 found that the transition from SOE employment to private sector employment was only a minor share of the increase in hiring and firing during this period. In the case of SOEs, a 9.8 percent net annual decline in employment stemmed from a 20.9 percent gross job destruction rate and 11.1 percent gross job creation rate, while in the private sector the peak reform period saw an average gross job creation rate of 53.4 percent, next to an 18.1 percent job destruction rate, leading to a 35.3 percent net job gain.[8]

A few things stand out from those figures. First, the transition from the state sector to more efficient industrial sectors was not as large as job churn within the state sector. This implies that the closure of bankrupt SOEs was not as large a factor in improving overall industrial productivity as the reallocation of labor within the state sector through liberal labor market policies. The authors of the above paper estimated that increased job churn within different ownership types accounted for as much as three-fourths of the total impact on industrial reform, and between 30 percent and 40 percent of total industrial productivity growth during this period. As discussed in Chapter 2, this increase in hiring and firing could only happen because of labor market reforms that moved the provision of social services and urban housing away from SOEs.

Second, while the state sector saw more gross job destruction than the private sector, the variation was much smaller than the disparity in job creation. In other words, the decline in SOE employment paled in comparison to the growth of private sector enterprises. As previously mentioned, these private sector enterprises were almost wholly dependent on either interregional or rural-urban migrants.[9]

Human Capital

Most studies of human capital growth as a share of China's growth story have focused on average years of schooling. As would be expected, these studies found a high rate of growth associated with human capital in the early stages of the reform period—as high as 24 percent of growth between 1978 and 1997—with a substantial slowdown later during the reform period.[10] This measurement, though, does not account for on-the-job learning and increased human capital utilization due to migration, which, when included, shows a substantially stronger performance during the Great Migration.

Annual years of education provides a conveniently concrete measurement of social investment into worker training, but it does not measure a variety of other features that impact how much a worker produces, such as the location of employment or job experience. A broader measure of human capital can be made by looking at the estimated lifetime output of workers under various conditions. Haizheng Li et al. from the Central University of Finance and Economics in Beijing did just that, in a report that estimated the lifetime income of China's population by comparing similar workers at different ages to get a measure of how income should be expected to develop over a lifetime under different conditions. The report found a substantially higher level of human capital growth after 1995, with the transfer of workers from rural areas to urban areas accounting for more than half of all growth. According to Li's findings, in 1997, human capital per capita grew 2.87 percent, with migration accounting for 1.86 of those percentage points and increased educational attainment accounting for 1.23 percentage points, while the aging of the population subtracted 0.2 percentage points.[11]

Even after accounting for migration, the ratio of human capital to GDP has declined precipitously over the course of the Chinese economic miracle, from 21.4 in 1985 to 12.9 in 2007. The growth of education's contribution to human capital plummeted in 2001, from 2.38 percent to 0.84 percent, bottoming out in 2005 at 0.29 percent, as children born in 1989 were entering the workforce. Though educational attainment has grown since then, this is still an area where China will have to invest more assets as the gains from migration disappear.[12]

Capital Investment

As China has recovered from the financial crisis of the late 1990s, fixed-capital investment has rapidly grown as a share of GDP, and has made an obvious contribution to the overall efficiency of labor in China. But there is a chicken-and-the-egg problem when attempting to determine how the interaction between labor migration and capital impacted overall economic growth. Investment in fixed assets could have encouraged workers to migrate to a region and increased overall labor productivity, or the availability of labor could have attracted more capital investment and increased the overall efficiency of capital.

This can be measured. There are two general measures of capital efficiency in an economy: productive efficiency, which looks at how much capital is necessary to produce a unit of GDP, and allocative efficiency, which looks at the extent to which investment is made in accordance with market demand— roughly, whether investments are profitable. These figures were calculated and broken down on a provincial level in a 2009 paper by Duo Qin and Haiyan Song, and found, predictably, that between 1992 and 2004 productive efficiency was highest in the most developed provinces with the strongest rates of migration—in order: Zhejiang, Shandong, Guangdong, Jiangsu, and Fujian.

Allocative efficiency in these regions, on the other hand, was extremely poor. Correcting for government investment, the provinces that saw the most overinvestment relative to market demand were, in order, Zhejiang, Guangdong, Jiangsu, Fujian, and Sichuan. In other words, capital in China generally chases productivity, not the other way around.[13]

When government investment is included in the calculations of allocative efficiency, overinvestment is shown to increase in commodity-producing areas, while several of the provinces in which the private sector overinvested show significantly better returns on capital. Between 1992 and 2004, Fujian, Jiangsu, and Shandong are shown as being underinvested relative to market demand, while Guangdong sees half the level of overinvestment as under non-government conditions. This reflects the still surprising infrastructure deficits in coastal provinces. Guangdong, for example, has less than 50 kilometers of rail infrastructure per million people, below Thailand and only slightly above Cambodia.[14]

This makes sense. One of the major roles the government plays in many economies is redistributing money away from richer regions toward poorer regions of the country. China's government in particular remains heavily invested in upstream industries like coal, oil, and mining, all of which are more prevalent in poorer inland regions. Nevertheless, it bears repeating that despite the substantial role of the state in China's economy, the Chinese government has systematically underinvested in some of the country's most prosperous regions.

Inflation

One aspect of China's economic miracle that has continually surprised market watchers has been the country's low trend inflation since 1996. Between 2000 and 2009, inflation in China grew at an average annual rate of 3 percent a year, compared to 6 percent in India, 7 percent in Brazil, and 13 percent in Russia, a period when China's average growth rate substantially outperformed the rest of the world.

This surprise has often veered into disbelief, as analysts reflect on the sky-high prices of luxury apartment complexes compared to the once modest price of living in Beijing's ancient *hutong* alleyways. Usually, this skepticism stems from analysts confusing increases in the standard of living with increases in the inflation rate. For example, the amount the average Chinese person pays for a phone has increased substantially in the past decade, but how much of that increase is due to substituting a 2G feature phone with a 3G smartphone is hard to determine. How much has the price of clothing changed because

Chinese are buying higher quality branded clothes rather than cheap knock-offs? Have food prices really risen, or are people substituting grains and vegetables with meats and fruits? *Hutong* housing often lacks both insulation and indoor toilets. How should we compare it to apartment blocks that have both?

In order to accurately assess inflation, you need to look at a single product that has maintained a relatively steady market presence over a long period of time—something like a McDonalds Big Mac. The *Economist* magazine's Big Mac index, which regularly looks at the price of Big Macs in forty-eight countries and the euro area, shows that the price of a Big Mac increased from RMB 10.2 in 2003 to RMB 14.5 in 2010, or an inflation rate of 4.4 percent annually. While higher than China's official inflation rate, it is not significantly so—the US, Japan, and the EU all see a similar divergence.[15]

There are two overlapping factors that have contributed to China's low inflation rate since the late 1990s. The first is directly linked to migration. China has seen regular short-term bouts of food price inflation, usually linked to supply shocks for pork production. In other countries, these events can turn into inflationary spirals as consumers, expecting higher prices, push their employers for wage increases. In China, this hasn't been an option, as competition for wages has weakened the negotiating position of workers.

More broadly, higher productivity and lower labor costs have translated into cheaper goods—though more expensive commodities—not only within China, but also outside of China. A report from Deutsche Bundesbank found that supply and demand shocks in China account for 5 percent of global inflation rates during the periods of those shocks, with a particularly strong impact on Australia, China's largest source of metals.[16]

But at the end of the day, inflation is always and everywhere a monetary phenomenon. If inflation is in fact as low as the figures indicate, money creation—in the form of higher bank lending or central bank-subsidized government spending—should be lower in China than in comparable countries with higher inflation rates. And that's exactly what we find. Growth in bank lending was only roughly 5 percent higher than GDP growth in China between 2000 and 2009, compared to nearly 15 percent higher in Brazil and over 40 percent higher in Russia. China is simply not a capital-driven growth story.

The Lewis Turning Point

The final major source of growth during China's reform period was the growth of the working age population. This demographic dividend accounted for 32 percent of total growth during the first decade of reform, then slowed to about 5 percent of total growth between 2000 and 2011, as children born under the one-child policy came of age.[17] In 2012, the number of working-age people in China declined for the first time. This decline will continue to be a drag on growth until China can bring its birth rate back up to the replacement rate—a point in time potentially very far in the future.[18]

The Great Migration is a cushion for this decline. While migrant workers aren't technically being added to the workforce, they are, for the most part, underemployed and can take up labor market slack for the first few years of China's demographic decline. According to calculations from the International Monetary Fund (IMF), China should transition from a labor-surplus to a labor-shortage country sometime between 2020 and 2025, with the country facing a shortage of over 100 million workers by 2030.[19]

This transition from a labor-surplus to a labor-deficit country is called the "Lewis Turning Point," named after Nobel Prize–winning economist Arthur Lewis. Lewis developed a theory of development where a "capitalist" sector grew by taking labor from a "subsistence" sector. This nearly unlimited pool of labor during the early stage of development keeps wages low and increases the return to capital, allowing entrepreneurs to reinvest wealth and further expand employment. At some point, this pool of excess labor is exhausted, and the country has to transition from a development model based on resource utilization to an economic model based on resource efficiency.

China has introduced a number of top-down reforms to help ease this transition. The country's economic policy has increasingly focused on supporting high-technology sectors and higher education in hopes that this sort of institutional support would be enough to allow Chinese companies to compete internationally. At first glance, these efforts seem to have produced results. University enrollments in China skyrocketed from about 400,000 in 1997 to over 30 million in 2010. In 2011, China surpassed the US as the world's top patent filer, filing nearly double the number of patents as in 2006.[20]

But quantity does not translate into quality, and a closer look shows that investments into higher education and high-tech production have not translated into industrial development. While China might produce more patents than the US or Japan, it receives less income on those patents.[21] University enrollments may soon surpass the population of Canada, but unemployment among young university graduates is twice as high as among high-school-educated workers of a comparable age.[22]

China has embraced an open market for labor, but it still lags well behind other countries in embracing the open market for goods, services, and particularly capital. Without the continuing influx of migrant workers, China will soon have to depend on a much more conventional model of development. The next two chapters will look at what advantages China has, and what disadvantages it has, as it tries to make that transition.

Why Factories Are Not Leaving China

ONE OF THE MORE obscure statistics monitored by the National Development and Reform Commission (NDRC), China's highest policy-making body, is the sales of pickled mustard greens, a cheap snack food for sale in convenience stores and train stations across China. While the NDRC has a broad sense of the size and location of China's "floating population," getting exact measurements can be difficult, so the policymaking body watches an array of secondary indicators to get a sense of how migration is progressing across the country. Pickled mustard greens are primarily purchased by poor urban residents who are frequently working or traveling, a neat description of China's migrant workforce. Where they are being purchased provides some indication of where migrants are living.

According to the pickled mustard index, in 2010, China witnessed one of the largest demographic shifts since the Great Migration began. Between 2009 and 2011, sales of pickled mustard greens in southern China fell from nearly half the national total to 30 percent, while the share of sales in central China grew from 3 percent to 10 percent. China's Great Migration had changed its center of gravity.[1]

This change had been a long time coming. During Hu Jintao and Wen Jiabao's decade in power, China's leadership focused on ending many of the more severe economic distortions that had caused Chinese migrants to rush to the city. Between 2006 and 2012, the government invested RMB 6 trillion (USD 1 trillion) in roads, water lines, power lines, telecom systems, schools, and hospitals in an effort to give rural dwellers more opportunities to escape poverty without leaving home.[2] While this did improve the quality of life in rural areas, the real beneficiaries were inland cities, which could take advantage of new infrastructure connections to coastal markets, government incentives for state-owned enterprises (SOEs) to invest inland, and a surge of unskilled labor that had returned to their home provinces as construction workers. Cities like Chongqing, Chengdu, and Zhengzhou were able to attract investments from major international electronics manufacturers, while companies in other inland cities picked up outsourcing contracts from coastal manufacturers looking to move up the value chain.

Like most government-engineered transitions, this one had some unforeseen consequences. The reversal of the Great Migration happened faster than anyone expected, putting sudden sharp wage pressures on coastal employers. Many companies had to fundamentally change the way they did business in order to survive, and many didn't even bother; they packed up and moved their factories inland or abroad.

Through most of the Chinese economic miracle, the country's development story had been overwhelmingly focused in coastal megacities, while inland regions had been left in relative poverty. Even today, roughly 160 million people in China's interior are living on under USD 1.25 a day measured by purchasing parity. The return of migrants to central China was an indication of hope for these people. Over the next twenty years, China has the opportunity to build a two-pole industrial economy: a low-skilled manufacturing economy based in central and western provinces like Chongqing, Sichuan, Henan, Hunan, and Hubei, and a coastal economy based on technology and services, in the old manufacturing powerhouses like Shanghai, Jiangsu, Zhejiang, Guangdong, and Shandong. At the moment, everything is going in the country's favor.

But China is working against the clock. Within fifteen years, China will begin to face its demographic decline. If the country has not developed by then, if people aren't working more with their brains than with their hands, if private businesses still can't access capital, and consumers still lack money to buy goods, the last stage of the Great Migration could sizzle into stagnation and decline.

Why Factories Are Not Leaving China

In 2010, Bloomberg's *Businessweek* published an article ominously titled "Why Factories Are Leaving China." The article featured interviews with a footwear manufacturer, the head of the textile trade association, and the head of a teddy bear manufacturing company, all of whom were broadly in agreement. Across China's manufacturing belt, wages were rising and workers were discontented. In low-end sectors, factories were getting ready to move abroad—according to the interviewees many of them already had.[3]

Two years later, the same year that the *New York Times* wrote, "China's vast takeover of world markets may be running out of steam," China surpassed the United States as the world's largest trading nation.[4] While much of this rise was fueled by a rapid growth in imports, Chinese exports still grew faster than all major trading nations. The only non-oil economies with faster growing exports were Turkey and Vietnam, the 31st and 34th largest exporters respectively. The value of the *expansion* in China's trade was nearly the same as all of Turkey's exports put together.[5]

The rapid growth of the export economy was consistent across a variety of product classes. Take textiles and clothing, for example. Textiles are a classic low-end industry, dependent on tight margins and low-cost labor. At the time these articles were published, Vietnam, Malaysia, and Bangladesh were all seeing rapid growth in textile exports, and textiles were probably cited more often than any other sector as an area where China was losing competitiveness. Yet, between 2010 and 2014, China's share of global textile exports grew from 31 to 36 percent, and its share of global clothing exports grew from 37 percent to 39 percent.[6]

Two other growing product classes are electronics and machinery manufacturing, which currently account for over half of all China's exports.[7] Again, there have been rumors of electronics manufacturers leaving China since 2010, when a number of worker suicides at the contract manufacturer Foxconn led to wage hikes and reports that the company was considering moving abroad, or at the very least expanding the use of machinery on its production line.[8] Samsung's USD 2 billion investment in a cell phone manufacturing plant in Vietnam in 2013 further drove home the point that if prices grew too high in China, manufacturers had other options.[9] Yet between 2010 and 2012, Foxconn expanded its workforce in mainland China from 900,000 people to 1.1 million people, and announced plans to open new factories in Guizhou and Shanxi Provinces.[10] Samsung opened a USD 7 billion factory in Xi'an in April 2014.

Stories about manufacturing leaving China are, more often than not, actually stories about export manufacturing expanding somewhere else. China has been the destination of choice for low-end manufacturing for so long that any success in this area in Mexico, Vietnam, or Turkey is seen as being directly at China's expense. But that's not how trade works. China did not take on its role as the world's largest manufacturer because it outcompeted other countries, it did so because it was able to find an underserved niche in the greater Asian supply chain and contribute to the growth of new product lines. With Japan and South Korea developing high-end gadgets, Taiwan producing components for those gadgets, and Hong Kong and Singapore providing shipping services, China with its hundreds of millions of people looking for work and its increasingly high quality infrastructure was able to provide final assembly work at a competitive price. Without any one country's involvement, all the other countries would have been poorer.

Another indication that factories aren't leaving China because of rapid wage growth is that . . . China is experiencing rapid wage growth. Workers in coastal China can demand higher wages because they are creating more value for the global economy, while jobs that create less value for the global economy are being pushed further afield where workers lack better options. China, in other words, is upgrading. People on the coast who were previously working in assembly plants have moved into producing machinery, components, or providing services. People elsewhere who previously had few local opportunities have suddenly found a growing number of assembly plants being built in their backyard.

Industrial upgrading in China has contributed to the boom in exports to Southeast Asia. In the three years following the passage of the China-Association of Southeast Asian Nations (ASEAN) free trade agreement in 2010—the same period when factories were supposed to be leaving China for Southeast Asia—China's exports to ASEAN grew by 37.2 percent, compared to a 26 percent increase in imports.[11] China's largest exports to the region—machinery and appliances, chemical products, and textiles—correlated with ASEAN's largest exports to Europe. During the period when Vietnam was developing into one of the world's largest textile exporters, it also became the fourth largest importer of Chinese textiles.[12] Factories weren't leaving China; China's supply chain was outgrowing its national borders, just as companies in Japan, South Korea, Taiwan, Singapore, and Hong Kong had previously found a way to expand their businesses using migrant workers in China.[13]

While Southeast Asian nations have clearly benefited enormously from industrial upgrading in coastal China, the largest beneficiary has been inland China, with several inland Chinese provinces seeing export growth well in excess of what has been seen in Southeast Asia. Between 2010 and 2014, exports out of Chongqing expanded from USD 7.5 billion to USD 63.4 billion. Henan Province in central China saw its total export manufacturing sector grow from USD 10.5 billion to USD 37.1 billion, with approximately 200 percent growth in the province's high-tech manufacturing sector in 2011 and 2012. By comparison, Guangdong, China's largest exporting province, exported USD 644 billion worth of goods in 2015, down 0.4 percent over the previous year.[14]

These points shouldn't downplay the opportunities for other developing countries in coming years. Coastal China's manufacturing machine is large enough that it could support industrial transfer to Southeast Asia without significantly impacting the amount of investment going to central China. Cambodia, which recently has seen a dramatic increase in industrial investment, has a population of 15 million—about half the size of Chongqing. Vietnam has a population breakdown similar to Henan. The GDP of Guangdong is roughly USD 1 trillion. The GDP of Vietnam and Cambodia put together is just over USD 150 billion. As Guangdong, Jiangsu, and Zhejiang upgrade, there is plenty of room for gains in both inland China and Southeast Asia.

Inland Chinese manufacturers will benefit from many of the same cluster effects that helped coastal China develop during the first decades of the Great Migration. While the US and Europe may be China's largest trading partners, foreign investment in China's manufacturing sector has traditionally mostly come from Hong Kong and Taiwan. Businesspeople who had a basic knowledge of the language, culture, and business environment in mainland China could leverage that knowledge in their investments and make China work for them in a way that companies from further afield often struggled to. As foreign companies have gained familiarity with investment procedures, hiring procedures, and local supply chains, China has gained a degree of flexibility on pricing. For example, as wages have risen in Suzhou, a city bordering Shanghai that hosts the largest concentration of Taiwanese businesses outside of Taiwan, investors have turned to Huai'an, a city of 5 million people 250 miles to the north, where disposable income levels are still only two-thirds of what's seen in Suzhou. In 2012, utilized foreign investment in Huai'an grew 31.7 percent with exports up 86 percent, the same year Suzhou's export growth slowed from 9.2 percent to 4.5 percent. Both cities are in the same province, enjoy similar regulatory benefits, and companies can even use the same port to ship their goods, which gives the cities a clear advantage over cheaper areas further afield.

This advantage is even more pronounced for domestic Chinese companies, which are less familiar with foreign business practices and have difficulties repatriating earnings due to China's currency controls. Private businesses in Zhejiang Province have already developed supply chains stretching into bordering Anhui and Jiangxi, just as Guangdong factories are making investments in Hunan and Guangxi. Transferring capacity to Southeast Asia or Africa would add several layers of institutional barriers to companies that are already working on thin margins.

China's long experience with infrastructure development and the recent completion of some major additions to the country's rail and highway systems are making some regions more viable than they were before. Despite being further from ports, shipping costs remain generally low in inland China. In 2012, the cost of shipping a container from Wuhan, a rising inland city on the Yangzi, to Los Angeles, was USD 2,000, while the price from Kuala Lumpur was USD 2,543 and from Bangkok it was USD 3,849.[15] Exporting cities off major water routes, such as Zhengzhou, Shenyang, and Xi'an, usually have access to better road systems than is typical in developing countries and have much better access to aviation infrastructure.

None of these factors though compares to the potential gains China could see from rising consumption. The growth of China's consuming class will bring more sales to companies that can produce low-cost products oriented toward the specific features of the Chinese market. Thousands of Chinese factories are ready to take up the challenge.

Financing Consumption

If there's one thing that most economists agree on about China, it is that the country needs to consume more. China's investment share of GDP has risen remarkably over the past decade, running for several years in excess of 50 percent. The fear is that all of this money is going into producing more goods for a weak consumer market and shrinking global markets, particularly after the 2007 global economic crisis when consumption from the US and the EU dropped dramatically.[16]

While economists are in broad agreement that China overinvests and underconsumes, there are substantial disagreements about why China invests as much as it does, as well as the current and potential consequences of this overinvestment.

Rising investment levels are a natural consequence of poverty alleviation. Thirty years ago, almost 800 million people in China were living under the global poverty line, struggling to buy the food and clothes they needed to survive. As the country developed, these people gradually earned more money, so they had something left after spending on the bare essentials—money to invest in housing, education, and new business, or just to put in the bank where it could collect interest from loans to other businesses. Experience from other developing countries, as well as China's own spending habits, shows that this period of increased savings ends when a household's annual income passes the USD 10,000 marker. By this measure, just over 25 percent of China's population is part of its "consuming class," and the number is quickly growing.[17]

The growth of consumer spending in China has, without question, been remarkable over the past few years. Since 2011, China has been the fastest growing consumer market in the world, and it is rapidly catching up with the US in terms of gross spending power. In 2009, China surpassed America as the world's largest automobile market. In 2012, the country surpassed America as the world's largest market for luxury goods. In 2013, it became the world's biggest smartphone market. As of 2013, China had surpassed Japan as the second biggest consumer in the world.[18]

The growth of China's consumer market is an unambiguous good for Chinese companies, and the greater Asian supply chain overall. More local consumption means that factories are closer to their final customers and can better experiment with new products and innovations. The introduction of new consumer groups could lead to the development of new products. It also gives workers the opportunity to develop experience in marketing and build the sort of soft skills necessary to develop a global business.

It is important to note that the Great Migration is so large that wealth accumulation in coastal China does not preclude a low-cost manufacturing base elsewhere in China. China's specialization in one area of the global supply chain—low-cost process manufacturing—was a consequence of its poverty and the labor-dependent structure of its development policy, but China is large enough that it can develop comparative advantages *within the country* just as well as it can develop comparative advantages with other countries. The return of migrant workers to Zhengzhou and Chongqing indicate that to some extent this process is already taking place.

This story has one weakness. China's dominance of the low end of the supply chain is stable. Even if other countries gain some benefits from coastal manufacturers exiting the low-cost part of the market, most capacity will be transferred to inland manufacturers, who continue to benefit from China's migrant workforce. For coastal manufacturers, however, the move up the supply chain is far from certain. China's financial sector remains severely underdeveloped, making it difficult for entrepreneurs to access capital, and China's weak intellectual property rights and uncertain regulatory environment can undercut the effectiveness of what little capital investment is possible. It remains to be seen how the government will address these problems. In the meantime, entrepreneurs are making do.

Shanzhai

China currently produces around 70 percent of the world's mobile phones.[19] Most of these are produced in giant outsourcing factories, like the iPhone factory run by Taiwan's Hon Hai Precision Industries (Foxconn) outside Zhengzhou. Others are locally developed high-tech phones like the Xiaomi, developed with venture capital funding and clever monetization tactics. In 2009, around a quarter of all phones produced in China were *shanzhai*, phones developed, engineered, and constructed in China to be produced quickly, sold cheaply, and marketed in a legal gray area in one of the most hotly contested intellectual property fields in the world.[20]

The term *shanzhai* literally means "mountain fortress," a reference to the hideouts of bandits in popular Chinese adventure stories. It took on its modern usage in the mid-2000s, when a host of Chinese companies were entering consumer electronics markets with goods that looked suspiciously like name-brand products but with a much lower price and somewhat lower quality. For emerging market consumers they were game changers. Sure, a shanzhai iPad made with cheaper parts running the Android operating system isn't the same thing as an Apple iPad, but, for USD 150, it's much more affordable.

The shanzhai market is not strictly—not even mostly—fakes. As the market for shanzhai phones developed, firms discovered that customers cared more about price and quality than the fake brand logo that left the company vulnerable to trademark lawyers. Shanzhai eventually took on another meaning: disruptive price innovation—that is, phones produced to "good enough" standards for dramatically lower costs.

The shanzhai phenomenon in many ways exemplifies China's development story at its best, and provides a glimpse at how China is moving up the value chain. The story goes like this: several large foreign investors enter the market, bringing with them basic technology and expertise that they aim to match with China's low-cost workforce. Chinese workers, either working for the company or suppliers, gain experience and find areas of the supply chain with low cost of entry. New companies are formed, training more workers and allowing companies to accumulate capital through retained earnings. This leads to further competition at the bottom that pushes companies to upgrade to higher-value-added goods or face diminishing margins. This story continues until the cost of entry—both in terms of rising wages and fixed capital costs—exceeds the expected returns.

This story has been repeated with some variation in a number of different sectors, including sectors that continue to feature a heavy state involvement. In thirty years, China has gone from soliciting foreign investment in its infrastructure sector in return for natural resources, to offering infrastructure investment to Africa in return for natural resources. In the highly politicized world of property development, a growing number of private developers have managed to become national brands by investing the owner's wealth and retained earnings into buildings that are built faster or with more attention to consumer demand than their state-supported counterparts.

The weakness of the shanzhai model is a perpetual shortage of capital and the constant threat of government interference, both of which present a challenge to companies attempting to upgrade from a low-margin commodities producer to a higher-value-added brand-name producer. Companies need capital to invest in research, development, and marketing, which isn't forthcoming from the state-owned banking sector. They also need to be sure that the rules of the game aren't going to change after they've made their investments, and that their path to riches would stand up to scrutiny if the owners became one of China's superrich.

• • •

Probably the most famous shanzhai company to try to make it big is BYD, the part-time battery, part-time automotive company that grabbed media headlines in 2008 with a USD 230 million investment from Warren Buffett.

At that time, BYD's development process was straight out of the shanzhai playbook. In an interview with *Caixin* magazine, Li Xuelin, an auto mechanic at BYD, described being called outside along with a half dozen of his colleagues to look at his boss's shiny new Mercedes Benz S300. Wang Chuanfu, BYD's CEO, drives up, gets out of his car, and then promptly orders the engineers to take the car apart to see how it works.

At first, no one moves, so Wang takes out his key and gouges the paint job. "Now you can start," he says.[21]

The company's business model was simple: reverse-engineer outside technology to see how it is made, make it cheaper using workers instead of machines, sell. In the early stages of the company's career, this sort of development process was incredibly effective. Within six years of putting out its first car, BYD produced the best-selling compact car in China—the 2009 F3.[22] The problem was that the car was similar enough to a Toyota Corolla that it could use spare parts produced for the Japanese car, and some dealerships went so far as offering to switch the logos.[23] It was the type of development process that can get a company dragged to court. Sanyo and Sony, both sued BYD—and lost—after the company admitted to reverse-engineering its competitors' batteries to learn the technology. The company has been involved in a long drawn-out legal battle with Foxconn for theft of trade secrets, with no end in sight.[24]

But BYD's innovation isn't in technology; it's in cost. BYD's insight in the battery market was that at a certain price-point, it paid off to replace precision machinery with masses of human labor. In 2013, the company employed 180,000 people, approximately the same number of people as Ford, which sells five times as many automobiles. The majority of these are production line workers, who, despite a higher rate of error—20 to 30 percent in the company's battery factories compared to about 5 percent in Japanese factories—can produce the same content at a substantial discount to mechanized factories abroad. BYD's F3 runs at half the price of the Corolla, while its batteries run at 30 percent off competitor's prices.[25] In the battery sector, this was the key selling point. BYD was able to dominate the market by approximating the quality of its competitors at dramatically lower prices. In the engineering-intensive automotive sector, things have been much more difficult. After an initial honeymoon period, the F3 fell to forty-ninth in the sales charts by 2012 as consumers reported an array of quality issues with the company's homegrown technology.[26]

The company has since stepped back from some of the more grandiose promises that its founder made about the company's future, including the claim that it would surpass Toyota by 2025, instead targeting incremental quality improvements in order to meet "foreign-OEM brand quality"—the quality of a contractor for a foreign company.[27] This has included more investment in machinery to meet customer-safety demands, and research and development, including efforts to differentiate their product's appearance in preparation for selling the car abroad where intellectual property rules are stricter.

While BYD fizzled out, other Chinese car companies have found success attacking the problem from different angles. Great Wall, China's second largest automaker by sales, once followed the shanzhai model of learning by replicating, which led to them being successfully sued by Fiat in 2006 to stop the export of the Great Wall Peri, which looked almost identical to the Fiat Panda, to Europe.[28] But the company was, in the meantime, building its own capabilities. Within a few years, the company not only had its own look, but also its own platform—every piece of its new subcompact and compact offerings are built to operate with the powertrain system that Great Wall designed in-house.[29] Geely, which produces China's best-selling domestic sedan, bought Drivetrain Systems International in 2009 and Volvo in 2010, bringing in not only technology but expertise to help them develop their products.[30]

It took both of these companies more than ten years to develop the capabilities to produce globally competitive vehicles. A lot of that time was spent copying and cost cutting, and building up experience and human capital.

The companies also had to save a lot of money in case the banks decided not to support them.

Does China Support Its Export Sector?

China's rise as an exporting power has been one of the defining stories of globalization. Hundreds of millions of poor Chinese have seen drastic improvements in their wages and their living conditions, just as global businesses have found ways to cut costs and introduce new product lines that decades ago would have been unaffordable to the average consumer. It has also been one of the most disruptive aspects of globalization, with the United States, Europe, and much of Latin America de-industrializing, as countries have found it easier to specialize in services or commodity extraction rather than try to beat the Chinese manufacturing Goliath.[31] Low-skilled workers who once had access to well-paid manufacturing jobs suddenly found themselves competing with hundreds of millions of people desperately fighting their way out of poverty.

If China is playing by the rules of free trade, then this is fine. Competition is how economies grow—by forcing businesses and workers to find their comparative advantage and encouraging companies to develop new products, new business methods, and new skills that allow them to solidify their competitive advantage. If China builds a world-beating textile sector, it makes the world a richer place, and creates more opportunities for people in other countries to either move up the value chain or enter other sectors. But if China isn't playing by the rules of free trade, then China's rise as an exporting power is more problematic. It implies that while China has disrupted the global economy, the businesses it has created are not sustainable and could easily disappear as soon as the government can no longer afford to subsidize the companies in question.

All countries, to some extent, support particular industries and particular companies. Every time a government decides to build a road instead of a rail line, it is supporting automotive manufacturers at the expense of rail manufacturers. Utilities, if not directly owned by the government, often enjoy an implicit government guarantee. Patent laws are generally seen as an acceptable way for the government to manipulate the market to reward innovation. But in China, the government not only owns many of the largest companies in the country, it also owns the banks, sets the exchange rate, and has the means to cheaply transfer land to preferred companies. The Chinese government's impact on its economy is enormous, and it is hard to argue that it hasn't had some effect on the country's exporting companies.

China's industrial policy is an easy target for WTO disputes. However, making the case that China's government actually supports its exporters on a large scale is more difficult than it might seem at first glance.

One common mistake made when discussing China's export sector is assuming that China's government supports exporters because exporters are state owned. Nothing is further from reality. The largest share of China's exports is produced by foreign-owned enterprises, many of them from the same countries that are protesting China's unfair business practices. In 2015 foreign-owned enterprises accounted for 44.2 percent of China's foreign trade, while privately-owned enterprises accounted for one-third of total foreign trade. State-owned enterprises account for a mere 18 percent of China's total exports, mostly in areas linked to China's bubbly construction industry, such as steel production and heavy machinery.[32]

While SOEs are not major exporters, they have consistently accounted for more than 80 percent of total borrowing from China's big four state-owned banks.[33] As discussed above, this is the reason why China has to maintain a closed capital account, preventing capital from entering or exiting the country, and by extension a fixed currency rate. SOEs are particularly bad borrowers, investing in projects that only see a return years down the line. If a significant amount of money were to go abroad, the banks would be threatened with a financial crisis. Export competitiveness has nothing to do with it.

In fact, the common complaint from foreign politicians that China undervalues its exchange rate is now rarely heard from the business community. An Economist Intelligence Unit survey found that the majority of foreign investors expected no impact on China's currency if it were to open the capital account, while Chinese investors were evenly split as to whether opening the capital account would cause the value of the RMB to decline (due to currency outflow) or increase (due to the country's trade surplus).[34] As China's economy has slowed over the past five years, consensus has quickly shifted to the RMB having been overvalued, not undervalued.

If China's closed capital account is not repressing the exchange rate, then it is easy to argue that capital controls are more harmful to exporting companies than helpful. Private-sector exporters face substantial problems accessing capital, are forced to invoice in a foreign currency, and can have difficulties repatriating money earned abroad. A lack of financial competition both increases the cost of funding and, for those who operate through retained earnings, decreases the return on savings.

Even if we make the assumption that China's currency is undervalued, it is unlikely that a countervailing tariff—the most often recommended solution—would have any effect on the decision making of Chinese political leaders. China controls its capital account and its exchange rate as a way to manage the risk associated with transferring capital from private enterprises, which are heavily involved in exporting sectors, to SOEs. Threatening exporters, which are overwhelmingly foreign and private enterprises, is merely increasing the damage that China is itself imposing.

There are very few good reasons for China's government to care about the export sector. While the Great Migration has had an outsized impact on world trade, its role in China's economy has been more diffuse. According to most estimates, the tradable sector accounts for somewhere in the realm of 10 to 20 percent of GDP, while housing and related industries account for as much as a third of GDP.[35] If foreign countries want China to allow the market to decide the value of its currency, they need to advocate for China to reform its state sector, open up its capital account, and meet its World Trade Organization (WTO) commitments to allow full foreign access to its financial services sector. These recommendations also have the advantage of being good for China.

The Value of Subsidies

The Chinese government does regularly support particular domestic private industries with tax incentives, discounted land sales, or access to government contracts or business deals with SOEs. The industries most often targeted are those necessary to offset some of the effects of the Great Migration: infrastructure, power production, real estate, and resource extraction. These subsidies have often been harmful to companies outside China, though they have often been equally detrimental to companies inside China.

Perhaps the best-known case of China's industrial policy at work involves China's support for its solar sector. As anyone who has traveled to China knows all too well, the country is choked in smog. The majority of the country's power and heating is produced by coal, and as the country's cities and industries have gotten larger, they have demanded more power to support their growth.[36] China looked for a solution to both its energy and its environment problems, and found it in the growing green-tech field.

Manufacturing solar panels is in many ways an ideal business for China. It is labor intensive, requiring some technical knowledge, but not as much as needed to produce the components that actually produce the power. It also meets a domestic demand—it's a source of clean energy, and one that can easily be applied in areas that are off the grid where a portion of the country's poor still live. Seeing this, China's central government began allowing local governments to support solar panel manufacturers through tax breaks, subsidized land sales, and targeted purchasing.

Between 2006 and 2012, global capacity for solar panel production increased tenfold, with China and Taiwan accounting for more than 70 percent of total output.[37] The rapid growth in production capacity led to a global price war that famously undid Solyndra, a California-based company that had received USD 536 million from the US government, as well as Suntech, China's largest solar-panel manufacturer.[38]

The US and the EU would both successfully bring antidumping complaints against China, which was necessary to protect those areas' own domestic industry. Ironically, however, it would increase the cost of solar panels for domestic consumption at the same time that the governments were subsidizing solar panel purchases. By 2013, China's solar sector was drastically consolidating in boom areas along the coast—particularly Jiangsu, which was at one point the center of China's solar industry—while the sector was continuing to expand in internal areas that were more eager to subsidize the expansion of industrial capacity in their regions.[39] China was still supporting solar installations, and unruly local governments would push solar farms to buy from local factories in order to encourage local employment and investment. At the end of that year, half of China's 600 cities had at least one solar panel factory, selling panels at a 60 percent discount to the price in 2010.[40]

Accepting the premise that China's strength in export manufacturing is dependent on government subsides requires us to ignore everything we know about how markets work. Governments "picking winners" isn't just a problem because decisions could go wrong and end up wasting taxpayer money. Subsidies distort markets, they encourage companies to create products that people don't want, and they undermine a company's ability to use price signals to determine how much return there will be on an investment. Subsidies can bring down the price of a product, but they cannot create a sustainable industry.

China's position in the global manufacturing supply chain remains strong. For countries competing with China, this can increase the lure of a national industrial policy and state subsidies to preferred industries. But industrial policy isn't how China grew into a major manufacturing power. China became a global manufacturing power because hundreds of millions of people came to China's cities looking for ways to support themselves, and because China implemented policies making it easier for them to do so. By comparison, China's industrial policy is a costly distraction.

6

China After the Great Migration

IN LATE 2009, a minor Chinese city in the middle of the Gobi Desert caught the attention of the international press and international investors. For more than five years, Ordos, a city of 2 million people at the center of China's coal belt had been constructing a major new city district that was supposed to house 300,000 people. When journalists first visited it, the Kangbashi New Area was found to be mostly empty, with official figures showing only 30,000 people living in the district by 2010.[1]

Ordos had all the makings of a great story: the visuals of large empty streets with brand-new buildings, a parable about the folly of state planning, and actionable implications for investors. The problem was that the story was specific to Ordos, a town whose largest investors were state-owned mining companies, and which was making money hand over fist from the growth in coal demand over the previous decade.[2] The city's experience was worlds away from the diversified economies of Shanghai and Beijing or the exporting cities along China's southern coast. In order for the story to be relevant, Ordos couldn't just be a single Potemkin village, it had to be a symbol for how a crisis was brewing in the nation's real estate sector.

In the following months, a number of other "ghost towns" were found. In 2010, one research company published satellite photographs of Zhengdong New District, a business district in the east of Zhengzhou (the capital of Henan Province) that had been under development since 2003.[3] The photograph showed mostly empty streets among mostly completed buildings. The company called it the "largest ghost town in China." Others were discovered in obscure areas of the country, seeming to show a national trend of wasting money on grand real estate projects, paying no heed to market demand.

Ordos and Zhengdong were developed along the same lines, with long-term planning and state incentives going toward promoting residential real estate construction and private and state-owned enterprise (SOE) investment. The consequences of these two building programs, though, could not be any more different. Real estate prices would plummet in the Ordos Kangbashi New District, which both proved the skeptics right and made the city slightly less ghostly. As of 2013, Kangbashi was home to around 100,000 people, or about one-third of its total capacity.[4] Over 1 million people live in Zhengdong New District; prices rose 20 percent in the first half of 2013, and more people are moving in every day.[5]

Between 2003 and 2010, China went through the biggest construction boom of modern times, contributing to the development of industries ranging from steel mills and concrete factories to Zambian copper mines and Australian iron ore companies. At its peak, as much as a third of China's economy was tied up in construction-related business. And then the construction boom slowed to a standstill, taking a fair amount of Chinese growth with it. The housing boom and the slowdown that followed contributed to an aggressive debate over the sustainability of China's growth story. In 2011, up to 50 percent of China's GDP came from investment, the majority of it going into housing and related industries. To many pundits, this sounded like lunacy. Investment at that level would quickly run into diminishing returns, and there was good reason to believe that China's Communist government didn't know how to let the market push companies into bankruptcy. Instead, state-owned banks would subsidize companies until the country faced a financial crisis.[6]

If you were to spend the next five years in Ordos, this argument would seem pretty convincing. Between 2006 and 2010, Ordos was a boomtown, seeing an average of 23 percent GDP growth a year on the back of the city's growing coal industry.[7] Then, in 2012 and 2013, nearly half of the city's coal mines were closed down due to declining steel demand, with another 20 to 30 percent not operating at full capacity. Real estate prices plummeted.[8] Between 2011 and 2014, service sector growth in Ordos fell by almost two-thirds from 13.2 percent to 5.1 percent. In 2014, completed real estate construction area was 60.5 percent smaller than the year before. The companies that had invested in housing would have to face smaller profits or losses on their investments. The thousands of people who had been involved in building that housing would have to find jobs elsewhere.[9]

If you spent five years watching Zhengzhou, the situation would look quite a bit different. Zhengzhou is the capital of a province of roughly 100 million people, which had, for a decade, been the largest source of migrant workers in the country. The Zhengdong New District was part of a multipronged strategy to bring migrant workers back to the province, both to help develop the local economy and to take urbanization pressure off coastal towns. The completion of the Zhengdong New District coincided with the opening of two major high-speed rail lines through the city, as well as several additional highways and freight lines. A major investment from Foxconn created an immediate demand for 300,000-plus workers and increased the city's visibility among contract manufacturers. This strategy, which had previously been successfully executed in Chengdu and Chongqing, helped transform Zhengzhou from an economically backward region that people wanted to leave to a place where people would plausibly want to return to. Since 2012, migrants have flooded the city, attracted by plentiful jobs and rising wages. There are plans to further expand development in the southeastern suburbs that have been prominently supported by Foxconn. Zhengzhou is on track to become one of the largest cities in China by 2020, with plans to integrate an additional 6 million rural dwellers into the urban area.[10] Between 2011 and 2014, service sector GDP growth was more than 8.5 percent a year. In 2014, completed housing area expanded by 27.9 percent. The population of the Zhengdong New District more than doubled.

For many analysts, Zhengzhou's lesson for the broader economy was clear. China was expecting another 300 million people to move to cities over the next two decades, and China's housing stock was still too small to meet the demand. There was clearly waste in the economy, but there was also clearly demand. China still had the capacity to muddle through.[11]

Other cities in China have followed a pattern roughly analogous to Zhengzhou and Ordos. The success of Zhengdong and other inland manufacturing centers such as Chongqing and Chengdu encouraged several other provinces to announce major urbanization plans for their capital cities.[12] In most cases though, the migrants simply didn't appear, leaving a city with a giant housing stock that would take years to reach capacity. On the other side, developed cities with large numbers of migrants have barely slowed at all. The fundamentals of China's economy continued to be strong, but poor fiscal incentives encouraged China to systematically misinvest capital, taking money away from cities like Shanghai, Beijing, and Guangzhou where there was a large demand for housing and pushing it toward inland regions where there was little.

Here again we see the major lesson from the Great Migration: *the efficiency of capital in China is heavily dependent on the mobilization of labor.* Without the immense economic gains from labor migration, capital in China is simply not very efficient.

The different performance of Ordos and Zhengzhou had its basis in the 1994 fiscal reform. As discussed in previous chapters, the 1994 fiscal reform created a number of incentives to encourage urbanization. After the reform, cities were heavily dependent on turnover taxes, infrastructure fees, and land expropriation for income, which helped align local government interests with the interests of migrants. For cities that benefited from the Great Migration, these incentives to urbanize made an important contribution to growth—migrants found places to live and places to work in dense urban centers where they could maximize their contribution to the economy. Though the income from land expropriation encouraged more urban sprawl than was economically efficient, the fact was that these places needed a lot more housing if they were going to absorb anywhere near the number of people who wanted to move there.

For regions that were losing workers to the Great Migration, the situation was different. There was some demand for housing to replace the old Maoist-era housing stock, and there was some demand for housing to accommodate local rural dwellers who wanted to move to a city closer to home, but the demand was much more modest. The fiscal incentives for urbanization, though, were the same everywhere.

It's worth spending some time looking at just how bad this moral hazard was, as it would affect much more than just the property market. After the 1994 fiscal reform package, the central government took a larger share of tax revenues, while local governments took a larger share of expenditures. As of 2010, local governments were responsible for 70 percent of government expenditures but only received 50 percent of revenues. This strengthened the central government's fiscal position, but forced local governments, which were not legally allowed to take on debt, to find other means of financing. The main mechanism they found was land expropriation, which, in 2011, accounted for upward of 30 percent of local government revenues in most Chinese prefectures, roughly RMB 3 trillion (USD 500 billion).[13]

This is, needless to say, a poor way to manage a government budget. The most obvious consequence of this system has been the rampant abuse of people's rights. In 2004, China's Ministry of Land and Resources found that 70 percent of all development zones across the country had illegally expropriated land.[14] In 2010, one anonymous online journalist mapped eighty-five cases of land expropriation with different symbols for cases with mass protests, self-immolation, or murder.[15]

Even if we set aside the ethical issues for a moment, the system opened up a number of avenues for abuse of the budgeting process. In order to get around the bar on local government borrowing, governments would incorporate small companies, known as local government financing vehicles, in order to take on debt to develop infrastructure or various other one-off projects. In order to convince banks—which were monitored by the more fiscally conservative central government—to lend to these companies, local governments would back their borrowing with the expected revenues from future land sales. As of 2013, predicted future revenues from land sales backed approximately half of new local government borrowing.[16] In other words, the ability of local governments to finance their debt would be dependent on the strength of the local property market.

China still has tools at its disposal that would allow it to muddle through these problems, but there is no good reason for Chinese people to suffer through this sort of mismanagement. Over the next decade, China has the opportunity to reform the economy to put the country's fiscal system on an even footing, but they are running out of time. A country that is growing at 10 percent a year can outgrow most fiscal problems, but as the country's demographics turn and economic growth slows, the government has less of a cushion to make mistakes. By the middle of the next decade, they might have no cushion at all.

The recent economic crisis should be a wake-up call. In order to prevent a hard landing, China needs to finish the reforms that it started more than thirty years ago. That means introducing full rural land rights, privatizing SOEs, ending the hukou system, and most importantly making sure that local governments have legitimate means to pay for legitimate costs. Absent these reforms, growth in China could quickly stagnate as debt and demographics take their revenge.

The Great Migration: The Next Ten Years

In March 2014, China introduced its much-awaited new urbanization plan—in fact, its first urbanization plan ever. While urbanization had been a backdrop for China's economic growth story for more than two decades, this was the first time China's government had made an explicit effort to coordinate population movements across provinces.[17]

The announcement came after a year of debating and several delays and compromises. The plan eventually set a headline urbanization target of 60 percent of China's population by 2020, up from 54 percent in 2013, roughly amounting to an additional 100 million people living in urban areas. Plans floated the previous year suggested that the government aimed to hit a more ambitious target of 70 percent urbanization by 2025.[18]

Alongside the government's plan to add 100 million people to China's urban population, the central government aims to put an additional 140 million people on local hukou lists, increasing payouts for social services by over 20 percent.[19] The plan also calls for "strict control of new urban construction land," drawing attention to the government's desire to maintain arable land use along China's grain belt, and protect water resources in the west of the country. This includes calling for stricter restrictions on what land is available for expropriation, and what processes local governments have to go through to expropriate the land.

Announcing plans to expand social services coverage and cut taxes is one thing, finding the money to pay for it is another. The new urbanization plan does not discuss how the government intends to increase revenue or decrease the costs associated with social services and urban construction. The only indication of how the government aims to reduce expenses is that it is encouraging urbanization in cheaper inland regions and smaller cities where the cost of living and social service benefits are lower, and by spreading local hukou registrations over ten to fifteen years—over 200 million people will not be registered by 2020. The plan, for example, mentions several times that migrants should be directed toward central and western China, both to new urban clusters and to various small- and medium-size cities outside of major industrial centers. Beijing, Tianjin, the Pearl River Delta (PRD) and the Yangzi River Delta (YRD) meanwhile are all mentioned as places where migration should be discouraged, and are given more lenience for restricting hukou transfers.

The plan does not specify why Beijing, Tianjin, the PRD, and the YRD deserve this special status, other than noting that they contain 18 percent of China's population on less than 3 percent of the country's land mass. There are certainly some legitimate reasons for wanting to discourage urbanization in these areas. Beijing and Tianjin are both facing severe water shortages, and though those shortages are mainly due to agricultural and industrial use and accentuated by mispricing, development in Beijing is still less sustainable than it is in the south of the country. Other complaints have less merit to them. In Shanghai, for example, the largest complaint about migrants is the inability to cover them on the city's pension system. In reality, Shanghai is the fastest-aging city in the country, meaning more migrant workers would only improve the sustainability of its pension system.[20]

Whether or not the concerns are reasonable, the problem is that migration patterns are subject to market demand, while government planning is not. The problem in Ordos did not stem from a lack of government support; it came from a collapse in coal demand. An effective migration policy needs to be responsive to changes in the market. Otherwise, the consequences are not just wasted investments, but also higher costs and less competitiveness for cities that the market might otherwise have rewarded.

The urbanization plan announced in 2014 is a good first step toward resolving some of the problems that have developed in the wake of the Great Migration. China's government is right to want to expand social services coverage for migrants, and it is right to want to spread the positive impact of the Great Migration to inland regions, where millions of people still suffer from extreme poverty. But the power of the Great Migration has been its use of markets, and it is that effective use of markets that China needs if it is going to finish its economic transition.

Agriculture

In the more than thirty-five years since China first began experimenting with rural land rights, the Chinese countryside has been transformed beyond recognition. In 1978, China was eager to keep rural dwellers on the land where they were, from the government's perspective, self-sufficient or, from their own perspective, impoverished. Even as the government introduced land rights that allowed rural dwellers to build wealth in the countryside, there was little interest in letting people come to the cities where they would disrupt strictly controlled labor markets. Three decades later, the government's biggest interest is moving people off the land, consolidating household farms into industrial farms, and claiming rural land on the outskirts of cities for urbanization. Today rural dwellers fight to protect their land rights; forty years ago they didn't have any.

China will make its last step toward full land rights when it allows individuals to sell, purchase, and rent land without the involvement of village political leaders. Those rights may be coming quite soon. While China's current land-rights system has been profitable to local governments, it has been one of the leading sources of unrest and corruption in the country, and it has undercut the modernization of the country's agriculture system. While China's agricultural output has increased dramatically over the past decades, it remains both labor intensive and water intensive, and is often not the best use of China's sparse land resources.[21] The transition to a market-based land-rights system is important not only as an incentive for investment in agricultural machinery, agricultural technology, and modern irrigation systems, but also because there is currently only a marginal ability to price the value of land. This makes it difficult to know where cities should restrict sprawl or where farming would be the most efficient use of land.

China will not be able to make this transition as long as it maintains its current food security policy. Since the Maoist era, China's government has demanded that 95 percent of all domestic grain consumption be produced locally.[22] This policy was originally seen as a way for the country to maintain its independence in the Cold War, but it has maintained consistent political support due to the memory of the Great Leap Forward. During the 1980s, when grain output grew 50 percent, China could exceed its target with land left over to spare for the cultivation of fruits and vegetables. Since the mid-2000s though, China has only maintained self-sufficiency by importing other products that compete for planting area, particularly oil seeds such as soybeans and rapeseed where China accounts for more than half of total world imports.[23] China requires provinces to maintain a steady area of land under cultivation, making up for any land converted to residential or industrial use by expanding cultivation elsewhere. As long as this policy remains in place, rural land rights will only be partial land rights—owners will have the right to benefit from the cultivation of the land, but not the right to convert cultivated land to other productive uses.

China's first rural land-trading system, which was introduced in 2008 in Chongqing and Chengdu, was developed as a workaround for this policy. The program operates like a carbon-trading system. The government awards villagers credits, known as *dipiao* or "land tickets," for transferring a portion of rural land over to agricultural cultivation. This could be done by tearing down a factory on the land or, more often, by condensing residential portions of villages into higher density buildings. Villagers can then sell these tickets to developers who need a *dipiao* to transfer rural land on the outskirts of cities to urban building land.

While this program has successfully helped distribute some of the gains from urbanization to rural population, it is not a system of land rights. Roughly 85 percent of the developer's payment goes to the holder of the *dipiao*, rather than to the government or the people losing their land. Villagers, in other words, are being paid for the efficient use of rural construction land, not for the loss of the rights associated with land ownership. Sales are also still mostly on a collective basis, leaving the program wide open to abuses. Nonetheless, the reports so far have been mostly positive, with villages and villagers using the money to upgrade village housing and other infrastructure.[24]

A more promising program was introduced in Anhui Province in November 2013. The trial program, which encompasses twenty counties, allows villagers to sell noncultivated land to private developers or private citizens for building factories, vacation homes, or other commercial products. While the scale of this program is fairly small, it is the first case of a Chinese government voluntarily giving up its monopoly power over the sale of rural land. As an extension of the plan, the province is looking at consolidating rural villages into townships, so villagers would have better access to infrastructure and public services, while profiting off the industrial use of their land.[25] Similar to the program in Chongqing and Chengdu, condensing villages into townships would also allow more land to be cultivated and land to be expropriated at the edge of cities.

The central government has also been developing a system to allow the trade of use-rights for agricultural land. The program was first announced in 2008, with an initial rollout in fifty counties. Villagers in these counties received registration documents for their agricultural land that they could rent or sell to others in the village or on a centralized exchange in Chengdu. The program has been successful enough that, in December 2013, the government announced that it planned to extend coverage to the entire nation by 2018.[26]

It is unclear how this reform will affect China's hukou regulations. China's hukou system and its land-rights system developed together to the extent that, in terms of rights and privileges, there is no advantage to a rural hukou other than land holdings. Allowing rural hukou holders to sell their land implies de facto permission for them to migrate, but only as second-class citizens without the services and social safety net given to urban hukou holders.

While both these programs are improvements over the current system, China still needs to find a way to disintermediate the government from the process of rural-urban land conversion and the conversion of rural construction land to rural cultivation land. The easiest and most environmentally friendly way to do this would be to end the policy of maintaining self-sufficiency in grain.

Relative to its population, China is extremely poor in agricultural resources, with 0.09 hectares of cultivated land per capita, compared to a global average of 0.22 hectares and an Organisation for Economic Co-Operation and Development (OECD) average of 0.35 hectares. The problem is made much worse by poor water resources. Because of a lack of irrigation systems, one ton of grain requires approximately 30 percent more water to produce in China than elsewhere.[27] Rainfall is highly variable per year and mostly centered in

the south of the country, some ways away from the more agriculturally productive North China Plain. China's self-sufficiency policy has a far-reaching
impact on global markets, creating exaggerated demand for Brazilian and US
soy, while discouraging imports of low-cost rice from Thailand.[28]

Without the stringent rules regarding how much land must remain
cultivated in each province, China could unify the markets for cultivated,
uncultivated, and urban land into a simple land-rights system, and allow
the market to determine the most efficient use of a plot of land. This would
allow China to transfer cultivation to more productive regions with sustainable water resources or, ideally, to foreign countries that don't face the same
environmental constraints that China does.

In order to do this though, China needs to reform local government
finances so they no longer have to make money off of land expropriation.
Luckily, it may be forced to do that anyway.

Fiscal Reforms

In 2008, China's government finances took an abrupt turn for the worse. As
part of the government stimulus package announced that year, the central
government lifted restrictions on bank lending, leading to a 129 percent increase in total loans to RMB 9.6 trillion (USD 1.6 trillion). Much of this went
to local governments, which by 2010 had racked up RMB 10.7 trillion in debt,
according to an official government audit. By 2013, this figure had risen to
RMB 17.9 trillion, indicating that, despite its best efforts, the government
was having trouble reining in lending.[29]

Absent strict government controls, there are very few reasons for banks to
stop lending to local governments and even fewer reasons for local governments to stop borrowing from banks. China's fiscal system and its financial
system are both structured in order to centralize risk in the treasury. Local
governments are not legally allowed to issue bonds, giving them limited means
of fundraising for special projects besides land sales, central government transfers, or borrowing from state-owned banks through SOEs. This allows China
to avoid the question of what would happen if one of its local governments
defaults, but makes the consequences of local government overreach an issue
of national importance.

It has been difficult for the government to clamp down on local government borrowing, in part because it is difficult to monitor. Just under half of all borrowing is channeled through off-balance-sheet local government finance vehicles (LGFVs). These local-government-owned SOEs can both raise money from state-owned banks—often using government land banks as collateral—and issue bonds on the domestic market (*chengtou* bonds). This is technically not local government debt, and has not historically been reported as such. These SOEs are expected to pay back any borrowing, though sometimes over a long time horizon. Historically, less than 20 percent of explicitly guaranteed debt and less than 15 percent of implicitly guaranteed debt has had to be covered by local governments. The bankruptcy rate is likely to be much higher for the recent surge of lending, though it is unclear how much higher.

The lending side is just as opaque as the borrowing side. When the central government tried to rein in bank lending following the completion of the stimulus program, banks pushed loans off balance sheet, funneling money through various trust companies, leasing firms, and wealth management products that are spun off of a bank's assets. Between 2010 and 2013, the share of local government debt made up by bank loans fell from 75 percent to only half. Issuance of *chengtou* bonds, on the other hand, expanded by 148 percent in 2012, with the value of bonds outstanding expanding by ten times since 2008.[30]

Because of the opacity surrounding how the money is raised, the risk could be either greater or smaller than the headline numbers suggest. Though the RMB 17.9 trillion figure has been widely used as a best estimate for the amount of debt held by local governments, any number of LGFVs could have fallen through the cracks. On the other side, LGFVs and local government–supported SOEs could show better repayment levels than critics fear. The government is trying to distance the banking sector from the crisis. State-owned banks are now forbidden from acting as guarantors for *chengtou* bonds, and the central government requires bankers to call the head office before purchasing these bonds.[31] If the government is able to push the damage from LGFV bankruptcies onto speculators, it could potentially reduce the larger harm to government finances, as it did during the Guangdong International Trust and Investment Corporation (GITIC) crisis discussed in Chapter 2.

Whether or not this is an immediate risk to the stability of China, it is quite clearly both a long-term risk to government finances and a horrible way to run a country. The central government is taking on all financial risk with very little control over how assets are spent. There is little in the way of feedback on government funding priorities, either through market-set lending rates at banks or through the ballot box. Meanwhile, Chinese households are forced to pay for spending through negative real interest rates or the loss of their land through expropriation.

The central government has taken two tacks on fiscal reforms. There have been some early experiments with bond financing, meant to distance local government funding from the state-owned banking sector and improve transparency. Over the longer term, the government has plans to centralize expenditures on social benefits in order to make them more portable and ease the spending burden on local governments. Neither of these reforms, though, will matter much if China cannot control its SOEs.

Bond Financing

As the local government debt problem came to public attention, China's central government began to experiment with local government bonds. At first, these bonds were issued through the Ministry of Finance (MOF) in the name of the region in question, which gave local governments a transparent source of capital, but did little to establish fiscal independence. Local governments were not allowed to independently issue bonds until November 2011, when the Ministry of Finance introduced a trial program giving Shanghai, Guangdong, Zhejiang, and Shenzhen allowance to borrow up to a MOF set limit. The program was extended to Jiangsu and Shandong in June 2013.[32]

The first independent local government bond issuance went noticeably wrong, with the four issuing governments receiving bid rates between 3.01 percent and 3.10 percent for three-year bonds, compared to 3.11 percent for central government bonds, and a 3.67 percent to 4.07 percent rate for MOF-issued local government bonds. Rates were brought down by aggressive purchases from state-owned banks, which were eager to see a successful issuance so as to attract more underwriting business in the future. The central government had done nothing to specify what would happen if the local governments failed to repay their debts, so the purchases were more or less risk free from the perspective of state-owned banks.[33]

The central government responded with a number of rules restricting banks' participation in this market. In July 2013, the MOF prohibited underwriters from purchasing more than 30 percent of a bond sale, and required an explanation if a bond's yield is lower than central government bonds. The document also gave guidance that cities should "actively create conditions to gradually promote the establishment of a credit rating system."[34] In 2015, China announced that it would allow the conversion of RMB 1 trillion (USD 160 billion) in *chengtou* bonds to municipal bonds, bringing down the yield and extending the maturities so the government had more time to develop a longer-term solution.[35]

Besides the introduction of local government bonds, China introduced a number of major changes to local government budgeting processes in 2014 and 2015 that could help them deal with this problem going forward. The simplest reform, and what will perhaps be the most effective reform, linked local government debt management to local bureaucrats' performance evaluations. The central government also laid out strict rules regarding what sort of projects local governments were allowed to finance through debt, how the debt was to be repaid, and who had final responsibility for repayment. The new rules specifically declared that local government debt would not be covered by the central government, instead requiring mismanaged provinces to restructure spending under an emergency management system.[36]

It remains to be seen what effect these reforms will have on land expropriation. The combination of a weak real estate market and the new mechanisms to raise funds should slow the pace of expropriation over the short term, but land sales are still a legitimate means for local governments to raise money. As long as local government expenditures remain larger than revenues, there remains a risk of abuse.

Social Services

China initially transferred coverage of social services to local governments in order to increase the amount of tax revenues that were being retained at the central level. As long as local governments had difficulty taking on debt, this policy was broadly successful at maintaining stability. The central government could bemoan poor social services coverage in distant underdeveloped provinces or push local governments to cover social services at the expense of local development projects, but at the end of the day, their balance sheets were covered and the only people hurt were China's poor.

As the Great Migration has expanded though, the problems with social services have reached the country's increasingly migratory middle class. Even without access to a ballot box, middle-class Chinese have been able to speak out about these problems and get enough support that the government feels it needs to respond to them. Poor social services have also had a noticeable effect on the larger economy, helping to propagate the SARS crisis in 2003, and leading to a burst of illiteracy since the education cuts after the 1994 fiscal reform.

China's current decentralized social services system also poses a barrier to China's long-term urbanization goals. If China expands social services payouts at the local level, the incentives that have led local governments to embrace poor migrants as a means of development would abruptly shift in favor of exclusion. Ending the hukou system so migrants could freely respond to the market demand for labor would be impossible.

Healthcare

The SARS epidemic was a turning point in China's healthcare system. Up to then, rural dwellers and rural-urban migrants had almost no access to public hospitals and lacked the money to afford private ones. In the immediate aftermath of the disease, China introduced two new trial programs, the new Rural Cooperative Medical Scheme and the Urban Resident Basic Medical Insurance Scheme, that allowed these groups to gain access to basic medical care with limited out-of-pocket expenses. In 2009, these programs were formalized and expanded nationwide, with coverage rates reaching 95 percent by 2011.[37]

These programs proved to be significantly more expensive than the government originally estimated. Though out-of-pocket spending would decline from 60 percent of total health spending to just 36 percent by 2010, total spending would jump from USD 124 billion in 2009 to USD 385 billion in 2011, and is expected to reach USD 1 trillion by 2020.[38] Premiums are split three ways among the central government, local governments, and policyholders, with the central government taking on the largest share. Additional spending was put into direct subsidies to the hospital for each service performed.[39]

Surveys conducted after the program was implemented found that poor Chinese, who had not previously been covered, were very happy with the accessibility of services, as were those with chronic illnesses. Inpatient services were used more regularly and spending on catastrophic care declined. On the other side, middle-class patients reported a decline in the quality of coverage, finding it more difficult to make appointments with doctors, while many of them said the overall cost of care had actually increased due to the wider coverage net.[40]

The decline in quality of coverage stems from how government payments are calculated. Hospitals are allowed to charge 15 percent markups on all medicines and receive a payment from the government per service performed, which encourages hospitals both to overprescribe high cost medicines and to cycle through patients, either by pushing patients out before they recover or readmitting patients so they can be billed twice. The government has admitted to cases where hospitals have turned away cancer patients because they would receive fewer subsidies for their care than short-term patients. The practice was formally banned in 2011, though reports continue to surface of cancer patients being denied care.[41]

The 2009 reform package was a step forward for basic medical coverage, which is important for reducing the risk of communicable disease, but the associated costs pose a substantial barrier to hukou reform. This problem is not insurmountable, but as experience in other countries has shown, it can often be difficult to structure a healthcare system that increases coverage for long-term diseases while controlling costs.

The most important change China needs to make to its current system is to shift government subsidies from the providers of healthcare services to the consumers of healthcare services, allowing insurance holders to see more of how their money is spent and decide on how to make the best use of it.[42] China's migrant workforce may be an underutilized resource on this front. If China were to centralize subsidies for basic medical coverage while leaving more expensive coverage to subsidized private insurance, migrants would be able to shop for healthcare across provincial borders and take advantage of differences in prices between cheaper inland regions or coastal regions with higher-quality services.

Pensions

Until 2009, China's pension system was broken into two programs that covered less than half of the population. Urban workers employed by larger private companies and SOEs were eligible to be enrolled in the urban enterprise pension scheme, which put aside the equivalent of 28 percent of their salary for retirement—20 percent paid by the employer, 8 percent by the worker. Workers then received monthly payments on retirement based on the amount saved divided by 139. Civil servants were enrolled in a separate program with defined benefits and no pay-in.[43]

In 2009, the government introduced two subsidized savings programs covering rural dwellers and contract employees (mostly migrant workers). Under the rural pension program, an individual can choose to set aside between RMB 100 and 500 a year (USD 16.4 and USD 82.2), with local governments providing an additional subsidy of at least RMB 30. On retirement, the worker gets RMB 55 a month, as well as a monthly payment amounting to the worker's total savings divided by 139. The urban employment scheme is broadly the same, except with a maximum annual payment of RMB 1,000.[44]

In February 2014, China's government announced plans to implement a unified basic pension program by 2020 that would be portable across regional borders. The basics of the scheme are similar to the rural and urban pension schemes that were introduced in 2009. Individuals will have the option to pay between RMB 100 and 2000 a month for at least fifteen years leading up to retirement. The pension program for urban employed workers will continue to exist alongside the new basic pension program, with new rules introduced in July 2014 allowing workers to transfer their pensions from the employed worker scheme to the basic scheme and back again. This will help overcome some of the restrictions the pension system placed on labor mobility. The plan also includes a consideration for local government finances, with the central government covering all subsidies for central and western provinces, and 50 percent of the subsidies for the rich eastern provinces.[45]

This new system is significantly more friendly toward migrants than the urban employed pensions program, and it is certainly more sustainable. The employer contribution to the urban employed pension program is managed on a pay-as-you-go (PAYGO) basis, with people paying into the system covering current retirees. PAYGO plans always face the risk that demographic decline or a slowdown in economic growth will lead to a decline in people paying into the system, both of which are an immediate concern for China. In fact, the failure of the urban employed pension program may have already happened. In 2009, over 90 percent of the money in personal savings accounts had been used to pay off the PAYGO portion of the program. This figure has improved somewhat in recent years, and it has likely been helped by the expansion in rural and migrant pay-ins, but the absolute amount missing from the individual savings accounts continues to grow. China will eventually have to either pay these expenses back from government funds or renegotiate payment amounts.[46]

To make matters worse, China's pensions are subject to the same financial restrictions as all other savers: limited to investment in the volatile stock market, low-yield central government bonds, or bank deposits. These savings vehicles often yield negative real returns, which can lead to a substantial decline in total assets over the lifetime of a pension program. Chinese workers are aware of this problem and have traditionally avoided pension programs in favor of investments in hard or productive assets.[47]

China's pension system seems to be going in the direction of subsidized personal savings accounts, which, with the approaching decline of China's working population, is a good thing. In order to make this program work, China will need to make it clear that prepaid pension plans will not be "borrowed" for the sake of paying off other pensions, and it will most likely have to change the conditions of the PAYGO program or directly subsidize the program as the country makes a transition toward savings accounts. Ideally, China will fully centralize the management of the pension system so migrant workers do not have to worry about transferring their accounts between different regions. Even if they do not decide to centralize the program, the central government should expand oversight of local government accounts to ensure that payment levels are in line with the funds that are available.

Education

Since 2003, China has legally required local governments to provide nine years of compulsory education to the children of migrant workers. While this law has increased coverage in some cities, migrant children continue to be discriminated against, with their families subject to arbitrary fees that are often several times larger than what local families have to pay and well out of reach for the poorest manual workers.[48]

While it is hard to get good statistics on enrollment levels for migrant children, the scale of the problem is visible in the various market-based and policy-based solutions that have been implemented in various cities. The most prominent of these is "migrant schools," private schools that serve migrant children exclusively, often for lower costs than the arbitrary fees set by public schools. Some local governments have embraced these migrant schools as a market-based solution to the problem. Shanghai, for example, officially licensed all 160 migrant schools known to exist in the city as of 2012. Though widely acknowledged to provide worse education than public schools, Shanghai's legitimization of the migrant schools has allowed many of them to improve the quality of their product. In 2009, the city distributed an average government subsidy of RMB 500,000 (USD 82,183) to each school for hardware upgrading, with an additional RMB 1,500 subsidy per student. By comparison, while migrant enrollment in Beijing is said to be better than in Shanghai, the city closes down a slew of unregistered migrant schools almost every year. The city was home to roughly 200 migrant schools in 2012, the majority of them unregistered.[49]

Beyond setting goals for local governments, the central government has shown no interest in addressing the ongoing problems facing migrant children. The government's 2010–20 education reform document dedicates one paragraph to the problem, which states "the task of ensuring equal compulsory education for children living with migrant worker parents in cities shall be ensured primarily by local governments." The paragraph then goes on to explain the new monitoring mechanism and boarding schools that will be set up to help children left behind in the countryside, implying that it does not expect urban governments to keep up their side of the deal.[50]

The government has made some positive moves since the release of the 2010 document. In 2013, the government passed a new reform package that, among other things, would allow migrant children to take the country's grueling college entrance exam in their home city, instead of moving to their hukou residency prior to taking the test. The new reforms also ban school officials from denying applicants for any reason other than their residency, separating children into "fast-track" and "slow-track" classes, or forcing families to purchase more than one type of secondary educational material besides textbooks. While many of these reforms were promoted as an effort to reduce stress in early education, they will have the secondary impact of helping migrants gain access to competitive urban schools at lower cost.[51]

Inequality in the provision of education is a fact of life for developed countries, and it will remain a fact of life in China. But China's current system, where students at ostensibly public institutions are charged arbitrary and often excessive fees, is discriminatory and inefficient. Children excluded from the formal education system will have fewer opportunities in life, will contribute less to the economy, and will have a harder time supporting family members who fall through the cracks of the pension system. Until fees are equalized, or preferably eliminated, China's education system will remain unreformed.

• • •

These reforms will be expensive, but the concerns that China has about paying for the expansion of social services reflect more on the inefficiency of its fiscal system than on the scale of the overall costs. The average additional cost of social services for an urban resident over a rural resident is between RMB 20,000 and RMB 100,000 (USD 3,000–15,000) over the lifetime of the migrant. Assuming that the expansion of hukou coverage is implemented over a fifteen-year time frame—roughly on par with the rate announced in the 2014 urbanization plan—this would cost the country approximately RMB 50 billion a year, or 0.1 percent China's GDP.[52]

China's government can afford this much; it is a question of how it sets priorities and how it separates responsibilities. Today the primary economic priority of China's central government is subsidizing its SOEs.

SOE Reforms

China's SOEs and their control over policymaking are far and away the largest threat to China's development. Despite receiving subsidies and benefiting from full or partial monopolies, China's SOEs are frighteningly inefficient and increasingly unprofitable. Selling off these companies would not only help the government pay for the immediate costs of urbanization, but it would also have the potential to increase growth and, eventually, tax revenue, helping to pay for a variety of long-term social services and discretionary spending costs.

SOEs have done poorly in the aftermath of the global economic crisis. Between 2008 and 2013, nonfinancial SOEs have made a combined annual return on assets of barely 3 percent, compared to a peak of 5 percent in 2007, and well below the cost of capital. The return on assets in the private sector has consistently been over two and a half times higher than the return on assets in the state sector.[53] While SOEs have been able to earn strong profits in some sectors—notably oil extraction, tobacco, and telecommunications—these profits are only maintained through inefficient monopolies, with the profitability of SOEs closely correlated with the lack of private sector penetration in the industry.[54] Since 2008, SOE spending has been increasingly debt financed, often with support from local governments aiming to promote local development goals. This has contributed to local government indebtedness and China's problems opening its banking sector.

China has faced this problem before. China's solution to the 1990s debt crisis was to let loss-making SOEs go bankrupt, while reforming profitable SOEs to make them act more like private companies with budget constraints and the ability to fire underqualified workers. This, combined with a bailout of the financial sector, was able to minimize the immediate risks in the system. As long as China was able to continue growing quickly and maintain control of its banks, this system was more or less sustainable, though the costs to the overall economy in terms of capital misallocation and economic waste would remain high.

It is important that China subject SOEs to bankruptcy proceedings if they are unable to pay their debts. While the immediate financial losses would go to the state-owned banks—which are already on uneven footing—bankruptcies would allow China to slow the mounting losses from the state sector and improve overall competitiveness in sectors where SOEs compete with the private sector.

While allowing bankruptcies would ease the immediate pressure on SOEs, China should get ahead of the curve and start privatizing companies in sectors where it already competes with the private sector. While China is unlikely to immediately privatize companies that still provide a substantial source of income—the aforementioned oil, telecoms, and tobacco industries—in other sectors, like steel (see box), many SOEs are bordering on bankruptcy while profitable private companies struggle with government anticompetition policies. Selling state-owned assets to private companies prior to bankruptcy would allow the government to both earn more off its assets and prevent further problems down the line.

This could be done over a few intermediary steps. The government would first set up a number of sovereign wealth funds (SWFs) that would split shareholdings in SOEs to reduce each fund's share to a minority holding. The SWFs could then gradually sell those holdings on the stock market and use the funds to diversify into offshore products, or liquidate the SWF to pay for national infrastructure projects.[55]

China's current plans are much less ambitious than this. In September 2015, China released an SOE reform plan that, rather than calling for a smaller role for SOEs in the economy, aimed to encourage mixed ownership of state-owned firms. The plan had some positives to it—it suggested a long-term goal to move toward a SWF model in order to distance the government from SOE management, and it opened up the possibility of fully divesting from competitive sectors—but the big message of the document was that the reforms would be slow and would not challenge the outsized role of SOEs in the economy.

The most sympathetic argument one could make for this reform is that the central government is signaling support for the entrenched interests that are defending SOEs, while slowly reforming the system to push management control toward the private sector. There is also, though, the real possibility that this reform could push the moral hazard associated with SOEs into the larger private economy, further undermining China's ability to reform its financial system and its fiscal system. If this were to happen, China would continue to struggle with poor capital efficiency, even as the returns from labor market mobilization slows. In a little more than decade, we might finally be able to call an end to the Chinese economic miracle.[56]

The exaggerated reputation SOEs have gained as global behemoths that can champion China's interests overseas is dangerously inaccurate. China's SOEs are drags on the economy, obstacles to reform, and increasingly pose a systemic risk to government finances. They also remain politically entrenched. It is yet to be seen whether China's leaders can push through the necessary reforms before country's fiscal system or its financial system reaches a crisis.

The Future of the Hukou

China has shown no sign of being interested in ending its hukou system. Instead, it has compromised, expanding access to local hukou coverage and expanding the central government's role in providing social services.

In the next decade, China is likely to unify the rural and urban hukou system into a single place hukou that specifies which region is responsible for providing a person with social services rather than specifying what social services an individual is entitled to.[57] This is certainly better than the system that China currently has in place, but it continues to be a system that values a stable labor market rather than a dynamic one. It's a system that rewards people for staying at home rather than lowering barriers for people who have the courage to migrate. China's migration policies are moving in the direction of the European Union, where they should be moving in the direction of the United States.

China has several reforms that it needs to enact over the next decade if it is going to become a country that fully supports migration and urbanization. First, it needs to bring the pension system and the healthcare system under the central budget, while more strictly enforcing school enrollment for migrant children. If it does this, the hukou will be little more than an identity card, just like the cards people are forced to carry in many other countries. The pension system and the healthcare system should be made more market driven in order to loosen the burden on government budgets and reduce distortions.

HEBEI IRON & STEEL

Hebei Iron & Steel is the largest steel producer in China and the third largest steel producer in the world. It was formed in 2008 from the merger of three SOEs: Tangshan Iron & Steel, Handan Iron & Steel, and Chengde Xinxin Vanadium & Titanium.[58] In 2010, it would forcibly acquire shares in twelve regional private steelmakers, under the agreement that the SOE would share its distribution network and technology in return from the right to negotiate with foreign iron-ore suppliers for the entire group.[59]

These mergers were part of a broader nationalization of China's steel industry that had been ongoing since 2007. Government-owned steel mills had been struggling with the rising cost of iron-ore due to high steel demand from the country's real estate sector. Private sector steel mills had consistently been willing to pay a higher price in negotiations with foreign mining groups, often going behind the back of government negotiators. "Consolidation" gave the country a unified voice to negotiate as well as a means to maintain SOE profit as the real estate sector slowed down. The government aimed to bring 60 percent of the sector under the ten largest companies by 2015, whether the acquired companies liked it or not.[60]

Since the merger, Hebei Iron & Steel has consistently struggled to make a profit. Shortly after the company took control of the provincial steel market, the government announced that it wanted to cut Hebei's steel production by 30 percent by 2020, the equivalent of 15 million tons of capacity a year.[61] There was a fair amount of sense to this demand. If an industry is unprofitable, then producing more steel will make it more unprofitable. Much of the steel was being produced with outdated technology that increased pollution, and Hebei is consistently ranked as China's most polluted province.[62] This could have benefited Hebei Iron & Steel. Private companies were expected to take the brunt of the closures because the SOEs had access to the sort of less-polluting production capacity that the government was demanding.

But the closures didn't happen. Through 2013, Hebei's steel industry was adding 30 million tons of capacity a year, both from private companies and smaller SOEs that were struggling to expand to meet the minimum size required under the consolidation plan. Local governments often supported the expansion of small steel mills, fearing that they would face lost tax revenues and lost jobs if the steel mills were to close—as many as 200,000 people are expected to lose their jobs if Hebei meets its capacity target.[63] Profit margins over the entire industry would fall to 0.48 percent in December of that year. Hebei Iron & Steel's net profit would decline 92 percent in 2012, turning to a loss in 2013.[64]

In December 2013, Hebei Iron & Steel also replaced its chairman. The new chairman, Yu Yong, admitted that there was widespread embezzlement going on throughout the company, saying that employees had treated the company as "a paradise for making personal fortunes," even as some of the company's subsidiaries relied on loans to survive.[65] Shortly after the leadership change, there were reports that some of the private companies that had formed partnerships with the company in 2010 were trying to get out of the agreement. An unnamed Hebei Iron & Steel executive told Chinese publication *Caixin* that there had been little cooperation between the two sides of the agreement, and the private companies were not eager to get management guidance from an SOE. "Why would any private company want to ask our people to manage their company?" the executive said.[66]

China has begun to change its tack. In 2012, China loosened requirements for registering a private steel enterprise. Then, in 2014, the government dropped its explicit target of consolidating 60 percent of the industry under SOEs. Xu Leijiang, the chairman of Baosteel, the country's second largest producer, said that the consolidation program had created "monsters" fighting with debt and unprofitable investments. These are the monsters that China will have to fight over the next decade.[67]

The government should end the nearly bankrupt PAYGO portion of the pension and focus the healthcare system on providing basic insurance for all and transferring funds that go to hospitals on a per-procedure basis to subsidize consumer choices on long-term care provision.

Second, China needs to substantially reduce the SOE share of the economy and continue with local government financing reforms that will allow cities and provinces to pay for infrastructure projects in a transparent way. Besides putting government finances on sounder footing, this will allow the economy to be more responsive to both market demand and the movement of migrants, with prices saying which cities should grow larger and which cities should be ignored.

Finally, the government should abandon its grain production targets so it can unify rural and urban land markets under a single land-rights system. This will allow the country to better determine what cities should be expanded and where food production should take priority. It would also disrupt local government's intermediation role in land markets, creating less opportunities for abusive land expropriation.

China's treatment of migrants is improving, but it is a long way from creating institutions that are responsive to the needs of migrants. For years, migrant workers have driven the Chinese economic miracle forward. They need to be encouraged, particularly as the population of China declines.

7

Zhengzhou

AS WENZHOU WAS one of the first cities to embrace the Great Migration, Zhengzhou, the capital of Henan province, is at the center of the most recent phase of the Great Migration. For a long time, Zhengzhou was seen as a backwater, where government intervention had led to ghost cities, health hazards and human rights violations. It was only when migrant workers started returning from the coast that Zhengzhou experienced the Chinese economic miracle.

• • •

Between 2011 and 2014, more than 300,000 people moved to Dazhai Village on the outskirts of Zhengzhou. The village, which a few years earlier was home to a few hundred peanut farmers, quickly filled up with construction. New roads are being built, new housing is going up, and the townsfolk have mostly become commercial vendors trying to make a few RMB off the new residents.

The new residents like to spend money; after all, most of them are young and have just found their first job after leaving home. The average age of the new residents is between 18 and 22, with very few of them passing 25, and Dazhai Village has come to reflect the interests of that age group. There are numerous Internet cafés on the main stretch of road through the town and there are cheap places to get food, clothes, and electronics. There are two Apple resellers in the town trying to catch the few people willing to splurge on a high-end phone, and repair people for the hundreds of mopeds that now fill the streets. There are karaoke parlors to go to on dates, and any number of short-stay hotels to go to afterward. More than one abortionist advertises services, just in case the dates have an unwanted outcome.

If you have bought an iPhone since 2012, it was almost certainly made by one of the young men and women living in Dazhai village. Foxconn, the company that does most contract manufacturing for Apple, transferred its main iPhone production facilities to the city in 2011, and has rapidly scaled up operations since then. In 2012, the factory tripled employment from 100,000 to 300,000 people. Dazhai was being built to accommodate this growth, with over a dozen new dormitories the size of apartment blocks under construction at the time of my visit in mid-2013.

Expanding payroll by 200,000 people in a year is not easy, no matter what country you are in. Add to that a conservative 20 percent employee turnover rate, and Foxconn has to hire roughly 700 people a day to staff this one factory.[1] In Zhengzhou, the company's employment efforts seem to be everywhere. Dotting the city, there are more than one hundred Foxconn recruiting offices that funnel potential workers to one of the company's dozen interview centers. The interviews aren't complicated. Foxconn has three requirements for new employees: they are over 18, they do not have any tattoos, and they were never previously fired from Foxconn. If they meet all those requirements, they are hired. But in the months prior to a new iPhone release, when recruiters have to push extra hard to meet their hiring targets, even those requirements are flexible.[2]

The entry of the Foxconn factory has fundamentally changed Zhengzhou's role in China's economy. In 2012, high-tech exports from the city more than tripled to USD 15.9 billion, putting Zhengzhou on par with other Western-technology manufacturing centers like Chengdu and Chongqing.[3] While much of this is simply the statistical effect of the new factory—the iPhone accounts for roughly a quarter of all smartphone production in China—industrial expansion is happening across the city, as companies take advantage of the new logistics infrastructure surrounding Foxconn and the growing supply of labor in the province. In 2015, the city produced one-eighth of all smartphones globally.[4]

• • •

Since the mid-2000s, Henan Province has been the largest source of migrant workers in China. It is, in many ways, the typical migrant worker province. The city of Zhengzhou sits in the middle of China's grain belt, surrounded by farms fed by the nutrient-rich water of the Yellow River. A 3000-year-old city wall that runs through the center of town testifies to the city's place at the beginning of Chinese history. Zhengzhou is 85 miles east of Luoyang, one of China's first capital cities. In the 1982 census, the province was deemed to be the most populous in China, with over 74 million people, the majority of whom worked in farming and associated industries like food processing and logistics. Even today, after the province's population has fallen behind both Guangdong and Shandong, it maintains China's largest rural population.[5]

While Henan's agricultural wealth helped it grow remarkably during Mao's time, the province quickly fell behind other regions in the decades following reform and opening. Zhengzhou was the diametric opposite of Wenzhou (see Chapter 3). While Wenzhou was an isolated city with few resources and could get by under the radar of the government, Henan was the country's insurance against famine. During the 1980s and 1990s, Henan fell behind other inland provinces like Hubei, Shaanxi, and eventually Sichuan, as the government pushed the provincial governments to maintain land and labor for farming.

By the 1990s, the province had come to symbolize all that was backward in China. In the decades since the introduction of the one-child policy, the province developed one of the worst sex-imbalance ratios in the country.[6] It was also the epicenter of an AIDS epidemic spawned by an illegal trade in blood. The province accounted for a disproportionate number of the poor and hungry living in major cities along the east coast like Beijing and Shanghai, encouraging widespread stereotypes about people from Henan being hicks and bumpkins. They were the Okies of China, forced by desperation to make a living on the richer coasts.

Unlike the Okies, who had migrated from Oklahoma during the Dust Bowl of the 1930s, Henan's migrants weren't running from natural disaster; they were running from government failure. Henan still had obvious potential. By 2010, when the population of the province was bordering on 100 million, the average pay was almost one-quarter of the going rate in coastal cities. Sitting on a large and broad plain nearly equidistant from Beijing, Guangzhou, Shanghai, and Xi'an, Henan was an ideal place to build infrastructure. The question was how to pay for the infrastructure. Unlike Wenzhou, the government wasn't willing to let workers turn their fields into highways and factories. Everything had to be done by the government.

In the early part of the 2000s, the province introduced two major plans to transform Henan from a rural backwater to an inland manufacturing center. The first was an "if you build it, they will come" plan. In 2001, the government set aside a 58 square mile plot of land for the construction of a new city district. Zhengdong New District was supposed to be a new modern business district that the city's broader urban area could be built around, paid for—like most major real estate projects in China—with a combination of local government investment and buy-in from property firms and larger corporations. Construction of Zhengdong was slow, and people moved in even more slowly, with real estate purchases in the area only really gaining steam in 2012, by which time another new city district was developing much faster in the area around Dazhai village.

The second plan was "they will build it if they come." In 2001, Zhengzhou announced that it would reform its hukou registration procedures to make it easier for rural migrants to switch to a local urban hukou. The program lasted for three years, over which time 250,000 new households were transferred to Zhengzhou, with a number of unregistered relatives living with them. A number of surveys found that the largest share of new migrants were children and the elderly, who could benefit from urban social services, rather than working-age adults who would have to pay more for the services than they would be taking out. Some schools in the city reported a one-third increase in new pupils in 2004, while newspapers expressed concerns about rising crime rates and traffic congestion. The program was cancelled in 2004, which forced most new migrants to the city to either leave their children in the countryside to stay at subpar rural schools or take them out of school all together.[7]

Zhengzhou's development story would have to wait until the end of the decade, when a number of new infrastructure projects would come online and manufacturers would struggle with rising coastal wages. By the early part of the 2010s, Zhengzhou had become the transfer point for the Beijing-Guangzhou high-speed railway and the Xi'an-Shanghai high-speed railway. Several new highways and several new freight rail lines would lower transportation costs to the coast.[8] Perhaps most importantly, during a period when migrant wages in Shanghai were approaching RMB 5,000–6,000 a month, wages in Zhengzhou were still hovering at about RMB 1,300 a month. The city was starting to look very good to investors. Foxconn was the first major investor to notice.

The Great Zhengzhou Labor Shortage

Foxconn is one of the largest employers in the world, and for most Chinese people that means Foxconn is an employer of last resort. For people under 30, it pays less than any other employer, it has lower hiring standards, and, though much of the Western news coverage is exaggerated, it is not known as a great place to work. Foxconn is a place you go to find a job when you're new in town and need to find work fast.

With the exception of working conditions, these facts are not something over which Foxconn has much control. Foxconn's massive demand for labor effectively means it can set wages for the entire city, as other companies have to compete with Foxconn's low hiring standards by increasing wages and improving workplace conditions. The hiring spree in 2012 forced Foxconn to raise wages for new hires from RMB 1,350 to RMB 1,800, with a moderate raise to RMB 2,000 for anyone who stayed longer than three months. Surrounding factories responded in kind, with most companies at local job fairs offering wages above RMB 2,000 and noting that their wages had nearly doubled in the three years since Foxconn arrived in 2011.[9]

Higher wages have not been enough for Foxconn to meet its hiring demands. The company enlisted the help of the local government, which had agreed in the initial investment contract to provide hiring support if the company needed it. After the announcement of the new hiring drive, the local government offered one-time subsidies to workers who stayed at Foxconn longer than three months and, according to Chinese media, went so far as to set hiring targets for surrounding cities.[10]

Despite the continued wage difference between Zhengzhou and coastal manufacturing cities, the city has been able to draw workers away from coastal regions as well as from other parts of Henan to help fill the gaping employment shortage. In Zhengzhou, being from Henan is not a disadvantage. Henanese workers in Zhengzhou are close to their families, which, besides offering comfort, allows them to more easily send remittances home. It is also easier to integrate into local social networks, since everyone is more or less from the same place, making networking and job advancement easier. One job fair in 2014 had 160,000 attendants lined up around the International Exhibition Center.[11] Few people complain that it's difficult to find a job. "In Shanghai, the pay is twice as high, but there's less work," one 22-year-old migrant worker says, "and Zhengzhou is closer to home."

The Center of China

As the cost of doing business in coastal China has risen, Zhengzhou has moved aggressively into the low-end manufacturing businesses that have become harder to sell in Guangdong. In 2010, alongside the opening of the Foxconn factory, Zhengzhou inaugurated the Xinzheng Free Trade Zone, based around the Xinzheng Airport and the nearby Foxconn factory, which would allow factories to import components and export finished products duty-free.

In March 2013, the central government approved a plan to build an "airport economic zone" in the Xinzheng district. The centerpiece of this plan is an expansion of the Zhengzhou Xinzheng Airport to 3 million tons of cargo throughput by 2025—on par with Shanghai Pudong's current throughput levels. The government hopes the zone will support a RMB 1 trillion (USD 163 billion) high-tech manufacturing cluster and 4 million residents.[12]

For all the government support given to this project, the Xinzheng Airport expansion is a demand-driven endeavor. Airfreight through Zhengzhou expanded nearly 64 percent in 2013, after expanding 47 percent the year before, making it by far the fastest-growing cargo airport in the country. The government expects the city's population to expand to 15 million by 2020, up from 9 million in 2012. Geographically, Zhengzhou has plenty of room to fit new workers and new employers, but it is still working to build the necessary infrastructure.

The city is receiving plenty of private sector support on this front. Foxconn has contributed both political support as well as technical advice regarding its own logistics operations. More broadly real estate companies have been rushing into the city, aiming to grab some of the new land up for development. Housing prices in the city increased 20 percent in the first half of 2013. Construction is literally everywhere in Zhengzhou, particularly in the rural suburbs that only a few years earlier were fields of wheat and corn. The first line of a 277-km (172-mile) subway system was completed in 2013, with another five lines under construction.[13]

Ruins

While urbanization has transformed Zhengzhou from a backwater to a manufacturing powerhouse, in a country with no land rights urbanization comes with significant human costs.

I arrive at the Sun Family Village outside of Zhengzhou, eight days after it was torn down. All the buildings are now a pile of rubble, except one—a two-story concrete block with three phrases scrawled across the front:

"Inside I have enough food for fifty years."

"Nothing can make me leave."

"There are weapons inside the house."

A blackened circle in front of the building marks the place where a Molotov cocktail was dropped earlier in the day. A sunburned and exhausted middle-aged woman is watching my guide and me from the top of the building, carrying a sleeping child in her arms. She won't talk to us. The police would negotiate with Molotov cocktails, but talking to the press would only lead to retaliation.

The Sun Family Village was built around a family of educated bureaucrats that played a major role in the late Qing dynasty government. One of the houses featured an inscription from the Kangxi emperor, and a sign saying that a high level official had lived there—that is, until the early morning of May 8, 2013, when the doors were beaten down, its residents dragged outside and tied up, and the house set on fire.

A week later, the house's former residents received an apology—not for the abuse they suffered at the hands of the government's thugs, but because the deputy director of the city district agreed with them that the house should have been preserved for its historic value. He promised that something commemorating the family would be built on the site.

I was introduced to the people of the village by Meng Xiaodong, a man who has taken it upon himself to bring as much media attention as possible to land-rights issues in Henan. He is officially a rural citizen, but like many of

A BAR IN ZHENGZHOU

The 7 Live House is the best-known rock club in Zhengzhou. It sits in a medium-size box-shaped room over a movie theater, large enough to fit a bit over one hundred people, with a small bar in the front and a stage in the back. It has been a good couple of years for the bar, as incomes have risen in the city and the usual crowd of college students has had more money to spend on entertainment and alcohol. "The city has changed a lot," says Sang Sang, the bartender. "Three years ago, I could get away with wearing anything, now I have to plan out my outfit."

The club was founded in 2008 by Shen Yi, a former engineer, who jokes that he got started in the music business because he "took a wrong turn somewhere." At the time, a rock scene was just starting to blossom in Xinxiang, a smaller city to the north, and Shen, who loved the music, thought there would be a market for it among college students in Zhengzhou.

For a long time, the club struggled to get by. Most bands went to Beijing if they wanted to get famous, and Zhengzhou was usually skipped over on national tours. While he found an audience among college students, the students were more interested in the music than the alcohol, which is where he can bring in his largest margins. Then his club was torn down as a part of the city's overhaul, prompting him to relocate to his current location.[14]

But he's cautiously optimistic. In the past few years, a number of coffee shops and independent bookstores have opened that offer more intimate folk concerts on the weekend. He's heard murmurings that more rock venues are on the way, meaning the market is picking up and there are more incentives for bands from Beijing, and increasingly international bands, to stop over in the city. Rising income levels also mean that his audience has more money to spend on drinks.

While few of the workers at the Foxconn factory make enough money to go to his shows, he thinks Foxconn and other low-end assembly factories will be good for Zhengzhou, because they keep migrant workers in the province and bring more wealth into the city. Still, he is concerned about the loss of green space and local color. "They cut all the trees down and replaced them with roads," he says, "but it's not their choice. All China is speeding up and Zhengzhou can't be left behind."

Sang Sang is less certain. "What's the Foxconn factory like?" she asks me. "I only know about it from Jon Stewart."

the rural dwellers in the suburbs of major cities, he works in town and makes his money as an engineer. Unlike most people, he spends his spare time playing politics. The local security bureau "invites him to tea" every few weeks, but as of yet, he hasn't gotten in trouble for anything. He insists that I use his real name if I write anything.

At the time I met him, he was actively involved in protesting three land expropriations going on around Zhengzhou. The pace isn't unusual. Since 2010, Zhengzhou's suburbs have been rapidly torn down to make way for high-density housing that developers and the local government could profit on. For those losing their land, the conditions were rarely fair. Usually, rural dwellers would get an apartment and a few thousand dollars in exchange for their plot of land and their two- or three-story house. Occasionally, people got even less.

The Sun Family Village, like many of the other villages that are being destroyed in Zhengzhou's rapid dash for modernization, was already too close to the city to grow many crops. Most of the villagers worked in factories, schools, and shops nearby in order to support themselves, and they would readily admit that the expansion of the city had been good for young people. For older people, the case was mixed. It was easy to find a job, but hard to find a good job. Pensions and healthcare remained at the same meager levels as back when Zhengzhou was rural backwater. Those who got caught up in a land expropriation could find themselves in penury.

For those in the Sun Family Village, the compensation had only barely been adequate. Villagers were moved into an unfurnished flat, which had better access to infrastructure than their previous residences (plumbing, heat, etc.), but they were required to pay condo fees that the villagers weren't sure they could afford. Most villagers complained that the compensation was not enough for them to replace the furniture that was destroyed when their houses were set on fire and bulldozed to the ground. Another complained that, per the conditions of his divorce, his ex-wife got everything and he would be left homeless.

The villagers lost other things. The village farmland afforded them all 400 liters of flour every year. Then there was the family history that was lost, the flowers and hearts drawn on the wall, and the inscriptions from a long dead Emperor commemorating a great-great grandfather's service to his country.

The village leaders—the officials that villagers elected after ten other candidates were crossed off the ballot list—made much more money than everyone else, selling land that they didn't own and then moving away to a home in the city where no questions would be asked of them. "We were stupid and blind for voting for them," one older woman said. "They were on the side of the government." The villagers' request to see the development plans for the land was not fulfilled. Most villagers are convinced that the government doesn't even have a developer lined up yet.

Zhengzhou is en route to becoming one of China's largest cities, and a major manufacturing center for global electronics companies. Much of the money the government uses to build this city will be stolen from the people who lived on its suburban fringes. It doesn't have to be this way, though. If China manages to reform local government finances and rural land laws, then more of the returns on development will be able to flow to Zhengzhou's poorest citizens rather than corrupt officials and international businesses—people who could be doing business, making money, and turning Zhengzhou into a place that migrants want to live.

As Meng Xiaodong and I left the Sun Family Village, we walked through a crowd of people looking through the rubble and cleaning out wires and other objects that could be recycled or reused. As we walked, Meng contemplated the scene with some disgust. "Everything in Henan is being destroyed," he muttered.

A man sitting on a pile of rubble laughs. "That's absolutely right," he says.

8

What Is China's Development Strategy?

> Sec. 2. No corporation now existing or hereafter formed under the laws of this State, shall, after the adoption of this Constitution, employ directly or indirectly, in any capacity, any Chinese or Mongolian. The Legislature shall pass such laws as may be necessary to enforce this provision.
>
> Sec. 3. No Chinese shall be employed on any State, county, municipal, or other public work, except in punishment for crime.
>
> —Article XIX of the California Constitution of 1879[1]

AH LOUIS ARRIVED in San Francisco in 1861, at age 21.[2] Like thousands of other Chinese at the time, he came from Guangdong looking to make money in the Gold Rush and escape the violence of the ongoing Taiping Rebellion. California at that time was the sort of place that would be called an emerging market one hundred years later. It was an economy that was transitioning from resource extraction—primarily gold and agriculture—to an economy based on agricultural processing, trade, and industry. It was also rapidly gaining migrants from the eastern United States, China, Mexico, Italy, Ireland, and Germany. When Ah Louis arrived in the state, the population was under 400,000; over the next three decades, the population would more than triple.[3]

Like most migrants to California at the time, Ah Louis failed at mining but eventually found other ways to make money, first working as a cook in a hotel in San Luis Obispo, then as a foreman and employment agent for the Pacific Coast Railroad. By the mid-1870s, he owned a brick-making factory and the main general store in San Luis Obispo's Chinatown. The Ah Louis store was a bank for the region's Chinese businesspeople, a supply center for local construction crews, and an employment office for Chinese workers. Soon he would be known as the primary recruiter for Chinese labor in central California, finding jobs for miners, road workers, and railroad teams.[4]

By all accounts, he was incredibly good at it. In 1877, the state awarded him two contracts to build roads that would later be integrated into California Route 46 and US Highway 101. In 1884, he received a contract to build four tunnels through the Cuesta Grade, connecting the Southern Pacific railroad with the land north of the Santa Lucia Mountains. According to most records, the tunnels were built over ten years, using the 2,000 Chinese laborers he supplied.[5]

This time was the high point of anti-Chinese agitating in the United States, with Chinese migrants increasingly blamed for poor wages in unskilled jobs, as well as an array of mining-town vices like drug addiction, disease, prostitution, and crime. In 1879, California passed a new constitution that banned corporations in California from employing Chinese workers—though these provisions would later be overturned by a U.S. Circuit Court as being in violation of the fourteenth amendment. A number of cities would follow with ad hoc rules closing down Chinese businesses. Starting in 1876, a number of boycotts were organized of San Luis Obispo's Chinese businesses, and the city council would try several times over the next ten years to close all of the Chinese laundries in town, which would have directly hit Ah Louis's banking operations. In 1886, the town of Arroyo Grande, just south of San Luis Obispo, forced all the local Chinese out of town on the threat of hanging.[6] The federal government responded in 1882 with the passage of the Chinese Exclusion Act, which barred unskilled Chinese laborers from entering the country. Chinese were barred from US citizenship, required to carry an identity card, and any person of Chinese ethnicity who left the country would be barred from reentry. The size of the Chinese population of the United States would barely change over the sixty years that the law was in place.[7] The Chinese share of the population of San Luis Obispo would never recover.[8]

Ah Louis continued to play a major role in San Luis Obispo's Chinese community. He owned half a block of Chinatown, and served as an unofficial mayor and postmaster of the Chinese community. He continued to make bricks until 1906, and he would continue to help itinerant Chinese laborers and long-time residents find jobs working in the region's fishing, mining, construction, and hospitality companies for most of his life. But his days of building California's highways and railroads were over. If not formally banned from taking contracts, the availability of Chinese labor was no longer a selling point, and many labor unions outright refused to work with companies that employed Chinese people.

In 1933, at age 92, Ah Louis decided to return to China to die in the same place he was born. He didn't stay very long. After seeing how little China had progressed in sixty-five years, he decided to return back to his adopted home. "My village has not changed for 800 years. I saw one woman carry water two miles. It's a very bad way to live," he told one reporter.[9] In San Luis Obispo, everything had changed. The city had been built on the bricks that he made, and connected to the world through his roads and his tunnels.

The mayor of the city had to intervene with immigration authorities in order to let him back into the country.

• • •

The value of migrants is one of the truisms of economics, yet every country restricts migration in some way, and most do so for sensible reasons. A nation is more than just an economy; it is a network of institutions that ensure that an economy functions, and it allows people to understand how that economy functions and how best to use their resources within the economy. Migrants challenge these assumptions: they add new rules to the game or ignore old rules, and for some, they make the game much more competitive. A nation's primary responsibility is to its citizens, and if migrants pose a threat to the prosperity of a country's citizens, then the government has a reasonable right to restrict their entry. The question is what constitutes a threat, and at what point are restrictions on migration more harmful to locals than comparatively more liberal migration laws.

The Chinese Exclusion Act was one of the first formal restrictions on migration introduced in the United States. While the law is now remembered as one sad moment among many in the history of race relations in America, at the time the Exclusion Act was positioned as a progressive law meant to protect workers in their battle with rapacious employers. Labor unions like the Knights of Labor compared employing Chinese to owning slaves, and argued that the

Chinese were destroying America's economy by bidding down the wages of the middle class.[10] As the Communists of China would argue in the 1950s, there seemed to be too many Chinese for the economy to support.

From the perspective of history, it's easy to point out that these arguments are ridiculous. Outside of the far West of the United States, Chinese made up an incredibly small percentage of the population—less than 400 people east of the Mississippi in 1870. In the western states, Chinese made up enough of the population that the US colonization of California would have been greatly slowed without them. They were paid for their work, and they were free to change jobs. In 1870, Chinese migrants accounted for 25 percent of the working population of California and owned a fair number of the state's businesses. The decline in immigration after the Chinese Exclusion Act would be a devastating hit to farms and canneries, not to mention the infrastructure companies that depended on people like Ah Louis to link the state together. Businesspeople would regularly petition for Congress to ease the ban on Chinese migrants well into the 1920s and 1930s, and would often ignore the law in order to fill out their workforce.[11] Today the population of California is nearly one hundred times higher than it was in 1860, while still featuring per capita personal income 5 percent higher than the national average.

But the immediate problem for working Americans wasn't economic growth or the rights of the Chinese. The immediate problem was that the Chinese were undermining various labor unions' attempts to restrict access to labor. They were changing the rules of the game in a way that strengthened the economy but made it more difficult for one politically privileged group to compete. Restricting people from hiring Chinese, purchasing from Chinese, or economically associating with Chinese was an expedient way to restore that group's economic privilege.

Maintaining a privileged space for locals is not necessarily wrong. A government is meant to advocate for the interest of its citizens, and modern migration barriers are based on the idea that a certain level of migration would be irrevocably harmful to the health of a place's institutions and its population. This is a real threat, even if the migrants are not usually the ones at fault. In China's case, increased migration pushed the country to the brink of bankruptcy; it undermined the delivery of social services and undercut efforts by the government to enforce state objectives ranging from ill-thought-out price controls to reasonable pollution controls. While migration in China was immensely profitable to everyone involved, Chinese institutions were often only barely able to manage the tide of new workers, with many institutions needing to be scrapped or greatly reformed in order to serve the country's growing urban workforce.

For politicians then, the question becomes this: how much migration can we accept before we put our political institutions at risk? For economists though, this question is backward. The more people we can trade with, the stronger our economy is. The more ways we can share work, the faster work can be done. If we accept that migration contributes to the economy, improves the lives of most everyone in the economy, and particularly provides the most efficient means of combatting global poverty, the question shouldn't be how much migration we can accept. Instead, the question should be, how can we change our institutions so that they are more friendly to migrants—and more friendly to economic growth?

Like tariffs and nontariff barriers in trade policy, there are hard barriers and soft barriers to migration. Most of the time when we speak about migration policy, we speak about the hard barriers—how many visas a country issues, the process for getting visas, the hukou—but soft barriers are often just as substantial a restriction on migration, and these soft barriers can often affect domestic migrants just as well as foreigners. At the most basic level, an anti-migrant law can be defined as a government restricting freedom of association so one group can have privileged access to the resources within a community. Beside blunt prohibitions on migration and hiring, these restrictions show up in a variety of domestic laws defining how many people can live in a city, what sort of property people are allowed to own and what they are allowed to do with that property, who people are allowed to trade with, and how public goods are distributed. In free-market economies like the United States, these indirect restrictions tend to be relatively mild. In developing countries like those in Africa, and formerly China, these indirect restrictions can be suffocating.

It is not always clear exactly what restrictions migrants face when entering a new community and what the larger consequences of those policies are. One of the lessons of China's experience with the Great Migration is that indirect restrictions on migrants—usually in the form of land-use and hiring restrictions—often have little impact on the resolve of migrants, but can have secondary effects on the economy, increasing the cost of restricted commodities and forcing migrants into a legal gray area that undermines the government's law-enforcement capacity. Even in the absence of international migrants, restrictions meant to protect local goods from outsiders will often have a distorting and detrimental effect on the local economy that harms those the law is meant to protect.

Many, if not most, of the problems created by migrants are a consequence of flaws in how the government delivers services rather than the migrant's interaction with these services. In China, politicians regularly blamed migrants for the failure of Maoist-era industrial policy and social services, while the real problem was that these systems were fundamentally unsustainable. As China has reformed services programs so that they are supportive of internal migrants and internally cost effective, the demand for direct restrictions on migrants decreased and China was able to enjoy the economic benefits of an open labor market.

China's experience with the Great Migration has provided some sense of how governments can go about experimenting with more liberal migration policies and what the potential gains and drawbacks are of particular liberalization strategies. The poor are an underutilized resource, and costs of barring them from local and global trade networks can be substantial. Even minor changes to make laws more supportive to migrants would make the world a much better place for millions of people.

The Economic Gains from Migration

When Candy Nichols moved from Idaho to California (see Chapter 4), the change in her salary reflected, in a rough sense, how much more she was adding to the American economy. In Ms. Nichols's case, she earned an additional USD 90,000/year by working in an area where demand for her services was higher; money that she would be able to spend on her mortgage, food service providers, auto mechanics, and the variety of other people who provide services necessary for a happy and productive life. Her impact on California's economy was even larger. California would be nearly USD 150,000/year poorer if Ms. Nichols had not decided to relocate—that's 3 million dollars over the course of twenty years.

Nearly 20 percent of the nurses in Northern California come from the Philippines, where the average salary is roughly USD 3,000/year. The average salary for a starting nurse from the Philippines in San Francisco is USD 60,000/year.[12] This is USD 60,000/year that is being created for the California economy and USD 57,000/year that is being created for the global economy. Where Ms. Nichols is increasing her contribution to gross national income (GNI) by a substantial 150 percent, a Filipino nurse is increasing his or her contribution to global GNI by an eye-popping 1900 percent.

Economic research on migration is still in its infancy, particularly relative to the voluminous literature on the benefits of free trade and open financial markets, but what research has been conducted has routinely found that the potential gains from lifting barriers to the movement of people is somewhere in the range of 50 to 150 percent of global GDP—between USD 36 trillion and USD 98 trillion. The scale of the benefits is large enough to border on the unbelievable. By comparison, the World Bank estimated in 2001 that a total liberalization of trade barriers would increase global GDP between 1.2 and 2.8 percent of GDP—between USD 1 and USD 2 trillion.[13]

While unbelievable at first glance, if we consider these studies in light of the experience of Ms. Nichols and the roughly 400,000 Filipino nurses living and working in the United States, the figures become difficult to dismiss. Migration massively improves the lives of migrants—migrants who then go on to spend money on goods and services and invest in new businesses. Even if the existing research did not account for some of the downsides of migration, the downsides would have to be overwhelming to offset the gains. While the political problems associated with migration are broadly understood, the economic arguments underlying opposition to migration are at best conjectural and imprecise.

They are also widely believed. While Ms. Nichols would, in most cases, be applauded for her decision to migrate, the migration of Filipino nurses is generally seen as a problem. Efforts to expand the temporary worker programs for nurses have been proposed and have failed to pass Congress almost every year between 2006 and 2011.[14] The laws were spoken against by the American

Nursing Association, the main nurses union, and the Center for Immigration Studies, an anti-immigration think tank, both of which expressed concern that Congress was overlooking local workers.[15] The laws were also relatively small in scope, proposing to expand temporary working visas for nurses to 20,000 a year, compared to a predicted nursing shortage of 1 million people by 2020, reflecting the country's increasingly elderly population. By 2020, total healthcare spending is expected to increase to 19.8 percent of GDP, up from 17.6 percent in 2010, largely on the back of rising wages.[16] Today the law allows only 2,800 temporary Filipino migrants to enter the country a year, though considerably more manage to enter under long-term green cards.[17] Some Filipino politicians also opposed the law. Jamie Galvez-Tan, the country's former secretary of health worried that if the United States expanded opportunities for migrants, then the Philippines healthcare system would "bleed to death."

Few countries in the world are as large and diverse as China and the United States, which means, for most countries, support for migration equates to support for immigration or emigration. While many people can acknowledge that migrants are better off for migrating, opponents of migration continue to argue that regions as a whole are worse off due to migration, particularly when one region is significantly poorer than another, with lower education standards, lower wages, and lower levels of institutional trust. Migrants, according to this line of argument, are selfish, maximizing their own welfare at the cost of their place of birth and their adopted home.

There are three arguments usually made as to how migrants hurt their departure points and their destinations. The most common argument is that immigrants, by working for less money, are undermining the wages of local workers, while conversely increasing the cost of necessary services in the country of origin. The second argument is that migrants are undermining human capital formation in the country of origin, taking educational resources from their place of birth without repaying those resources in the form of labor. The third argument is that receiving countries lack the political or institutional capacity to absorb migrants, either because anti-migrant sentiment would translate to lower electoral support—if not nationalist violence or institutional collapse—or because the strength of an economy is predicated on limiting the distribution of social services. All three arguments are based on questionable reasoning.

Labor Market Responsiveness

A large part of the case against Filipino nurses rests on the idea that there are both too many of them and too few of them. There are too many Filipino nurses for the American hospitals to absorb without significant declines in local wages and employment, and too few Filipino nurses for Filipino hospitals to lose without experiencing a significant decline in quality of the country's healthcare industry.

The impact of mass migration on wages is well recorded and detailed in previous chapters of this book. The mass migration of Europeans to the United States during the late nineteenth and early twentieth centuries repressed wage growth by approximately 1 to 2 percent a decade across the country, and for a brief period led to negative wage growth in New York. It similarly led to a rise in wages in major émigré countries like Ireland and Italy.[18] Researchers have found that the migration from Mexico to the United States between 1970 and 2000 directly led to an 8 percent increase in average wages in Mexico.[19] China may be unique in that wages grew much faster in migrant-receiving provinces than migrant-sending provinces, reflecting the government's continued restrictions on rural-urban migration relative to the rapid growth in the country's urban economy.

This impact on wages all but disappears in modern developed economies, where immigrants are usually complementary to local workers rather than direct competitors. In the UK, for example, studies have found that the high levels of immigration brought about by opening to the European Union had a statistically negligible effect on wages. A 1 percent increase in the share of immigrants in the workforce was found to lead to a 0.6 percent decline in the wages of the poorest 5 percent, with the largest negative effect seen by previous migrants, who were competing directly with new migrants for jobs. Skilled workers saw an immediate gain in their earnings, while the impact on unskilled wages disappeared after ten years.[20] Others studies have found that a removal of 10 percent of immigration barriers leads on average to a 2.5

percent decline in wages in migrant-receiving countries; by comparison, a similar expansion of female employment in the workforce is accredited with a 3 to 5 percent decline in male wages.[21]

The declines in unskilled wages are usually found to be only a temporary consequence of mass migration rather than a long-term impact of population mobility. The reason for this can be seen with some back-of-the-envelope math: if the workforce expands by 10 percent, and wages decline by 3 percent, net worker income increases by 6.7 percent. This is money that is spent on consumer goods and services, and is invested back into the economy. Absent institutional barriers, the economy adjusts relatively quickly to meet the demand from this new spending, often with investments by the migrants themselves. Immigrants in America are disproportionately entrepreneurial, accounting for 20 percent of small business owners and 50 percent of top start-ups, despite only making up 13 percent of the population.[22]

The expansion of the workforce to meet new spending needs also contributes to maintaining job growth. Immigrants are usually found to have a negligible or net positive impact on local employment level. With the UK studies, some decrease in employment was found in local-born populations with an intermediate education, while workers who had passed higher education saw their employment prospects improve. Again, negative effects disappeared after ten years, while positive effects remained.[23] In the United States, the effect of immigrants on local employment has been shown to be positive, because immigrants compete more with outsourced low-skilled labor—for example, in China—than with local labor in the United States. By lowering the cost of local production, immigrants allow companies to stay onshore and employ domestic workers in higher-skilled jobs.[24]

For the most part, higher wages in developing migrant-supplying countries should be seen as a good thing, and are unlikely to challenge the sustainability of services provision. In the Philippines, higher demand for nurses has translated into higher demand for nursing education, with the number of nursing schools growing from 127 in 1995 to 300 by 2004. There are approximately six times as many nurses per capita living in the Philippines than in any other country of comparable income levels, as well as many countries that are significantly richer.[25] As of 2013, the most recent health secretary, Enrique Ona, was warning of a glut of nursing students.[26] In Africa, countries experiencing the largest outflows of doctors and nurses have systematically better health conditions than other parts of the continent.[27]

So while mass migration does seem to have an immediate impact on the price and availability of labor, the labor market response is generally much quicker and more efficient than any legal response. If liberalization is approached incrementally, the economic gains should consistently outweigh the costs.

The "Brain Drain"

Migration is much easier for the wealthy and the educated. They have more resources to make the trip, enjoy more opportunities at their destination, and often face less legal restrictions to migration than workers with fewer resources. This has often been framed as a barrier for developing countries, which lose their best and brightest to countries where the returns on their skills are higher. The assumption is that skilled workers provide important services, improve productivity of workers around them, and have been educated using public resources that have not yet been paid back through taxes.[28]

Though the freedom to emigrate is enshrined in the Universal Declaration of Human Rights of the United Nations and broadly enforced by international law, developing country governments have used the "brain drain" argument to pressure immigrant-receiving countries to bar certain skilled professionals from migrating. For example, the United Kingdom's National Health Service is prohibited from recruiting medical staff in developing countries, unless those countries give explicit permission for them to do so—permission that they have so far only received from the Philippines, India, and China.[29] The chairman of the British Medical Association described encouraging health professionals to emigrate from poor to rich countries as "the rape of the poorest countries." Others have suggested that companies that hire medical professionals from poor countries should be tried for crimes against humanity.[30]

It should be stated upfront that the Universal Declaration of Human Right protects emigration, and not immigration, for a reason. Denying workers the right to emigrate from their country of origin implies that nations have property rights over their citizens. Whether the denial comes in the form of direct restrictions as practiced by countries like North Korea and Cuba, or indirect restrictions through collaboration with receiving countries, the basic premise of controls on emigration is that citizens are property, and that their "owners" deserve compensation if they are to transfer ownership. Whatever the utilitarian argument for restricting emigration is, the moral argument is deeply questionable.

The utilitarian argument, it seems, is questionable as well. Research into the impact of emigration on development has shown up conspicuously empty-handed. While there is a correlation between poor development outcomes and emigration, the evidence points to causation going the other way: poor development outcomes lead to emigration, emigration does not lead to poor development outcomes.

Take the Filipino nurses again as an example. While nursing graduates are plentiful in the Philippines, the country's healthcare system continues to perform poorly, with high rates of maternal and child mortality. The reasoning for this is fairly straightforward, the Philippines is a poor country that struggles to invest in hospital infrastructure. In 2009, only 38.8 percent of pregnant women delivered their child in a hospital, while the ratio of hospital beds to the population is lower than it was in the 1980s.[31] The value that a Filipino nurse has to the Philippines depends not only on his or her presence within the country, but also to what extent the nurse can utilize his or her skills within the local market conditions.

And the Philippines is a best-case scenario. Skilled workers are often underemployed in developing countries due to barriers on hiring and private enterprise, similar to those seen in China prior to the Great Migration, or other less explicit prohibitions. For example, in some countries, nurses are banned from opening a clinic without the supervision of a physician, even if the alternative for a disadvantaged community is no healthcare services at all. Skilled female workers are significantly more likely to emigrate to Organisation for Economic Co-operation and Development (OECD) countries than skilled male workers, due to a lack of opportunities for women in many developing countries.[32]

While it seems intuitively obvious that there should be some positive gains associated with skilled workers remaining in a country, in practice these gains have been hard to measure, particularly relative to the large and certain gains that the migrant enjoys from emigrating. Research into the impact of increased educational investment on national productivity levels has found no statistically significant gains outside of the individual who is being educated—that is, nurses are no more productive if three doctors are around than if one doctor is around—implying that institutional restrictions on productivity are much more significant than human capital restrictions on productivity.[33]

Even if we assume that there are substantial gains to restricting educated workers from migrating out of developing areas, the extent that we would have to restrict migration in order to achieve these gains is unclear. In both Kenya and Mozambique, more than half of the country's physicians live in the capital city, while only approximately 8 percent of the population lives in the city. Without a hukou-like system of regional employment, there is no system where restrictions on skilled emigration are inherently helpful to the poor, and the consequences of such severe restrictions would almost certainly outweigh the benefits.[34]

All of these factors were at play in the story of Ah Louis. Ah Louis clearly was a talented man who was able to contribute to the development of California, but it does not follow that he would have contributed equally well, or at all, to China's development if he had decided not to emigrate. During the beginning of his career, Ah Louis's productivity would have been deeply constrained by the Taiping Rebellion. Even if he wasn't one of the roughly 20 million people to be killed during the conflict, any attempt to invest in local development would have been constrained by the threat of violence or various institutional barriers associated with the war effort, such as claiming of provisions, enforced conscription, or the redistribution of property to political allies. Even following the Taiping Rebellion, China failed to develop in the sixty years that Ah Louis lived in America. Ah Louis was an unskilled worker when he first arrived in America, and there were certainly millions more similarly talented people living in China at the time, but their decision to stay in the country had no substantial effect on the deterioration of the country's fortunes.

Skilled emigration also has positive spillovers for places of origin, many of which were detailed in previous chapters of this book. Many migrants return to their home country after some time abroad, particularly in situations where movement between countries is relatively easy. Besides returning their domestically earned education to the country, these returnees bring with them experience and knowledge of foreign business practices, technical skills from working with foreign technology, and knowledge of free-market institutions. Often they also bring with them significant amounts of money, which can be used to invest in a business utilizing international trade contacts. Even without returnees, the prospect of emigrant wages can be a motivation for others to pursue an education, though the reality of international immigration restrictions means that many, if not most, people who desire to emigrate from developing countries will be forced to remain at home.[35]

Institutional Barriers

While there are few legitimate economic reasons to restrict migration, supporting migrants does come with political consequences, particularly rapid migration into an area where migrants are directly competing with locals for wages. Migrants are, almost by definition, a group that lacks political representation, meaning that pro-migrant policymaking is dependent on the extent that policymakers can gain the support, or at least avoid the ire, of politically represented groups.

This consideration is particularly relevant in developing countries like those in South Asia or Africa, where the citizens in the receiving area do not have substantially more access to capital or skills than the migrant population. But even in developed countries, rising income inequality and advancements in technology that allow capital to substitute for skilled labor have increasingly made pro-migrant development policy difficult. Add to this various cultural, religious, and nationalist pressures, and pro-migrant development policy can come across as irredeemably idealistic and politically suicidal.

The politics of migration can change rapidly. Thirty years ago, it would have been unthinkable for workers from Poland to have large-scale access to employment opportunities in the rest of Europe. Today it's enshrined in European law. Since 1990, the number of Chinese-born Americans has nearly tripled while the number of Indian-born Americans has quadrupled, in both cases without significant political backlash.[36] The world has managed to overcome restrictions on the labor mobility of women, slaves, serfs, rural Chinese, and South African blacks, and there are no a priori reasons why international migrants are different.

Even modest changes to emigration policy can have a significant impact on the wealth of a nation. Research from Zahid Hussain at the World Bank found that Bangladeshis working in the Middle East on temporary work permits made on average six times Bangladesh's average GDP per person. Though the average Bangladeshi had to pay USD 3,150 to intermediaries—substantially more than the average household income—the average return on investment was roughly 117 percent annually over a three-year employment period. If governments were to remove only some of the barriers that force migrants to hire an intermediary, the returns would be even higher.[37] If the Bangladeshis were able to move to a developed country instead of the Middle East, the gains would be higher still.

The most common proposal for addressing the political costs of migration is to tax it and use the tax revenues to subsidize social services for the poor—the typical losers from high migration rates. Even if migration taxes were linked to tax cuts elsewhere, this could provide enough of a positive externality that voters would be willing to support a larger influx of migrants. Similarly, the government could auction off work permits, which would give systematic preference to workers with capital that could invest in job-creating enterprises—though this would do little for low-skilled workers who are the most likely to engage in illegal migration.

There are some low-hanging fruits that policymakers can attack prior to addressing the question of how many or how few migrants should be allowed across a border. As China's experience with the Great Migration has shown, many of the most severe barriers to migration are domestic policies that regulate how migrants are allowed to interact with the local economy. These barriers can harm intranational migrants as much, if not more, than international migrants and can accentuate the economic and political costs of migration. These programs should be reformed for the sake of political constituents, even if the benefits are more pronounced for migrants.

Namely, a pro-migrant domestic policy would focus on five points:

1. Strengthen property rights in migrant-supplying regions to improve migrants' access to capital.
2. Ease restrictions on hiring and new company formation so changes to the labor market could be quickly absorbed by the receiving region.

3. Reduce the cost and improve the responsiveness of infrastructure construction, with a particular focus on housing.
4. Improve the sustainability of basic social services.
5. Lift direct barriers to migration.

These, of course, are the same issues that China had to deal with over the course of the Great Migration, issues that form the core of what should be understood as China's basic development strategy. While China's situation was somewhat unique due to the policy infrastructure it inherited from Mao, each of these problems has parallels in other developing or developed countries, often with severe consequences for the citizens of those countries. If a politician is looking for low-hanging fruit, then this is a good place to start.

Agriculture

China's government has been struggling with the issue of rural land rights for the better part of a millennium. Under Mao, China's government came up with a solution that was unique in its horribleness. People were tied to their land, and forced to work for a commune whose leaders were well within their rights to sell all of a village's food, leaving workers to starve or subsist on what they could scavenge. Starting in the early 1980s, China implemented a system of basic land-use rights that was slowly strengthened to the point where it is currently approaching a full land-rights system.

While China's struggle with rural land rights was certainly unique, rural land rights continue to be a problem across a large segment of the world. South Africa and Zimbabwe both have long-standing land reform programs that aim to transfer land from the white population to the black population in order to redress the abuses of those countries' apartheid governments. Both laws are widely considered to be failures, though problems with the Zimbabwe law have been accentuated by the government's use of force to expropriate landholdings.[38] In Brazil and Colombia, there are long-standing campaigns to expropriate land from agribusiness companies and redistribute it to the rural poor. While neither campaign has gotten political support, they continue to be high on the agenda of those governments.[39] In India, many rural dwellers are barred from leasing their land, and throughout Africa rural dwellers are often barred from selling land without the permission of their tribal leader.[40] Recently, global controversy has arisen from land-shortage countries like Saudi Arabia, South Korea, and China purchasing land for agribusiness from countries that have been willing to sell their land, including Myanmar and much of Africa.[41]

Tensions run high in these debates, but they are often short of real substance. Land can be treated with almost mythical reverence in political discourse, but there is little sense as to why poor people would be better off owning a piece of land than they would be from the sort of tax-and-transfer schemes that are enjoyed by poor people in developed countries. In fact, land ownership may be significantly worse, as land redistribution focuses welfare income in one volatile industry rather than spreading costs across several income streams. And, as China found out, efforts to maintain even land distributions will always be undermined by population growth.

This isn't to say that rural land distribution isn't an important issue for the rural poor, rather it is to say that the underlying issue is *how* people are being transferred out of agriculture rather than *if* they should be transferred out of agriculture. The central conceit of a market economy is that an individual should know better than the government what is best for him and his property under conditions of shortage. Rural dwellers need to be able to decide for themselves whether it is more profitable to stay on their land or leave for the cities without legal pressure from policymakers.

Policymakers do have a role in supporting these decisions, though. An effective rural land-rights policy would ensure that poor rural dwellers have secure rights to their land, including the ability to sell and lease their land to their neighbors or agribusiness concerns. The government could help ensure that poor farmers have access to the same markets as rich farmers. Finally, farmers who lose their land either through expropriation or a poorly considered investment need to have access to the same opportunities in the industrial economy and the same social safety net that other workers have access to.

The majority of Africa still has laws that recognize the rights of tribal chiefs to control the sale of land within area designated as part of a village, even if customary land rights are held by a specific member of the village.[42] This gives chiefs an easy opportunity to profit off of other's property, which, as development picks up across Africa, has become a constant temptation. Similarly, governments can use a lack of precision regarding land rights to expropriate land in order to support development projects or foreign agriculture projects that provide more direct revenues to government coffers.

Expanding private land rights in Africa is an old idea. Many countries have tried and most have failed to at least loosen the control of traditional tribal chieftains over the country's legal system. The problem is usually accredited to "culture," which is to say a difficult mix of politics and poor legal enforcement.[43] Difficult—but also a problem that has been solved in many countries before.

One possible path forward would be to establish a set of best practices that agricultural companies should abide by when investing overseas, with a focus on ensuring that people who had previously used the land that they are investing in received the majority of compensation. An index of what countries have the best and worst enforcement of land rights can help companies and activists identify at a glance if they are likely to have problems following these best practices—land rights are already a component of the American NGO Freedom House's annual Freedom in the World rankings. This would increase oversight of projects that could cause political problems, while allowing projects that are positive for those selling their land to continue unimpeded. With investment linked to reform, governments would have an incentive to improve legal protections for the poor while foreign countries would keep their hands clean from accusations of landgrabs.

China originally faced a very different problem when reforming its agriculture system. While many African countries are willing to let the victims of expropriation wander landless, living in shantytowns, and surviving on whatever work they can find, China's number one priority was to restrict urbanization. Agriculture acted as a sort of social safety net, which allowed China's government to send people home when the cities didn't want them, with the assurance that at least they wouldn't starve.

While few other countries are as explicitly concerned with urbanization as China is, agriculture's role as a safety net has been widely recognized by development experts, and investment in agriculture has been touted by the World Bank as a means of reducing the impact of economic shocks.[44] One consequence of agriculture's role as a safety net is that land-rental markets can play a particularly important part in the transition from a rural to an urban economy. Renting rural land allows workers to engage in short-term migrant labor while still maintaining residency in rural areas, or alternately can provide basic funds that can support the worker's establishment in an urban area. Besides China's experience, this can be clearly seen in the case of Mexico, where researchers found that households receiving a land certificate between 1993 and 2006 were 28 percent more likely to have a migrant member.[45]

Improving farmers' access to capital, physical infrastructure, and markets would help this transition process. China, for example, still maintains a largely positive role in agricultural markets as a supplier of crop insurance, and subsidizes access to agricultural technology and some infrastructure construction. This is an area where developed countries can help. Agricultural subsidies and trade barriers in developed markets' agricultural sector disproportionately hurt small-scale farmers, and any reduction in these market distortions should be applauded.[46] Investment from foreign companies in developing-world agricultural markets, as long as they are cautious about land expropriation issues, should also be applauded.[47] Foreign investors bring money, technology, machinery, and know-how into the sector, and can be particularly helpful for increasing access to developed-world consumers.

The problems associated with rural land laws decline significantly in countries with robust industrial employment and a basic social safety net, meaning, to some extent, these reforms are likely to be ongoing alongside larger reforms to the economy and the treatment of migrants.

Hiring and New Company Formation

In 2012, the radio show *This American Life* covered a one-man play by Mike Daisey recounting his experience visiting the Foxconn factory in Shenzhen and talking with workers about the working conditions at the factory. He claimed to have witnessed widespread use of underage labor, guards carrying guns, mangled workers, and some who claimed to have been beaten, using these stories to advocate for a change in how Apple produces its popular products. Two months after the radio show was aired, *This American Life* issued a retraction after they found that Mike Daisey's experience had been largely fabricated. The radio show was widely believed and reported on by several other news and entertainment channels, including in *The Daily Show with*

Jon Stewart episode referenced by the bartender in Zhengzhou (see p. 130). Even well after the retraction, there was a widespread belief that Foxconn was abusing its workers.[48]

Foxconn is not a great place to work. It generally pays the lowest wages of any employer in a city, with only meager benefits. There's a reason for this. Foxconn hires so many people that surrounding companies have to raise their wages and improve their working conditions in order to compete for labor, a competition that cannot continue indefinitely. Foxconn is also not a horrible place to work. The company is regularly vetted against abuse, and workers are free to work elsewhere—a right that many thousands of the company's workers partake of every day. Manufacturing hiring continues to be robust in the country, and workers, as previously mentioned, have access to a social safety net in the form of their land. Why, then, were the producers of *This American Life* so eager to swallow a story that fact-checkers were able to, fairly quickly, establish as false?

Shortly after the first *This American Life* show aired, the *New York Times* began a run of articles that aimed to explain why Apple made its products abroad rather than employing more Americans. The series, which would go on to win the Pulitzer Prize, went over many of the features of the greater Asian supply chain that has cemented China's role as a global manufacturing leader: the concentration of component suppliers, the ability to hire large numbers of workers quickly, the flexible working hours, and, of course, an article providing anecdotal examples of worker abuse (much better substantiated than the claims in *This American Life*). A few months after the series ran, the *Times* ran a story about improvements to working conditions supposedly brought about by their story, completely ignoring the possibility that in an atmosphere of rising wages, workers might have been able to negotiate for themselves.[49]

There's something deeply appealing about the idea of the helpless migrant —migrants who are not able to make decisions for themselves, who are vulnerable to exploitation because they don't know any better, who would be better off at home where their poverty is comfortably in the collective blind spot rather than working at the low-end of the global supply chain in full view of consumers. Poverty is ugly, and it is easy to find fault with a situation where the most profitable company in the world pays its workers one of the lowest wages in China, even if it only pays the lowest wage because other factories have to raise their wages to compete. And certainly abuses of migrants still happen: the audit Apple conducted of its suppliers following the controversy found at least one factory that regularly used child labor, a sign of systematic exploitation rather than a forged ID or an occasional willingness to look the other way. Migrants are also vulnerable to being forced into slavery, as happened in a series of cases in Shanxi in 2007. The risk of abuse is even worse for international migrants who often have less legal rights than domestic migrants, and face a hostile cultural environment.[50]

But that wasn't what was happening here. The *New York Times*, writing at the height of the worst economic crisis since the Great Depression, was asking why poor people deserve to have jobs that could be filled by people who are much more wealthy. This argument was passed off with claims that migrants were open to exploitation, because, like children, they were unable to make decisions about their own employment.

The restrictions on private employment that China maintained until the mid-1990s were based on the same patronizing argument. From the perspective of a worker, it does not matter whether his or her employer is a state-owned enterprise (SOE), a private enterprise, a large conglomerate, or a feisty start-up; what matters is that the worker is able to make a decision about what job offers the best opportunities for compensation, career building, working conditions, and long-term security. Communism took that choice away and forced workers to work for a single employer that usually failed to satisfy those demands.

The proliferation of small factories, construction companies, and services companies after 1978 gave workers the opportunity to negotiate with their employers for a higher salary with the real threat that they might quit for another job elsewhere. Many took advantage of the right to quit, leading to a continued high rate of employee turnover in Chinese factories, particularly at low-end employers like Foxconn.[51] Despite the fact that almost every rural-urban migrant has the opportunity to return home where a basic income from farming should be waiting for him or her, very few choose to return to farming.

If we don't buy into the myth of the helpless migrant, then improving the situation of workers in developing countries means improving the scope of their choices. As long as people still need to work, an economy with 1,000 companies that are able to hire whom they please will put workers in a better negotiating position than an economy with 100 companies who can only hire some workers. Most countries do not have SOEs, but all countries place some restrictions on market access and employee contract rights, which a migrant-friendly development policy should target for reform.

A particularly strong example is South Africa, which in recent years has experienced both high levels of unemployment—often over 25 percent—and rapid wages increases. The number of self-employed in South Africa rose by 2 million between 1995 and 2005, while the number of privately employed fell by 150,000.[52] While the wage increases are certainly good for the people who have jobs, a 25 percent unemployment rate in a poor country is a tragedy. Rapid wage gains in an economy with a 25 percent unemployment rate is a scandal.

There is no clean answer as to why South Africa faces a substantially larger unemployment rate than other countries at the same income level, but there are a few likely culprits. The most commonly mentioned is South Africa's strong unions. South African law allows unions to impose collective agreements reached by bargaining councils to all companies in a particular industry—meaning that a start-up with no immediate cash flow has to pay its workers the same amount as a large company that produces regular dividends for share-holders. These agreements cover about 25 percent of formal sector employees. In 2005, union wages were 17 percent higher than wages of nonunionized workers, while wages per unit of output would almost double between 2003 and 2006, indicating that unionized workers were taking much of the income that could have otherwise been directed toward new employment.[53]

The trade unions naturally dispute this analysis, instead blaming government economic policy and free trade, particularly China's dominance of the textile market, as a proximate cause of high-unemployment rates in manufacturing.[54] These arguments don't hold up to much scrutiny. In 2006, the country imposed restrictions on imports of Chinese clothing, which led to the total value of imports from China dropping by 50 percent the following year. This provided no net benefit to local industry, with the gap left by China quickly filled by imports from Vietnam, Pakistan, and Mauritius, while it had a real cost to consumers as these new suppliers had higher prices than China.[55] Foreign direct investment in the sector has also declined, as profit margins have been low or negative due to rising wages and lower sales.[56] South Africa is simply not able to produce textiles at a cost that can be absorbed by the market.

The typical left-wing argument for unionization is that workers need to restrict access to labor in order to advocate for political representation against privileged holders of capital. In countries where there is high labor market turnover, though, this is counterproductive. Workers in China have been able to advocate effectively for both higher wages and better working conditions by threatening to quit. In an economy where there are fifty companies doing the same thing, this is an effective threat, and even in poorly functioning economies, it's a threat with some traction. Strong unions and restrictions on new company formation have pushed roughly 10 percent of Nepal's workforce out to foreign countries.[57] Expanding the workforce allows for new companies to form and provides more economic leverage for workers to negotiate with companies for wages rather than turn every wage negotiation into a drawn-out political fight. Unions, however, are fighting against demographics and against migrants; without prudent regulations, they contribute to the shrinking of the labor market rather than the growth of labor's share of the market.

Making this argument would be easier if it wasn't for the fact that so many developing countries restrict new business formation as much as they do labor. These restrictions take forms ranging from bureaucratic hurdles for new company formation and strict licensing restrictions to laws passed to protect incumbents and subsidized use of state assets. These laws slow new company formation and restrict opportunities for workers to sell their skills elsewhere.

While there is a role for licensing in any economy, there is a strong argument to be made that developing countries need weaker regulatory barriers than developed countries. Licensing increases the costs of services. In developed countries, this usually means that consumers consume less of the services, or, in the case of necessary services, they transfer money from another spending area. In a developing country, that implies that many consumers will not be able to access a service at all. If a nurse is banned from opening a clinic without a physician present in Maine, then patients have to go to a more expensive hospital; if a nurse is banned from opening a clinic in Mozambique, patients go without basic healthcare.[58] This extends to employment barriers: a rich economy has more business activity to absorb workers and a stronger safety net for those who fall out of the workforce; a poor economy has poverty. Poorly defined permit and licensing systems are also a breeding ground for corruption, as they allow bureaucrats to level arbitrary fees and aid preferred clients. And while most developing countries do not have SOEs running the economy, many of the richest businesspeople in the developing world enjoy government-supported monopolies that are no less harmful.[59]

The easiest way for developed countries to help developing countries create jobs is to ease tariff and nontariff barriers to trade. This is particularly a problem in agriculture, where developing-country workers have an obvious comparative advantage, but often can't access developed-world markets because of tariffs, subsidies to incumbents, or pseudoscientific bans or labeling laws. A study from the University of Lausanne in 2010 found that ending market distortions associated with the European Union's Common Agricultural Policy would increase global GDP by EUR 33 billion (USD 45.5 billion), with the majority of the benefits going to Europe itself (EUR 18.6 billion) followed by Latin America (EUR 6.4 billion).[60]

Poverty means a lack of choices, not the lack of the ability to make choices. People who grow up in poverty have poor access to education and healthcare, they don't have enough money to start companies, and even if they are qualified for a job, they often face difficulties getting to and from their workplace. Employment restrictions can help workers who are already employed, but for those making the transition out of poverty, restrictions on which companies can hire will only make their position more difficult.

Infrastructure

If you manage to miss the traffic, it takes just under two hours to drive the hundred miles from Sacramento in California's central valley to Fremont along the coast of San Francisco Bay. Both cities cover roughly the same land area, but people choose to live in Sacramento at almost twice the rate that people choose to live in Fremont. Some of the people who work in Fremont will even commute from Sacramento so they don't have to live in Fremont. If we assume that people make rational decisions, then we have to say that Sacramento is objectively a better place to live than Fremont.

By almost any other measure, though, Sacramento is an objectively worse place to live. Sacramento sits in the middle of the state's agricultural heartland, the city is home to nearly 500,000 people, earning on average USD 50,013 per household. More than 22 percent of the city's population lives below the US's official poverty line, compared to a rate of 15.3 percent nationally. The city's average high temperature in June is a scorching 93 degrees. Fremont is a city on the outskirts of Silicon Valley. It's a growing destination for tech companies, and the home of the Tesla Motors factory. The median household income is just over USD 100,000. Only 6.3 percent of the population lives under the US official poverty rate. The city's average high temperature never exceeds a temperate 77 degrees.[61]

The reason why people choose Sacramento over Fremont by such an overwhelmingly high margin is not a mystery. In August 2016, the average rent for a one-bedroom apartment in Sacramento was USD 2,156. The average rent for a one-bedroom apartment in Fremont was USD 4,372.[62] The government of Fremont, which strictly manages the size and location of new building, has decided that the city should be a luxury good. High rents keep out poorer residents and minimize expenses on social services, while maximizing tax revenues. This presents a cleaner image to residents and investors, but it directly harms the economy, forcing companies to subsidize high rents through wages and preventing many companies from forming in the first place.

Fremont's decision to restrict density is usually defended with a sort of Yogi Berra logic—"if it gets too crowded, no one will want to come here." The reality is somewhat more subtle. In most cities, people who own property only own partial rights to their land. A parcel is like a unit in a condo building; you are free to change the interior, but any changes that might affect other residents have to go through the condo board—except in this case the condo board is the city government. Higher density buildings can require changes to existing infrastructure that can sometimes be costly, and it requires co-opting homeowners who consider their neighborhood as part of their property rights.

While zoning laws are supposed to support long-term residents at the expense of short-term residents, in Silicon Valley they seem to have done the opposite. Despite the sky-high cost of rent, the San Francisco Bay Area has the highest price/rent ratio in the lower forty-eight states.[63] Silicon Valley locals, the sort that want to own property and settle down for the long-term, face substantially higher costs of entry than short-term migrants who can make do with rental housing. Tech companies, unsurprisingly, prefer to hire workers from abroad, whose wage demands are generally lower because they do not have to invest in housing.[64] In most parts of the country, one high-paying tech job supports five local services jobs. In the Bay Area, the number is closer to two.[65]

When these sort of anti-density measures are applied in the developing world, the result is not only slower growth, but much higher rates of poverty. When people think about developing countries around the world, one of the images that tends to come to mind are the large urban slums in Mumbai, Rio de Janeiro, and Johannesburg, where the poor seem to live on top of each other in search of a piece of the urban economy. The horrendous poverty in these slums contributes to the myth that migrants would be better off in rural areas, and that leaving rural areas was either forced on them or is an indication of poor decision-making skills. What's wrong with this argument is that outside of China, developing countries simply aren't that dense.

Take India, for example. In 1980, 25 percent of India's population lived in cities, compared to 20 percent in China. By 2015, India's urbanization rate had grown to 32 percent, China's had grown to 53 percent. The reason being, India simply doesn't build enough. Mumbai's cost per square meter of real estate was over USD 11,000 in 2015, higher than Tokyo. Shanghai, China's most expensive real estate market, sells a square meter of real estate for under USD 7,000—less than Taipei. Incomes in India are less than half the levels of China, putting housing even further out of reach of the average Indian.[66] Johannesburg and Rio are less dense than Los Angeles.

Opportunities for the poor and urban density go hand in hand. The easier it is for a worker to live in a city, interact with other people in the same field, and put face time in with potential employers, the easier it is for that person to find a job. In cities where housing is more expensive, there's more competition for a seat closer to the table and the poor get left on the sidelines.

For most Chinese, their first trip to the city involves living in a dormitory, working at a factory, and eating at cheap noodle stands along the side of the road. For almost all migrants, this spare existence is preferable to living in the countryside. They earn more money, have a sense of independence, and have a chance to build a career rather than accepting the poverty they were born into. There is no point where someone is better off because they are not able to afford the housing they want. Access to cheap housing gives the poor more opportunities to make decisions about how best to improve their lives, which in almost all cases leads to real improvements in their living standards.

While urban areas are wonderful tools for expanding market access and employment opportunities for the poor, another lesson from China is that reducing the cost of infrastructure can be as important as increasing density. The political barriers to urbanization can often be higher than barriers to rural development, and as was seen during the township and village enterprise (TVE) period in China, reducing the cost of housing, roads, rails, piping, and electricity so that poor people can engage with distant markets and employers can work with the rural poor can transform the countryside from an impoverished supply station for urban development to an independent engine of growth. And even in cities, development can abruptly stop because the cost of new subways, roads, and bridges climbs too high for the government to manage.

While there is an assortment of best practices associated with infrastructure construction—most of which are routinely not followed—in countries with high corruption and poor government capacity, it is important to get the private sector involved.[67] Public-private partnerships (PPP) and fully private infrastructure construction can provide both a crucial source of capital and market oversight of budgeting. Encouraging the private sector to approach the government with infrastructure projects will also improve the government's ability to respond to market demand.[68]

China has famously built world-class infrastructure often while working under serious fiscal constraints. During the reform period, politically ignored cities like Wenzhou and distant rural areas would use private sector funds almost exclusively. Rural areas were able to maintain Communist levels of infrastructure investment with only private sector funds, while Wenzhou jump-started a decade of nearly 20 percent annual growth.

These projects had a few big things going in their favor. The most important was access to capital, originally through unofficial markets, then increasingly through subsidized bank loans. The second was a relatively blank-slate regulatory system. Licensing and registration procedures were nearly nonexistent, while the government was quick to embrace private sector fundraising mechanisms like toll roads as a means of encouraging investment. Low wages and low-priced inputs also helped keep the costs down.

While subsidized bank loans would be unadvisable, once proof of concept has been established, finding funding through bond issuances should not be difficult. Infrastructure projects can provide a steady income over a long term, with private-public projects often a preferred low-risk investment for pension funds. Linking construction to surrounding industrial projects—a road to a factory, for example—should further increase financial support both from the industrial projects themselves and because the associated guaranteed income would assist fundraising through traditional channels.[69]

China has also used land sales as a means to raise money for infrastructure projects. While China's expropriation system is not recommended, other governments, most notably Hong Kong, have sold commercial real estate around major transit hubs as a way to raise money for surrounding infrastructure.[70] This does not provide the same transparency benefits that PPPs provide, but it does help with the fundraising process and encourages more stakeholders to get involved.

Social Services

The delivery of social services in a developing economy is a difficult task that defies a simple solution. It also matters quite a lot for the sustainability of any pro-migrant program. In China, poor healthcare coverage for migrants contributed to the 2003 SARS epidemic, while poor educational opportunities for migrant children contributed to growing levels of illiteracy during the 1990s. Rural Chinese workers have also benefited from indirect social services, being better able to migrate and take risks than workers in other economies due to the minimum basic income provided by their land.

Higher social services payments can undermine migration's positive role in the economy. One problem contributing to South Africa's struggle with unemployment has been the extension of the generous pension system enjoyed by whites under apartheid to the entire economy. This extension has been a clear disincentive for workers struggling under the country's weak labor market, with "retired" workers regularly reentering the workforce when employment can be found that pays them higher than state pension benefits. While this is fine for the workers as long as the government can keep paying pensions, it has opportunity costs for the larger economy, as lower paid jobs are not being filled. The transition from apartheid has also greatly expanded the level of education among black workers. This is undoubtedly a good thing, but, like any labor market shock, it has driven down the once high wage premium enjoyed by high school graduates, and may have contributed to high wage expectations among the unemployed.[71]

In terms of affordability, migration usually has a negligible or net positive effect on social services programs, with a 2013 OECD study finding that immigrant households on average contribute 0.3 percent of GDP more than they receive in benefits. The main reason for this is that international immigrants tend to migrate for the sake of employment, not for the sake of social benefits. As such, they tend to be younger than the average population in developed countries, and create more income for payouts to older beneficiaries. On the other hand, immigrants tend to experience unemployment at higher rates than native-born workers, which can increase social services payouts under more generous social safety net schemes or in situations where spending is influenced by significant regulatory distortions. In the United States, for example, migrants make a net contribution to the country's pension system amounting to 0.5 percent of GDP, which is almost entirely cancelled out by payments for health services to migrants. In Germany, on the other hand, migrants have a net cost to the pension system of 1.3 percent of GDP, but a net positive contribution elsewhere. These estimates do not include increased tax revenue arising from migrants' impact on economic growth.[72]

The Great Migration has forced China to dismantle and restructure several social services programs in order to make them sustainable with larger population flows. Early on, China had to end both government grain stipends and government housing provision due to the pressures and distortions brought on by migrants. More recently, China has introduced private pension savings accounts and centralized healthcare subsidies in order to improve fiscal flows into these programs. Still, China is hardly a model for the world. The country still restricts access to social services for a large percentage of its population, with serious costs to the country's health and welfare.

China has eased the pressure on its social services system somewhat, because of the minimum basic income available to rural-urban migrants due to guaranteed rural land rights. While this barely provides a subsistence income for most workers, it is enough that migrants can take chances in the big city without worrying that they will lose everything. China's restrictive land-rights system is hardly a model for other developing countries, but developing a similar basic income system through taxes and transfers could be just as effective.

The idea of a minimum basic income has a long association with rural land rights. One of the oldest incarnations of this idea was proposed in 1797 by the American revolutionary Thomas Paine as a means of redistributing some of the wealth associated with rural land ownership, which still maintained an association with landed nobility, while maintaining strong land rights. His proposal was to give 15 pounds to all people at age 21 (USD 17,500 today), and 10 pounds a year to all people over 50, with the money taken from a 10 percent tax on inherited land.[73]

The advantages that this proposal has over the land redistribution schemes that have been enacted in South Africa and Zimbabwe are obvious. Landowners would be able to guarantee the ownership of their property, while the poor would have more assets to support migration and find jobs in more modern areas of the economy. A minimum basic income program also has a lot going for it as a social safety net, particularly in countries with poor government capacity or high levels of corruption. Payments could be made directly through a taxation authority and paid to cell phones, retail or postal banks without building a new social services bureaucracy. If explicitly framed as a social safety net for people living in extreme poverty rather than a reparations program or a means of redistributing wealth, then payments could be kept low enough that they wouldn't have a significant negative impact on unemployment, while taking some pressure off of other more generous safety net programs.[74]

The International Hukou

The policies detailed above are all targeted toward improving the situation of locals, with the added benefit of lowering the costs and consequences of migration. The largest economic returns, though, will come from easing direct barriers to migration: immigration laws.

As China's experience has made clear, the problems created by open borders are real and substantial, even if the economic balance sheet is overwhelmingly positive. Large-scale movement across borders weakens the capacity of social services ranging from law enforcement, education, and healthcare to housing, heating, and water. This is particularly true when migration is responding to a sudden event, so institutional mechanisms and markets do not have time to adapt.

But the substantial gains from migration are not limited to countries with open borders. When Candy Nichols migrated to California, she wasn't dependent on other migrants for her decision to be economically valuable. There is no reason to think a country that incrementally expands the number of immigrants allowed to access its labor markets would not see economic gains proportional to the number of workers immigrating. Maintaining predictable migration numbers, through quotas or other restrictions, will allow services markets (such as housing) and social services to adapt and better integrate a growing population.

This is, more or less, how the United States manages its immigration policy. America takes in roughly 18 percent of the world's immigrants through one of a variety of visa categories, including separate numerically controlled visas for workers, refugees, asylum seekers, spouses and children of green card holders, and siblings of American citizens, as well as 55,000 people chosen randomly as part of the diversity visa lottery. Alongside this, the US sees a predictable flow of nonnumerically controlled visas for the spouses, children, and parents of US citizens. In total, roughly 500,000 people permanently relocate to the United States every year along with 85,000 temporary skilled workers (H1b).[75]

If we are to take the economics literature on migration at face value, then one of the easiest ways to fight poverty in the developing world and improve economic performance back home would be to expand the diversity visa system. Diversity visa applicants need to meet four qualifications to get a US visa: they must have never committed a crime, to not be found a threat to the United States, to have a high school diploma, and to have a place to stay in the US. That's it. The visa numbers are also limited to countries with lower numbers of immigrants in the United States, with each country receiving no more than 7 percent of total issuances to prevent a single country from having outsized influence on the American political process.

Much of the advocacy to increase visa numbers focuses on skilled immigration. Many developed countries make it tragically difficult for master's and PhD students from foreign countries to transfer to a working visa after graduation. This effectively bars them from contributing to the economy that educated them and, in most cases, significantly reduces their lifetime earnings.[76] There is no good reason for this policy. Educated workers both contribute more to fiscal revenues and contribute more to job creation than noneducated workers, they have a positive impact on the wages of unskilled workers, and whatever impact they have on the wages of skilled workers is negligible, particularly in the era of outsourcing.[77]

But reforms should not only focus on skilled workers. Even in developed countries, unskilled workers remain a crucial part of the workforce and, over the long term, contribute significantly more to the economy than they take out in terms of social services. Immigration policy is an unusually effective form of development aid, providing workers from a developing country with an income significantly larger than they would receive in their home country, skills that they can transfer back home, and a debt of gratitude to the country that took them in. Expanding the diversity visa lottery by a set amount every year—or creating it in countries where it doesn't exist—would allow countries to adapt to the additional burden on social services and improve the demographics of aging countries while avoiding the political risk associated with large amounts of migration from single countries. It would also be very good for the poor.

In developing countries that are already struggling to create jobs for the local population, unskilled immigration is a harder sell, but China's experience in the Great Migration shows that the advantages can easily outweigh the disadvantages. Immigrants, whether they are skilled or unskilled, create connections with communities in other countries that contribute to trade linkages and the development of specialized industrial clusters. Immigration also allows workers to "vote with their feet," often providing much-needed feedback on the effectiveness of local economy policies.

The value of an open labor market is one of the truisms of economics. Giving people the opportunity to cross borders and pursue economic opportunities creates wealth for migrants, those around them, and the global economy. The largest barrier to migration is political, but political opinions can change rapidly. Fifty years ago, a common labor market in Europe would have been unthinkable; there is no reason that changes on a similar scale could not happen globally over the next fifty years.

• • •

In January 1979, one hundred years after California wrote a constitution banning Chinese labor, Deng Xiaoping made his first historic visit to the US. Early in the trip, the new chairman and US President Jimmy Carter had a now-famous exchange about their country's relative migration policies. The United States had granted China diplomatic recognition earlier that month, but had refused to grant normal trading relations. The problem, Carter explained, was that US law prohibited granting most-favored nation status to centrally managed economies unless they allow free emigration.

Deng Xiaoping smiled and asked, "Well, Mr. President, how many Chinese do you want? Ten million? Twenty million? Thirty million?"[78]

The numbers were small compared to what Deng Xiaoping and his successors would have to deal with in the coming years, but it was enough to make Deng's point. The topic was quickly changed.

This conversation encapsulates much of the world's migration policy. Instead of looking to the market to see how much labor is in demand and how that labor can be supplied, politicians say a number, sometimes an arbitrary number, and almost always one that severely undervalues migrants.

In the following three and a half decades, those 30 million Chinese and many more like them would contribute to the greatest development story in human history. They would build the largest manufacturing economy in the history of the world, one that many Americans would blame for their own country's loss of jobs overseas.

How many did we want? Ten million? Twenty million? Thirty million? How many more remain unwanted?

Notes

Introduction

1. United Nations, *The Millennium Development Goals Report 2015*, New York: United Nations, 2015, 15.
2. *Economist,* "Good Tidings from the South," December 3, 2011; Nick Miroff, "Latin American Equality: Free Markets or a Left-Wing Success?," *Global Post,* December 1, 2012.
3. Acha Leke, Susan Lund, Charles Roxburgh, and Arend Van Wamelen, "What's Driving Africa's Growth," McKinsey & Company, June 2010.
4. William Easterly, *The White Man's Burden: Why the West's Efforts to Aid the Rest Have Done So Much Ill and So Little Good*, New York: Penguin, 2006, 7; Dambisa Moyo, *Dead Aid: Why Aid Is Not Working and How There Is a Better Way for Africa*, New York: Farrar, Straus and Giroux, 2010, 8.
5. The Organisation for Economic Co-operation and Development (OECD), "State Owned Enterprises in China: Reviewing the Evidence," January 26, 2009, 8–9. World Bank and the Development Research Center of the State Council, *China 2030: Building a Modern, Harmonious and Creative Society*, Washington, DC: World Bank, 2013, 4.
6. *CRI Online,* "Zhōngguó tiělù chūnyùn 40tiān fāsòng lǚkè 2.4yì réncì" [China's trains saw 240 million passengers during the 40 days around the Spring Festival], March 10, 2013; Xu Jin, "Quánguó 2yì yóukè chūnjié chūxíng shànghǎi shìmín xuǎnzé chūjìng yóu zhàn bǐwéi 39.85%" [Across the country 200 million people travelled during the spring festival, including 39.85% of Shanghai residents], *Eastday,* February 19, 2013; *Shanghai Railway Bureau,* "Shànghǎi tiělùjú tíqián zuò hǎo chūnyùn chēliàng zhǔnbèi gōngzuò" [Shanghai Railway Bureau prepares for the Spring Festival], December 27, 2012; *Shanghai Railway Bureau,* "Chūnjié huángjīnzhōu shànghǎi tiělùjú sòngkè 569.6Wàn rén" [Shanghai Railway Bureau: During the Spring festival 5.696 million people travelled], February 16, 2013; *Shanghai Railway Bureau,* "Shànghǎi tiělùjú chūnyùn 40tiān ānquán sòng kè 4113wàn rén" [Shanghai railway bureau: in 40 days around spring festival 41.13 million people travelled safely], March 7, 2013; *BBC,* "China Snow Strands 'Nearly 100,000' at Guangzhou Station," February 2, 2016.
7. Wang Xinye, "Migrant Workers in Shortage After Spring Festival holiday," *CCTV,* February 19, 2013.

8. Leslie Chang, *Factory Girls: From Village to City in a Changing China*, New York: Spiegel & Grau, 2009, 20.

9. Sierra Stoney and Jeanne Batalova, "Mexican Immigrants in the United States," *Migration Information Source*, February 28, 2013: 3; *Eurostat*, "European Social Statistics Pocketbook," July 2013, 3.

10. Department of Economic and Social Affairs of the United Nations, "The Number of International Migrants Worldwide Reaches 232 Million," September 2013, 1.

11. Michael Clemens, "Economics and Emigration: Trillion-Dollar Bills on the Sidewalk?," *Journal of Economic Perspectives* (Summer 2011): 84.

12. See Chapter 4 note 3 for a discussion of Chinese growth accounting and where these figures come from.

13. George W. Bush, *Decision Points*, New York: Crown, 2010.

14. Jonathan Anderson, "Five Persistent Myths About China's Banking System," *Cato Journal* 26, no. 2 (Spring/Summer 2006): 245.

15. Haiyan Deng, John Haltiwanger, Robert McGuckin, Jianyi Xu, Yaodong Liu, and Yuqi Liu, "The Contribution of Restructuring and Reallocation to China's Productivity and Growth," *Economics Program Working Papers* 07-04, The Conference Board, December 2007.

Chapter 1

1. Jia Lingmin, in discussion with the author, May 2013. Her story was extensively covered in local media; *Xiaoxiang Morning News*, "Zhùle 700duōtiān dìsān gè wōpéng yòu bèi chai" [After living there for 700 days, Jia Lingmin's third shack is destroyed], August 23, 2012; "Jiǎ língmǐn zìshù: Shíbā dà qíjiān bèi bǎngjià, ōudǎ hé qiújìn de jīngguò" [Jia Lingmin: While the Eighteenth Congress of the Communist Party was happening, I was kidnapped, beaten and imprisoned], *Boxun*, November 14, 2012; "Zhèngzhōu duō rén bèi rēng ní gōu hòu fāxiàn fángwū yǐ bèi qiángchāi" [After being thrown in a ditch, Zhengzhou people return to find their houses destroyed], *Boxun*, October 25, 2010.

2. Ezra Vogel, *Deng Xiaoping and the Transformation of China*, Cambridge, MA: Harvard University Press, 2010, 429.

3. Organization for Economic Cooperation and Development/Food and Agriculture Organization (OECD-FAO), *OECD-FAO Agricultural Outlook 2013–2022*, 2013, 34.

4. Violent conflicts relating to agricultural land rights and tenancy are one of the overriding themes of Chinese history and feature prominently in many narratives about China's reform policies. The tenant problem was most notably invoked by the early Communist Party, but it also features in more recent analyses of China's reform such as Joe Studwell, *How Asia Works*, New York: Profile, 2013, 3–70. That said, there is a significant amount of evidence suggesting that Chinese peasants were better off than peasants in other countries. Until Mao came to power, Chinese peasants were subject to less restrictions on their movements than, say, Russian serfs, and the country was notable for its large number of small-scale freehold farms. This argument was made persuasively by Gang Deng, *The Premodern Chinese Economy: Structural Equilibrium and Capitalist Sterility*, London: Routledge, 1999, 48–72, 301–06, appendix H. Deng

further argues that a lack of consolidation on farms discouraged urbanization and industrialization, and delayed China's development until the collapse of the commune system (71–72).

5. Deng, *Premodern Chinese Economy*, 24.

6. Kenneth Pomeranz, "Land Markets in Late Imperial and Republican China," *Continuity and Change* 23 (2008): 101–50.

7. Chris Bramall, "Chinese Land Reform in Long-Run Perspective and in the Wider East Asian Context," *Journal of Agrarian Change* 4 (2004): 107–41.

8. There is some fuzziness in the numbers, but most research has found that the government figure of 3.8 percent average growth between 1952 and 1956 is roughly accurate. See Bramall, "Chinese Land Reform," 117.

9. Tiejun Cheng and Mark Selden, "The Origins and Social Consequences of China's Hukou System," *The China Quarterly* 139 (1994): 644–68.

10. Ibid.

11. Ibid.

12. Ibid.

13. Ibid.

14. Ibid.

15. Ibid.

16. Ibid.

17. Yang Jisheng, *Tombstone: The Great Chinese Famine, 1958–1962*, New York: Farrar, Straus and Giroux, 2012, chapter 11.

18. Cheng and Selden, "Origins and Social Consequences," 666.

19. Ronald Coase and Ning Wang, *How China Became Capitalist*, London: Palgrave Macmillan, 2012, 7.

20. Coase and Wang, *How China Became Capitalist*, 46–53.

21. Ibid.

22. Ibid., 77.

23. Ibid., 68; Robin Dean and Tobias Damm-Luhr, "A Current Review of Chinese Land-Use Law and Policy: A 'Breakthrough' in Rural Reform?," *Pacific Rim Law and Policy Journal* 19, no. 1 (2010): 121–59.

24. Dean and Damm-Luhr, "Chinese Land-Use Law," 127.

25. Kevin J. O'Brien and Lianjiang Li, "'Accommodating Democracy' in a One-Party State: Introducing Village Elections in China," *China Quarterly* 162 (June 2000): 465–89.

26. Ping Li, "Rural Land Tenure Reforms in China: Issues, Regulations, and Prospects for Additional Reform." Chapter in *Land Reform: Land Settlement and Cooperatives*, special ed. Food and Agriculture Organization of the United Nations, 2003.

27. Loren Brandt, Scott Rozelle, and Guo Li, "Tenure, Land Rights, and Farmer Investment Incentives in China," *Agricultural Economics* 19, no. 2 (1998): 63–71.

28. Dean and Damm-Luhr, "Chinese Land-Use Law," 133.

29. Tianjin Shi, "Village Committee Elections in China: Institutionalist Tactics for Democracy," *World Politics* 51, no. 3 (April 1999): 385–412.

30. Allen Choate, "Local Governance in China: An Assessment of Villagers' Committees," *Asia Foundation Working Paper Series*, February 1997; Allen Choate, "Local

Governance in China II: An Assessment of Urban Residents Committees and Municipal Community Development," *Asia Foundation Working Paper Series*, November 1998, 36–37.

31. Zhu Keliang and Roy Prosterman, "Securing Land Rights for Chinese Farmers: A Leap Forward for Stability and Growth," *Development Policy Analysis* 3, Cato Institute: Center for Liberty and Prosperity, October 15, 2007, 10.

32. Kam Wing Chan and Will Buckingham, "Is China Abolishing the Hukou System?" *China Quarterly* 195 (September 2008): 582–606.

33. Chan and Buckingham, "Hukou System"; James Barth, Michael Lea, and Tong Li, "China's Housing Market: Is a Bubble About to Burst?," Milken Institute report, (December 2012): 3.

34. Chan and Buckingham, "Hukou System."

35. Dean and Damm-Luhr, "Chinese Land-Use Law," 126-27.

36. Ibid., 151.

37. China Development Research Foundation, *China's New Urbanization Strategy*, New York: Routledge, 2013, 47–49.

38. Lixing Li, "Land Titling in China: Chengdu Experiment and Its Consequences," *China Economic Journal* 5, no. 1 (February 2012): 47–64.

39. Yinqiu Lu and Tao Sun, "Local Government Financing Platforms in China," *IMF Working Paper* no. 13, October 2013, 11.

40. Verna Yu, "A Blow for Freedom: The Campaign in Memory of Sun Zhigang, 10 Years On," *South China Morning Post*, May 14, 2013.

41. *China Daily*, "Sun Zhigang's Brutal Killers Sentenced," June 10, 2003; Qianfang Zhang, "Chinese Legal Reforms in the Aftermath of the Sun Zhigang Incident," *Asia Law Review* 4 (2007): 1–39; Chan and Buckingham, "Hukou System," 599.

42. *China Central Television*, "Party and Government Organs at All Levels Have Introduced Countermeasures," December 15, 2003.

43. *Xinhua*, "Zài hù nóngmín gōng tóng zhù zǐnǔ míngnián jiāng quánbù miǎnfèi jiēshòu yìwù jiàoyù" [All children of migrant workers living in Shanghai will get free compulsory education next year], December 18, 2009.

44. *Wall Street Journal*, "What Worker Shortage? The Real Story of China's Migrants," *China Real Time Report* (blog), January 4, 2013.

45. Coase and Wang, *How China Became Capitalist*, chapter 1.

46. Chinese Human Rights Defenders, "Jia Lingmin," December 24, 2014. https://www .nchrd.org/. *Boxun*, "Zhùmíng wéiquán rén jiǎ língmǐn, liú de wěi fēnbié bèi pàn 4 nián hé 1 nián bàn qǐng kàn bóxùn rèdiǎn: Qiángxíng chāiqiān" [Well-known activists, Jia Lingmin, Liu Dewei, sentenced to four and a half years], November 6, 2015.

Chapter 2

1. *Chinasmack*, "Anti-Mainlander Hong Kong Ad Parodied, Becomes Internet Meme," February 4, 2012. www.chinasmack.com. The border between Shenzhen and Hong Kong is the most traveled border in the world, in part because of the extremely different regulatory environments on each side. On one hand, Shenzhen is in the middle of the largest manufacturing economy in the world, and thus an easy place to buy cheap clothes, electronics, and plastic goods. Hong Kong, on the other hand, has zero tariffs

on most goods and a first-world social services system, making it a cheap place to buy imports and luxury goods, as well as to go to the hospital. Shortly before this ad came out, one of China's largest milk companies was caught putting chemicals into its milk to increase the volume, leading to the death of several infants. Chinese in Shenzhen went to Hong Kong to buy all the foreign milk powder that they could get their hands on in order to meet the demand from concerned parents. "Crippled Chinese" is a reference to writing in simplified Chinese characters.

2. Ibid.

3. Ibid.

4. London had building regulations prior to the Industrial Revolution, but they remained mostly unenforced until an 1844 building law. A. J. Ley, *A History of Building Control in England & Wales 1840–1990*, Coventry, UK: RICS Business Services, 2000, 29.

5. Jewish Women's Archive, "Pauline Newman Organizes Influential New York Rent Strike," jwa.org.

6. New York City Rent Guidelines Board, *Rent Regulation Prior to the Establishment of the Board*, last updated June 1, 2016, www.nycrgb.org.

7. Edward Glaeser, "Urban Colossus: Why Is New York America's Largest City?," *National Bureau of Economic Research Working Paper* no. 11398, June 2005.

8. Robert Allen, "Pessimism Preserved: Real Wages in the British Industrial Revolution," *Oxford University Department of Economics Working Paper* 314, 2007, 14; Simon Szreter and Graham Mooney, "Urbanization, Mortality, and the Standard of Living Debate: New Estimates of the Expectation of Life at Birth in Nineteenth-Century British Cities," *Economic History Review* 51, no.1 (1998): 84–112.

9. John Milholland, "Immigration Hysteria in Congress," *Forum*, January 1921, 68–76; Madison Grant, "America for the Americans," *Forum*, September 1925, 6.

10. Ted Robert Gurr, "Historical Trends in Violent Crime: Europe and the United States," in *Violence in America—Volume 1: The History of Crime*, ed. Ted Robert Gurr, Newbury Park, CA: Sage, 1989, 31.

11. John Saville, *Rural Depopulation in England and Wales*, Abingdon, UK: Routledge 1957, 10.

12. Ibid., 11

13. Son-Thierry Ly and Patrick Weil, "The Antiracist Origin of the Quota System," *Social Research* 77, no. 1 (Spring 2010): 45–79.

14. Ronald Coase and Ning Wang, *How China Became Capitalist*, London: Palgrave Macmillan, 2012, 56–59.

15. Coase and Wang, *How China Became Capitalist*, 57.

16. Ibid.

17. Zhejiang is the most notable example of an area with poor per-capita agricultural yields converting to private industry early. Fujian, Guizhou, and mountainous regions of Guangdong were also early to embrace private industry; Jiajian Chen, Robert Retherford, Minja Kim Choe, Li Xiru, and Cui Hongyan, "Population Policy, Economic Reform, and Fertility Decline in Guangdong Province, China," *East-West Center Working Papers* no. 120, May 2009; Yasheng Huang, "The China Boom: Rural China in the 1980s," *The China Boom Project*, Asia Society Center on US-China Relations, June 1, 2010. chinaboom.asiasociety.org.

18. Yasheng Huang, *Capitalism with Chinese Characteristics*, Cambridge, UK: Cambridge University Press, 2008, 64.

19. Coase and Wang, *How China Became Capitalist*, 54–56.

20. Ibid.

21. Ibid.

22. Jing Jin and Heng-fu Zou, "Soft-Budget Constraint on Local Governments in China," in *Hard Budget Constraint on Local Governments*, ed. J. Rodden, G. Eskeland, and J. Litvak, Cambridge, MA: MIT Press, 2003, 288.

23. Chunli Shen, Jing Jin, and Heng-fu Zou, "Fiscal Decentralization in China: History, Impact, Challenges, and Next Steps," *Annals of Economics and Finance* 13, no. 1 (2012): 1–51.

24. Jin and Zou, "Soft-Budget Constraint," 3.

25. Ibid., 296.

26. Ibid., 297.

27. Ibid. China went through an inflationary crisis during this period that contributed to nominal GDP growth. Still, real GDP grew by an impressive 40 percent.

28. Jin and Zou, "Soft-Budget Constraint," 34–37.

29. Adam Wagstaff, Magnus Lindelow, Shiyong Wang, and Shuo Zhang, *Reforming China's Rural Health System*, Washington, DC: World Bank, 2009, 29.

30. Coase and Wang, *How China Became Capitalist*, 105.

31. Huang, *Capitalism with Chinese Characteristics*, 164.

32. Coase and Wang, *How China Became Capitalist*, 92.

33. Ibid.

34. Ibid., 115–26.

35. Ibid., 130.

36. This was the basis of the grain procurement system, which was also canceled at this time.

37. Coase and Wang, *How China Became Capitalist*, 129–33.

38. World Bank and the Development Research Center of the State Council, *China 2030*, 104.

39. Robert Pozen, "Tackling the Chinese Pension System," *Paulson Policy Memorandum*, The Paulson Institute, July 2013, 1; Sarah Barber and Lan Yao, "Health Insurance Systems in China: A Briefing Note," *Background Paper* 37, *World Health Report*, World Health Organization, 2010, 6.

40. Coase and Wang, *How China Became Capitalist*, 133–34.

41. The exact share of expenditure varies from year to year, but it generally hovers in the realm of 70 to 80 percent of total spending. See Shen, Jin, and Zou, "Fiscal Decentralization." The gap between local government income and local government expenditure is primarily made up by one-off income from land sales and a few other fees but not debt, which local governments are legally forbidden to take on. The expansion of local government debt during and after the 2009–2010 stimulus package was mostly related to off-balance-sheet projects.

42. Shen, Jin, and Zou, "Fiscal Decentralization," 11–12.

43. James Kai-sing Kung, Chenggang Xu, and Feizhou Zhou, "From Industrialization to Urbanization: The Social Consequences of Changing Fiscal Incentives on Local

Government Behavior," in *Law and Economics with Chinese Characteristics: Institutions for Promoting Development in the Twenty-First Century*, ed. David Kennedy and Joseph E. Stiglitz, Oxford: Oxford University Press, 2013, 491–510.

44. Shen, Jin, and Zou, "Fiscal Decentralization," 3.

45. Huang, *Capitalism with Chinese Characteristics*, 245; Pozen, "Chinese Pension System," 5.

46. Shen, Jin, and Zou, "Fiscal Decentralization," 24.

47. Carl Walter and Fraser J. T. Howie, *Red Capitalism: The Fragile Financial Foundation of China's Extraordinary Rise*, Singapore: John Wiley & Sons, 2011, 40.

48. Ibid., 41.

49. Ibid., 57–60.

50. World Bank and the Development Research Center of the State Council, *China 2030*, 21.

51. There are some problems with this statistic. China classifies ownership status in five ways: state-owned enterprises, collectively owned enterprises, shareholding firms, private firms, and foreign-owned firms. The first two classifications are unambiguously state owned and the latter two classifications are unambiguously private; shareholding firms are mostly, but not entirely, majority state owned. The total lending breakdown varies from year to year, but private firms and foreign firms generally receive between 15 and 25 percent of total bank loans, and account for over half of all economic output. See James R. Barth and Gerard Caprio Jr., "China's Changing Financial System: Can It Catch Up with, or Even Drive Growth," *Policy Brief* 2007-PB05, Networks Financial Institute at Indiana State University, March 2007, 22; Gangming Yuan, "Non-performing Debts in SOEs and the Effect of Policies Aimed at Their Solution," in *China in the Global Economy*, ed. P. J. Lloyd and Xiao-guang Zhang, Cheltenham, UK: Edward Elgar Publishing, 2000, 125–45; Richard C. K. Burdekin and Ran Tao, "China's State-Owned Banks' Lending Practices, 1994–2005: Empirical Tests and Policy Implications," *Open Economics Journal* 1 (2008): 14–24; Eve Cary, "Reforming China's State-Owned Enterprises," *Diplomat*, June 19, 2013.

52. Haizhou Huang and Shuilin Wang, "Exchange Rate Regimes: China's Experience and Choices," *China Economic Review* 15 (2004): 336–42.

53. Ming Lu, Jianyong Fan, Shejian Liu, and Yan Yan, "Employment Restructuring During China's Economic Transition," Bureau of Labor Statistics, *Monthly Labor Review* (August 2002): 25–32.

54. Lu, Fan, Liu, and Yan, "Employment Restructuring," 30; Chang kon Choi, "The Employment Effect of Economic Growth: Identifying Determinants of Employment Elasticity," 2007.

55. Yeqing Huang and Neng Wan, "Dynamic Changes of Labour Market and Employment Opportunities of Migrant Workers in Transitional China: Evidence from Three Metropolises." (Paper presented at the Global Development Network's 13th Annual Global Development Conference, Budapest, Hungary, June 16–18, 2012.)

56. Chan and Buckingham, "Hukou System," 603.

57. Rachel Murphy, "Domestic Migrant Remittances in China: Distribution, Channels, and Livelihoods," International Organization of Migration, *MRS* 24, 2006, 8.

58. Ibid.

59. Lu, Fan, Liu, and Yan, "Employment Restructuring," 4; "Self-employed, Private Firms Create a Third of Jobs in China," *Xinhua*, February 8, 2016.

60. Kevin Gallagher, *The Dragon in the Room: China and the Future of Latin American Industrialization*, Stanford, CA: Stanford University Press, 2010, Chapter 1.

61. Tony Hines. "Globalization: An Introduction to Fashion Markets and Fashion Marketing," in *Fashion Marketing: Contemporary Issues*, ed. Tony Hines and Margaret Bruce, Oxford: Butterworth Heinemann, 2001, 1–24.

62. Kjeld Erik Brodsgaard, "Foreign Direct Investment in China: Origin, Distribution, and Impact on the Economy," in *China: Business Opportunities in a Globalizing Economy*, ed. Verner Worm, Copenhagen: Copenhagen Business School, 2008.

63. Edwin Cheng and Tsan-Ming Choi, eds., *Innovative Quick Response Programs in Logistics and Supply Chain* Management, Berlin: Springer, 2010.

Chapter 3

1. Li Zhang, *Strangers in the City: Reconfigurations of Space, Power, and Social Networks Within China's Floating Population*, Stanford, CA: Stanford University Press 2001, 48–62.

2. Ronald Coase and Ning Wang, *How China Became Capitalist*, London: Palgrave Macmillan, 2012, 58.

3. Li Minghuan, "'To Get Rich Quickly in Europe!' Reflections on Migration Motivation in Wenzhou," in *Internal and International Migration: Chinese Perspectives*, ed. Frank N. Pieke and Hein Mallee, Richmond, UK: Curzon, 1999, 181–99.

4. Bradley Gardner, "China's Black Market City," *Reason*, December 2011.

5. "The Jinhua-Wenzhou Railway." Accessed August, 7 2016. baike.baidu.com.

6. Interviews in Wenzhou were conducted by author in January 2010 and January 2011. Interviewees' names are not listed to protect their identities.

7. "Rui'an: China's Capital of Car and Motorcycle Spare Parts, the Forging Base of China," 2010. http://www.gasgoo.com/promotion/ruian-popularization/.

8. Jonathan Watts, "The Tiger's Teeth," *Guardian*, May 24, 2005.

9. Lu Shi and Bernard Ganne, "Understanding the Zhejiang Industrial Clusters: Questions and Re-Evaluations," *International Workshop Asian Industrial Clusters*, Lyon, France, 2006, 246.

10. Wendell Cox, "China's Top Growth Centers," *New Geography*, June 1, 2012.

11. Economist Intelligence Unit, "Zhejiang," *Access China*, February 2014.

12. Gardner, "China's Black Market City," 1.

13. *China Daily*, "Banking Goes Underground on Tightening," December 28, 2010.

14. This information was provided by several interviewees who requested to remain anonymous.

15. Tang Xiangyang and Ruoji Tang, "Considered Opinion: The Wu Ying Case," *Economic Observer*, April 19, 2011.

16. *BBC News*, "Convicted Chinese Businesswoman Wu Ying Given Reprieve," May 12, 2012.

17. Interviews in Wenzhou conducted by author, January 2010 and January 2011.

18. Li, "Get Rich Quickly."

19. Hu Weijia, "China's First Private Bank Begins Operation," *Global Times*, March 26, 2015.

20. Bin Wu and Valter Zanin, "Exploring Links Between International Migration and Wenzhou's Development," *Discussion Paper* 25, University of Nottingham, China Policy Institute, November 2007, 3; C. Bonifazi, F. Heins, S. Strozza, and M. Vitiello, "Italy: The Italian Transition from an Emigration to Immigration Country," *IDEA Working Papers* no. 5, March 2009.

21. Vinicio Bacio (Investitalia), in discussion with author, January 2011.

22. Interviews in Wenzhou conducted by author, January 2010, January 2011.

23. Joseph Fewsmith, "Chambers of Commerce in Wenzhou and the Potential Limits of 'Civil Society' in China," Stanford University, *China Leadership Monitor* 16 (2005): 4.

24. Kate Zhou, *China's Long March to Freedom: Grassroots Modernization* (New Brunswick, NJ: Transaction, 2009), 278; Simon Rabinovitch. "Wenzhou Factories Adapt to the Times," *Financial Times*, July 10, 2011.

25. A pseudonym.

26. Gianluca D'Agnolo (partner at Chiomenti Studio Legale), in discussion with author. Confirmed in interview with Investitalia.

27. Wu and Zanin, "International Migration and Wenzhou's Development."

Chapter 4

1. Robert W. Fairlie, "Immigrant Entrepreneurs and Small Business Owners, and Their Access to Financial Capital," United States Small Business Administration/Office of Advocacy, May 2012, 38; Rebecca Burn-Callander, "Migrant Entrepreneurs Driving Job Creation Across Britain, Study Shows," *Telegraph*, March 4, 2014.

2. Siskind Susser, "Chart of Physician Licensing Requirements by State," 2014, http://www.visalaw.com/IMG/physicianchart.pdf.

3. The literature on growth accounting in China is large and rowdy with some fairly major disagreements about how to use the data. The consensus figure for labor-reallocation's share of overall economic growth is 20 percent, with some higher estimates and some lower estimates. In all cases, though, the authors acknowledge that the impact of migration is significantly larger than the measurable impact of labor reallocation.

   The starting point for the research included in this chapter was the World Bank report, "Integration of National Product and Factor Markets: Economic Benefits and Policy Recommendations," June 13, 2005. The report estimated that moving 5 percent of China's population out of agriculture into other industries would increase GDP by 3.3 percent. This, it noted, is consistent with previous research by Fang Cai and Wang Dewen, "The Sustainability of China's Economic Growth and Labor Contribution," *Journal of Economic Research* 10 (1999). Cai and Wang would cite their 1999 research again in "Impacts of Internal Migration on Economic Growth and Urban Development in China," in *Migration and Development Within and Across Borders: Research and Policy Perspectives on Internal and International Migration*, eds. J. DeWind and J. Holdaway, International Organization for Migration and the Social Science Research Council, 2008. In this article, they also noted that the 20 percent figure probably underestimated the contribution of labor reallocation because it did not account for human capital growth. Jane Haltmaier, "Challenges for the Future of Chinese Economic Growth," *Board of Governors of the Federal Reserve System International Finance Discussion Papers* 1072, January 2013, found that changes in sectoral employment accounted for 22.3 percent of economic growth between 1989 and 2000 and 21.2 percent between 2000 and 2010.

The 33 percent figure comes primarily from Kang H. Cao and Javier A. Birchenall, "Agricultural Productivity, Structural Change, and Economic Growth in Post-Reform China," *Journal of Development Economics* 104 (2013): 165–80, which measured the gains from labor reallocation between 1978 and 1998 based on reconsideration of agricultural output growth. This argument was taken from a different direction by Loren Brandt, Chang-tai Hsieh, and Xiaodong Zhu, "Growth and Structural Transformation in China," in *China's Great Economic Transformation*, eds. Loren Brandt and Thomas G. Rawski, Cambridge, UK: Cambridge University Press, 2008. Brandt, Hsieh, and Zhu argue that more than three-quarters of growth from reallocation came from labor moving from the state sector to the private sector, with only one-quarter coming from rural-urban migration. Their argument is largely based on the high rate of agricultural productivity growth dampening the impact of rural-urban migration.

An important note of dissent from these estimates comes from Louis Kujis and Tao Wang, "China's Pattern of Growth: Moving to Sustainability and Reducing Inequality," *World Bank Policy Research Working Paper* 3767, November 2005, who argued that labor reallocation only accounted for 10 percent of growth between 1993 and 2004, because migrants were mostly absorbed by the services sector rather than the more productive industrial sector. Kujis and Wang admitted, though, that reallocation could account for a substantially larger share of economic growth in the following years, which correlates with the findings of the World Bank, "National Product and Factor Markets."

4. Mitali Das and Papa N'Diaye, "Chronicle of a Decline Foretold: Has China Reached the Lewis Turning Point?," *IMF Working Paper* no. 13, January 2013, 15.

5. Cao and Birchenall, "Agricultural Productivity."

6. Das and N'Diaye, "Chronicle of a Decline Foretold," 3.

7. Haltmaier, "Future of Chinese Economic Growth."

8. Haiyan Deng, John Haltiwanger, Robert McGuckin, Jianyi Xu, Yaodong Liu, and Yuqi Liu, "The Contribution of Restructuring and Reallocation to China's Productivity and Growth," *Economics Program Working Papers* 07-04, The Conference Board, December 2007.

9. The role of migration in industrial reform was particularly visible in the case of the Northeast, which had been an industrial base in the 1970s and 1980s, then stagnated after the reforms.

10. John Whalley and Xiliang Zhao, "The Contribution of Human Capital to China's Economic Growth," *China Economic Policy Review* 2, no.1 (2013) 28.

11. Haizheng Li, Yunling Liang, Barbara M. Fraumeni, Zhiqiang Liu, and Xiaojun Wang, "Human Capital in China." Paper presented at 31st General Conference of the International Association for Research in Income and Wealth, St. Gallen, Switzerland, August 11, 2010.

12. Li, Liang, Fraumeni, Liu, and Wang, "Human Capital," 55.

13. Duo Qin and Haiyan Song, "Sources of Investment Inefficiency: The Case of Fixed-Asset Investment in China," *Journal of Development Economics* 90, no. 1 (September 2009): 94–105.

14. Lin Ling, "Guǎngdōng tóuzī jìn 2 wàn yì gōulè lùlù jiāotōng yòu rén qiánjǐng" [Guangdong to invest Rmb2 trillion to upgrade transportation infrastructure], *Yancheng Evening News*, November 15, 2012.

15. Jonathan Anderson, "Settling Another Old Debate on Chinese (and Argentine) Inflation," *UBS Investment Research*, January 24, 2011.

16. Sandra Eickmeier and Markus Kuhnlenz, "China's Role in Global Inflation Dynamics," *Deutsche Bundesbank Discussion Paper* No. 07/2013, April 2, 2013, 19.

17. Haltmaier, "Future of Chinese Economic Growth."

18. *Economist*, "Peak Toil," January 26, 2013.

19. Das and N'Diaye, "Chronicle of a Decline Foretold," 15.

20. Lee Chyen Yee, "China Tops U.S, Japan to Become Top Patent Filer," *Reuters*, December 21, 2011.

21. Yee, "China Tops U.S., Japan," 1.

22. Bob Davis, "Chinese College Graduates Play It Safe and Lose Out," *Wall Street Journal*, March 25, 2013.

Chapter 5

1. I was originally told about the pickled mustard index by Zhang Hong, an editor at the *Economic Observer*, in May 2013; *Economic Observer*, "Chéngzhèn huà de zhàcài zhǐshù" [Urbanization's mustard index], August 10, 2013.

2. Jamil Anderlini, "Rural Investment Pays Off in China," *Financial Times*, September 11, 2012.

3. Dexter Roberts, "Why Factories Are Leaving China," *Bloomberg Businessweek*, May 13, 2010.

4. Eduardo Porter, "China's Vanishing Trade Imbalance," *New York Times*, May 1, 2012; Michael Forsythe, "China Eclipses U.S. as Biggest Trading Nation," *Livemint*, February 10, 2013.

5. World Trade Organization, *World Trade Report 2013*.

6. World Trade Organization, *International Trade Statistics 2011*, World Trade Organization, *International Trade Statistics 2015*. Russell Flannery, "Where's China's Growth? Textile Industry Is Weaving Expansion," *Forbes*, September 2, 2013.

7. China Customs Data http://info.hktdc.com/; *Xinhua*, "2013 Nián wǒguó jìn chūkǒu zǒng zhí zēngzhǎng 7.6% Shǒu pò 4 wàn yì měiyuán guānkǒu" [In 2013 China's export value grew 7.6% broke the $4 trillion mark for the first time], January 10, 2014.

8. Tim Worstall, "Now Apple's Manufacturing Is Leaving China," *Forbes*, July 24, 2012.

9. Jungah Lee and Jason Folkmanis, "Samsung Shifts Plants from China to Protect Margins," *Bloomberg Technology*, December 11, 2013.

10. *Want China Times*, "Foxconn Expanding into China's Third- and Fourth-Tier Cities," December 10, 2013. www.wantchinatimes.com.

11. China Customs Statistics. http://info.hktdc.com/.

12. *Fibre2Fashion*, "US, Japan Lead in China's Textile Exports: CCCT," January 20, 2014.

13. Directorate-General for Trade (EU) Trade Statistics Report, "European Union, Trade in Goods with ASEAN," April 16, 2014.

14. *Guangdong Provincial Bureau of Statistics*, "Guangdong 2015 statistical report," February 29, 2016.

15. Overseas Research Department, Japan External Trade Organization, "The 22nd Survey of Investment Related Costs in Asia and Oceana (FY 2011 Survey)," April 2012.

16. *Xinhua*, "Overcapacity Poses Major Risk to China's Economy," November 30, 2013.

17. Tom Miller, *China's Urban Billion*, London: Zed Books, 2012, 154–61.

18. Tian Ying, "China Ends U.S.'s Reign as Largest Auto Market," *Bloomberg Business*, January 11, 2010; Vinicy Chan, "Chinese Shoppers Overtake U.S. as Top Luxury Buyers," *Bloomberg*, December 11, 2012; Gao Yuan, "China Now World's Biggest Smartphone Market," *China Daily*, November 6, 2013; *Xinhua*, "China to Become World's Largest Consumer Market in 2015: Commerce Minister," May 28, 2012; Zheng Yangpeng, "China Projected to Remain Fastest-Growing Consumer Market," *China Daily*, December 22, 2015; *Economist,* "The World's Second Biggest Consumer," February 18, 2014.

19. *Economist*, "Made in China," March 14, 2015.

20. This figure declined somewhat after 2009 due to the transition to smartphones, but is expected to tick up again; W. Lin, "'Shanzhai Culture' and Its Cultural Value Identification with Adolescents" [in Chinese], *Journal of China Youth University for Political Sciences* 5 (2009): 46–50; Dylan McGrath, "China Cracking Down on Gray-Market Handsets," *EE Times*, July 11, 2010; Greg Lindsay, "China's Cell Phone Pirates Are Bringing Down Middle Eastern Governments," *Fast Company,* June 14, 2011.

21. Liang Dongmei, Yang binbin, Fu Yanyan, and Wang Duan, "How Manufacturing's Mockingbird Sings," *Caixin*, February 10, 2010.

22. *Global Times*, "2009 Top 10 Best-Selling Sedans in China," January 22, 2010.

23. Xiang Hansong (automotive columnist for ifeng.com), phone interview, July 2012.

24. "Trade Secrets Dispute Continues Between Foxconn and BYD," *Want China Times*, June 26, 2012. www.wantchinatimes.com.

25. Liang, Yang, Fu, and Wang, "Manufacturing's Mockingbird," 1.

26. "Most Popular Cars in China: The 2012 List." China Auto Web.

27. Sherry Li (representative for BYD), phone interview, July 2012.

28. Jamil Anderlini and Vincent Boland, "China Car Group Sues Fiat in Copying Case," *Financial Times*, October 20, 2009.

29. Bill Russo (senior adviser, Booz & Co.), phone interview, August 2012.

30. Bill Russo, Tao Ke, and Edward Tse, "An Inorganic Approach to Globalization: The Marriage of Geely and Volvo," Booz & Company Perspective Report, 2009, 5.

31. Kevin Gallagher, *The Dragon in the Room: China and the Future of Latin American Industrialization*, Stanford, CA: Stanford University Press, 2010, 6.

32. China Customs statistics. http://www.chinacustomsstat.com/.

33. Ming Lu, Jianyong Fan, Shejian Liu, and Yan Yan, "Employment Restructuring During China's Economic Transition," Bureau of Labor Statistics, Monthly Labor Review (August 2002): 30; Chang kon Choi, "The Employment Effect of Economic Growth: Identifying Determinants of Employment Elasticity," 2007.

34. Bradley Gardner, "Renminbi Rising," Economist Intelligence Unit, 2014, 9.

35. John Horn, Vivien Singer, and Jonathan Woetzel, "A Truer Picture of China's Export Machine," *McKinsey Quarterly* (September 2010): 2; Jonathan Anderson, "Is China Export-Led," *UBS Investment Research*, September 27, 2007.

36. Charles C. Mann, "Renewables Aren't Enough. Clean Coal Is the Future," *Wired*, March 25, 2014.

37. Arnulf Jager-Waldau, "*PV Status Report 2013*," European Commission, JRC Scientific and Policy Report, September 2013.

38. Keith Bradsher, "Chinese Solar Panel Giant Is Tainted by Bankruptcy," *New York Times*, March 20, 2013; Jim Snyder, and Christopher Martin, "Obama Team Backed $535 Million Solyndra Aid as Auditor Warned on Finances," *Bloomberg*, September 12, 2011.

39. Economist Intelligence Unit, "China's Solar Storms," *Access China*, December 6, 2012.

40. Feifei Shen, "Chinese Zombies Emerging After Years of Solar Subsidies," *Bloomberg Real Clear Energy*, September 8, 2013.

Chapter 6

1. The early articles about Kangbashi had a number of inaccuracies in them. Articles couldn't agree about whether the district was meant to hold 300,000 people or 1 million people (the smaller number is accurate). A number of articles also associated the construction with the 2009 stimulus package, despite the district being under development since 2004. Additionally, the articles claimed either that the district was built exclusively with government funds or with capital from property speculation (only government buildings were funded by the government).

   Tom Miller of Gavekal Dragonomics has done particularly extensive work correcting some of the misunderstandings surrounding ghost cities, including dedicating a chapter in his book *China's Urban Billion* to the topic. See also Miller's "Time for a Reality Check on China's Ghost Cities," *China Dialogue*, August 10, 2013.

   Early articles on Ordos include Graham Smith, "Where Is Everyone? The Derelict Majesty of Chinese Ghost Town Built to House One Million but with Less than 30,000 Residents," *Daily Mail*, July 24, 2012; Kevin Hamlin, "China's Desert Ghost City Shows Property 'Madness' Persists," *Bloomberg*, June 23, 2010; Melissa Chan, "China's Empty City," *Al Jazeera*, November 10, 2009.

2. Eli Bildner, "Ordos: A Ghost Town That Isn't," *Atlantic*, April 8, 2013.

3. KPMG Huazhen, *Zhengzhou Zhengdong New District, Investment Environment Study 2009*; Chandni Rathod and Gus Lubin, "And Now Presenting: Amazing Satellite Images of the Ghost Cities of China," *Business Insider*, posted December 14, 2010.

4. Song Fuli and Hu Dan, "Build It and They Will Come," *Economic Observer*, March 25, 2013; Wang Kaihao, "Kangbashi Thrives Despite Perceptions," *China Daily*, December 24, 2012.

5. *Zhengzhou Evening News*, "Zhèng dōng xīnqū rénkǒuguò bǎi wàn!" [Masses of people occupy new neighborhood in Zheng Dong!], August 16, 2013; Economist Intelligence Unit, "Zhengzhou," *Access China*, February 2014.

6. Noriel Roubini, "China's Unbalanced, Unsustainable Growth Model." Email.

7. Tom Miller, *China's Urban Billion*, London: Zed Books, 2012, Chapter 5.

8. *Global Times*, "When the Ordos Bubble Burst," July 12, 2013.

9. Ordos Prefectural Statistical Bureau, "Ordos 2011 Statistical Report" and "Ordos 2014 Statistical Report."

10. *Zhengzhou Evening News*, "Zhèngzhōu píngjūn měitiān chūshēng 300 rén 2020 nián rénkǒu jiāng dá 1500 wàn" [In Zhengzhou, 300 people are born per day, population will reach 15 million by 2020], November 27, 2012.

11. Miller, *China's Urban Billion*, 126.

12. Tania Branigan, "China Becomes an Urban Nation at Breakneck Speed," *Guardian*, October 2, 2011.

13. Yinqiu Lu and Tao Sun, "Local Government Financing Platforms in China," *IMF Working Paper* no. 13, October 2013, 6.

14. *China Daily*, "Illegal Land Development Zones Cut," June 26, 2004.

15. Josh Chin, "China's Blood-Stained Property Map," *Wall Street Journal*, China Real Time (blog), October 29, 2010.

16. National Audit Office of the People's Republic of China. "Audit Results of Nationwide Government Debt," December 30, 2013.

17. *Xinhua*, "Guójiā xīnxíng chéngzhèn huà guīhuà (2014–2020 nián)" [National New Urbanization plan (2014–2020)], March 16, 2014; Ian Johnson, "China Releases Plan to Incorporate Farmers into Cities," *New York Times*, March 17, 2014; *Economist*, "Moving on Up," March 22, 2014.

18. Ian Johnson, "China's Great Uprooting: Moving 250 Million into Cities," *New York Times*, June 15, 2013.

19. *Xinhua*, "Guójiā xīnxíng chéngzhèn huà guīhuà (2014–2020 nián)" [National New Urbanization plan (2014–2020)], March 16, 2014.

20. Wang Hongyi, "Aging Population May Be Catalyst for Change," *China Daily*, June 24, 2010.

21. OECD, *OECD-FAO Agricultural Outlook 2013–2022*, 2013.

22. *Economist*, "Daily Bread," October 26, 2013; *Xinhua*, "China Vows Sufficiency in Grain Production," January 22, 2013.

23. Robin Dean and Tobias Damm-Luhr, "A Current Review of Chinese Land-Use Law and Policy: A 'Breakthrough' in Rural Reform?," *Pacific Rim Law and Policy Journal* 19, no. 1 (2010): 144; OECD, *OECD-FAO Agricultural Outlook 2013–2022*, 2013.

24. Miller, *China's Urban Billion*, 76–83.

25. Langi Chiang, "Anhui Tests Land Reform in Wake of Plenum Vow on Rural Property Rights," *South China Morning Post*, November 13, 2013; *Xinhua*, "Rural Land Reform Means Bigger Profits for China's Farmers," February 2, 2014.

26. *Xinhua*, "Beijing to Complete Land Use Rights Registration by 2018," December 27, 2013.

27. *OECD-FAO Agricultural Outlook 2013–2022*, 2013.

28. *OECD-FAO Agricultural Outlook 2013–2022*, 2013; *Xinhua*, "China Expected to Bolster Rice Import," October 18, 2013.

29. National Audit Office of the People's Republic of China. "Audit Results of Nationwide Government Debt."

30. *Economist*, "Counting Ghosts," January 4, 2014; Qu Hongbin, Sun Junwei, Paul Mackel, and Wang Ju, "The Rise of the Redback II," HSBC Global Research Guide, March 2013.

31. *Jinrong jiewang*, "Yínjiānhuì jìxù qiánghuà róngzī píngtái xìndài jiānguǎn chéng tóu zhài bǎochí jiào dà fā háng guīmó" [CBRC supervision of credit financing platform to continue to strengthen], March 28, 2013. http://bond.jrj.com.cn/2013/03/2814191518 3909.shtml.

32. Simon Rabinovitch, "Strong Demand for China Local Bond Sale," *Financial Times*, November 15, 2011; *Xinhua*, "China Allows 2 More Local Gov'ts to Issue Bonds," July 5, 2013.

33. Nicholas Borst, "China's Carefully Managed Local Government Bond Issuance," Peterson Institute for International Economics, November 30, 2011.

34. Ministry of Finance of the People's Republic of China, "Guānyú yìnfā '2013 nián dìfāng zhèngfǔ zìxíng fā zhài shìdiǎn bànfǎ' de tōngzhī" [On the issuance of 'The approach to the launch of 2013 local government bonds], July 2013. gks.mof.gov.cn.

35. *Bloomberg News*, "China Lets Local Authorities Convert Debt into Muni Bonds," March 9, 2015.

36. Wang Tao, "China Unveils Local Government Debt Solutions," *UBS Investment Research*, October 7, 2014.

37. Yanzhong Huang, *Governing Health in Contemporary China*, China Policy Series, New York: Routledge, 2013; *Economist*, "Feeling Your Pain," April 27, 2013.

38. Karen Eggleston, "Health Care for 1.3 Billion: An Overview of China's Health System," *Stanford University Working Paper Series on Health and Demographic Change in the Asia-Pacific*, January 9, 2012; Franck Le Deu, Rajesh Parekh, Fangning Zhang, and Gaobo Zhou, *Health Care in China: Entering 'Uncharted Waters'*, McKinsey & Company, November 2012.

39. Central government share of coverage varies across regions and different insurance programs, but currently it accounts for the majority of spending. See Sarah Barber and Lan Yao, "Health Insurance Systems in China: A Briefing Note," *Background Paper 37*, *World Health Report*, World Health Organization, 2010. Also see Ke Priyanka Saksena Xu, Xie Zhe, Huang Fu, Haichao Lei, Ningshan Chen, and Guy Carrin, "Health Care Financing in Rural China: New Rural Cooperative Medical Scheme," *Technical Briefs for Policy-Makers 3*, World Health Organization, 2009.

40. Yanzhong Huang, "What Money Failed to Buy: The Limits of China's Healthcare Reform," *Forbes*, March 4, 2014.

41. Eggleston, "Health Care for 1.3 Billion," 5.

42. This argument is treated in more depth in Huang, *Governing Health*.

43. Robert Pozen, "Tackling the Chinese Pension System," *Paulson Policy Memorandum*, The Paulson Institute, July 2013, 5.

44. Xuejin Zuo, "Designing Fiscally Sustainable and Equitable Pension Systems in China" (Powerpoint), *Designing Fiscally Sustainable and Equitable Pension Systems in Asia in the Post Crisis World*, January 9, 2013. www.imf.org.

45. Liyan Qi, "China to Create Unified Pension System," *Wall Street Journal*, February 7, 2014; *Xinhua*, "China Seeks Unified Pension Scheme Before 2020," February 2, 2014.

46. Pozen, "Chinese Pension System," 14; Zuo, "Sustainable and Equitable Pension Systems," 32.

47. Pozen, "Chinese Pension System," 10.

48. Kam Wing Chan and Will Buckingham, "Is China Abolishing the Hukou System?" *China Quarterly* 195 (September 2008): 583; *Xinhua*, "More Regions to Reform Migrant Education System," January 4, 2013.

49. Holly H. Ming, *The Education of Migrant Children and China's Future: The Urban Left Behind*, New York: Routledge, 2014, 32–33.

50. Ministry of Education of the People's Republic of China, "Outline of China's National Plan for Medium- and Long-Term Education Reform and Development (2010–2020)," October 12, 2010.

51. Valerie Strauss, "China's 10 New and Surprising School Reform Rules," *Washington Post, Answer Sheet* (blog), October 30, 2013.

52. Kam Wing Chan, "A Road Map for Reforming China's Hukou System," *China Dialogue*, October 22, 2013. www.chinadialogue.com.

53. Andrew Batson, "Treat Different SOEs Differently," *Caixin*, January 14, 2014; Nicholas R. Lardy, "China's State-Owned Enterprises: Transformation of State Firms' Role Likely to Accelerate," *Bloomberg Brief: China's Reform Plan*, November 2013.

54. Andrew Batson, "The SOE Irritant in U.S.-China Relations," *Wall Street Journal*, July 7, 2013; Gao Xu, "State-Owned Enterprises in China: How Profitable Are They?" World Bank, *East Asia & Pacific on the Rise* (blog), March 2, 2010.

55. For a longer discussion of this proposal, see World Bank and the Development Research Center of the State Council, *China 2030: Building a Modern, Harmonious and Creative Society*, Washington, DC: World Bank, 2013.

56. Wang Tao, "Something Positive from the SOE Reform Plan," *UBS Investment Research*, September 21, 2015; Gabriel Wildau, "China's State-Owned Enterprise Reform Plans Face Compromise," *Financial Times*, September 14, 2015; Lingling Wei, "China Unveils Overhaul of Bloated State Sector," *Wall Street Journal*, September 13, 2015.

57. Chan and Buckingham, "Hukou System," 605; A. Melander and K. Pelikanova, "Reform of the Hukou System: A Litmus Test of the New Leadership," *ECFIN Economic Brief* 26, July 2013.

58. Kathrin Hille, "Hebei Steel Merger Prompts Doubts," *Financial Times*, December 30, 2008.

59. Zhang Boling, "Government Backed Consolidation of Hebei Steel Industry Melts Away," *Caixin*, January 15, 2014.

60. Dexter Roberts, "To Fix Overproduction, China Wants to Supersize Industries," *Bloomberg Businessweek*, January 23, 2013.

61. Economist Intelligence Unit, "Hebei," *Access China*, February 2014.

62. Ibid.

63. Chuin-Wei Yap, "China's Steelmakers Adding, Not Cutting, Capacity," *Wall Street Journal*, February 26, 2014.

64. *Steel Orbis*, "Hebei Steel Co.'s Net Profit Down 92 percent in 2012," April 15, 2013; Du Juan, "Steel Companies See Profits Drop," *China Daily*, December 23, 2012.

65. Toh Han Shih, "Hebei Iron Resignation Reveals Firm in Crisis," *South China Morning Post*, December 14, 2013.

66. Zhang, "Hebei Steel Industry."

67. David Stanway "China Ditches Steel Industry Consolidation Targets in New Plan," *Reuters*, March 25, 2014.

Chapter 7

1. Jass Yang and Chenyan Liu, "Turnover Rates at Chinese Factories," CSR Asia, posted November 8, 2005. www.csr-asia.com.
2. According to interviewees, the most commonly "stretched" rule of the three is the ban on hiring people who had previously been fired. The most common reason for a worker at the Zhengzhou factory to lose employment is fighting on the job, and workers caught doing so usually have friends to advocate for them with recruiters. Despite all the concerns about underage workers in China, workers at the factory said they very rarely saw people under 16, which is the legal age of employment in China, while 16- to 17-year-olds were a bit more common during rush periods. The no-tattoo rule is due to concerns about gang involvement.
3. Zhengzhou Municipal Bureau of Statistics, Zhengzhou 2012 Statistical Report, March 10, 2013.
4. Shepard, Wade, "On China's Central Plains, an 'aerotropolis' grows near Zhengzhou," *Citiscope*, May, 6, 2016. www.citiscope.com.
5. OECD, *OECD Rural Policy Reviews: China 2009*.
6. Official figures are not published, but estimates usually are in the realm of 130 men to 100 women at birth; Shuzhuo Li, "Imbalanced Sex Ratio at Birth and Comprehensive Intervention in China" (paper presented at 4th Asia Pacific Conference on Reproductive and Sexual Health and Rights, United Nations Population Fund, Hyderabad, India, October 2007).
7. Que Aimin and Yin Jiangyong, "Hùjí xīnzhèng jiào tíng zhèngzhōu míngquè biǎoshì hū hùjí gǎigé bù huì zhǐbù" [Though the new policy has halted, Zhengzhou has shown the *hukou* system needs reform], *Henan Newspaper*, September 22, 2004; *China News Weekly*, "Zhèngzhōu hùjí gǎigé shòucuò fǎnsī wénjiàn hòu xū shēnkè zhìdù biàngé" [Zhengzhou household registration setback reflects the need for profound institutional change], April 23, 2007.
8. Interviews conducted by author with local logistics companies. May 2013.
9. Local interviews conducted by author. May 2013.
10. *Global Entrepreneur*, "Guōtáimíng wú jiě nántí: Fùshìkāng chāojí dà gōngchǎng de sìjié" [Guo Taiming has no answers for the difficult problems of Foxconn factories], November 5, 2012.
11. *Zhengzhou Evening News*, "Hénán liǎng chǎng zhāopìn huì xīyǐn 16 wàn qiúzhí zhě xiāoshòu xūqiú gāojū shǒuwèi" [160,000 people queue for Henan job fair], February 17, 2014.
12. Shi Baoyin, "Nation's First Airport Economic Zone Taking Off," *China Daily*, May 18, 2013; National Development and Reform Commission, "Zhèngzhōu hángkōnggǎng jīngjì zònghé shíyàn qū fāzhǎn guīhuà (2013–2025)" [Zhengzhou's airport economic zone development planning (2013-2025)], April 2013. http://www.ndrc.gov.cn/zcfb/zcfbghwb/201304/W020140221372408841861.pdf.
13. Zhengzhou Urban and Rural Planning Bureau, "Zhèngzhōu shì chéngshì guǐdào jiāotōng xiàn wǎng guīhuà xiū biān" [Zhengzhou City Rail Transit Network Planning Revision (2015–2050)], March 8, 2016.
14. He used the term "*Chai-na*," a pun meaning "torn down" in Chinese but sounding like the English "China."

Chapter 8

1. *The Statutes of California*, (Sacramento: State Office, 1880).

2. His Chinese name was Wong On. There is some debate over the exact year of his arrival, but 1861 is the most-often cited date; Lynn Landwehr, "The Ah Louis Store," *History in San Luis Obispo County*, 2004. http://www.historyinslocounty.org/.

3. US Census Bureau, "Resident Population and Apportionment of the U.S. House of Representatives: California," https://www.census.gov/dmd/www/resapport/states/california.pdf.

4. Landwehr, "The Ah Louis Store."

5. Chester Newton Hess, "What California Means to Its Oldest Living Chinese," *Westways* 26, no. 3 (March 1934).

6. Susie Lan Cassel, *The Chinese in America: A History from Gold Mountain to the New Millennium*, Walnut Creek, CA: AltaMira Press, 2002. *Los Angeles Herald*, "Chinese Laundrymen Boycotting San Luis Obispo," April 6, 1887; *Daily Alta California*, "Anti-Chinese Crusade," February 12, 1886.

7. Campbell Gibson and Kay Jung, "Historical Census Statistics on Population Totals by Race, 1790 to 1990, and by Hispanic Origin, 1970 to 1990, for the United States, Regions, Divisions, and States," US Census Bureau, *Working Paper Series* 56, September 2002.

8. San Luis Obispo actually had a relatively small Chinese population at that time because most of the local work was seasonal. There were only 21 Chinese for every 1000 white people in 1880, or roughly 2 percent of the population, compared to 10 percent in San Francisco and 20 to 25 percent in the gold country. Today there are 1,710 Chinese or Chinese-Americans living in San Luis Obispo County, 0.6 percent of the population. In 1880, Chinese accounted for nearly 9 percent of the population of California and roughly a quarter of the working population—they were almost entirely young men. In 2010, Chinese or Chinese-Americans accounted for less than 2 percent of the population of the state.

    See Sandmeyer, Elmer Clarence, *The Anti-Chinese Movement in California*, Champaign, IL: Illini, 1973.

9. Hess, "What California Means."

10. Horton, Carol A., *Race and the Making of Modern Liberalism*, New York: Oxford University Press, 2005, 81–87.

11. Peter Andreas, *Smuggler Nation: How Illicit Trade Made America*, New York: Oxford University Press, 2013, Chapter 12.

12. These figures are taken from online discussion boards, particularly allnurses.com. I used a high estimate for salaries in the Philippines and a low estimate for salaries in San Francisco.

13. Clemens, "Economics and Emigration."

14. H.R. 1929 (112th): Emergency Nursing Supply Relief Act
    H.R. 5687 (111th): Underserved Area Nursing Relief Restoration Act of 2010
    H.R. 1001 (111th): Nursing Relief Act of 2009
    H.R. 1358 (110th): Nursing Relief Act of 2007
    H.R. 6418 (109th): Nursing Relief Act of 2006

H.R. 1285 (109th): Nursing Relief for Disadvantaged Areas Reauthorization Act of 2005

15. The American Nurses Association was careful not to outright oppose the bill, but stressed that they did not believe more nurses from abroad would alleviate the nursing shortage; Bill Allen, "House Subcommittee Holds Hearing on the Need for Visas for High-Skilled Employees," *Washington Labor & Employment Wire*, June 12, 2008.

16. Oncology Nursing Society, "Oncology Nursing Society Position on the Impact of the National Nursing Shortage on Quality Cancer Care," *ONS Positions*, January 2013; Chris Fleming, "U.S. Health Spending Projected to Grow 5.8 Percent Annually," *Health Affairs* (blog), July 28, 2011.

17. Between 2000 and 2008, the US received roughly 40,000 Filipino immigrants a year, one-quarter of whom were nurses and one-half of whom moved to California; Aaron Terrazas and Jeanne Batalova, "Filipino Migrants in the United States," *Migration Information Source*, April 7, 2010.

18. Timothy J. Hatton, "International Migration and World Development: A Historical Perspective," *Historical Paper* 41, National Bureau of Economic Research, September 1992.

19. Clemens, "Economics and Emigration."

20. Martin Ruhs and Carlos Vargas-Silva, "Briefing: The Labour Market Effects of Immigration," The Migration Observatory, March 5, 2014.

21. Clemens, "Economics and Emigration"; Jonathon W. Moses and Bjørn Letnes, "If People Were Money: Estimating the Gains and Scope of Free Migration," in *Poverty, International Migration, and Asylum*, ed. George J. Borjas and Jeff Crisp, New York: Palgrave Macmillan 2005, 188–210.

22. John Dearie and Courtney Geduldig, "More Immigration Means More Jobs for Americans," *Wall Street Journal*, December 29, 2013.

23. Ruhs and Vargas-Silva, "Labour Market Effects."

24. Gianmarco I. P. Ottaviano, Giovanni Peri, and Greg C. Wright, "Immigration, Offshoring, and American Jobs," *Working Paper* 16439, National Bureau of Economic Research, October 2010.

25. World Health Organization. Density of nursing and midwifery personnel (total number per 1000 population).

26. *Philippine Daily Inquirer*, "What Went Before: Glut of Nursing Graduates," July 9, 2013.

27. Clemens," Economics and Emigration."

28. Clemens, Michael, "Skill Flow: A Fundamental Reconsideration of Skilled-Worker Mobility and Development," *Working Papers* 180, Center for Global Development, August 2009.

29. NHS Employers, "Developing Countries—Recruitment," March 18, 2014. www.nhsemployers.org.

30. Clemens, "Skill Flow."

31. Enrique T. Ona, "Universal Health Care in the Philippines: Gains and Challenges" (Powerpoint), accessed November 12, 2013. csis.org.

32. Frederic B. Docquier, Lindsay Lowell, and Abdeslam Marfouk, "A Gendered Assessment of the Brain Drain," *IZA Discussion Paper* 3235, Institute for the Study of Labor, 2007.

33. Lant Pritchett, "Does Learning to Add Up Add Up? The Returns to Schooling in Aggregate Data," in *Handbook of the Economics of Education*, ed. Eric A. Hanushek and Finish Welch, New York: Elsevier, 2006.

34. Clemens, "Skill Flow."

35. Ibid.

36. Kristen McCabe, "Chinese Immigrants in the United States," *Migration Information Source*, posted January 18, 2012. www.migrationpolicy.org; Monica Whatley and Jeanne Batalova, "Indian Immigrants in the United States," *Migration Information Source*, posted August 21, 2013. www.migrationpolicy.org.

37. Zahid Hussain, "New Evidence Reaffirms that Migration Is Costly but Still Worthwhile for Bangladeshis," World Bank, *End Poverty in South Asia* (blog), posted May 15, 2010; Michael Clemens, "Migration Is a Spectacularly Good Investment for Most: New Study from Bangladesh," Center for Global Development, posted May 21, 2010. www.cgdev.org/blog.

38. Andrew England, "South Africa's Black Farmers Struggle with Land Reform," *Financial Times*, December 5, 2013; *Economist*, "Seeds of Change," accessed June 20, 2013. www.economist.com/blogs/baobab; Eddie Cross, "The Cost of Zimbabwe's Continuing Farm Invasions," *Economic Development Bulletin* No. 12, Cato Institute, May 18, 2009.

39. *Economist*, "Peace, Land, and Bread," November 24, 2012; *Economist*, "This Land Is Anti-Capitalist Land," April 26, 2007.

40. R. S. Deshpande, "Current Land Policy Issues in India," *Land Reform* 3, Food and Agriculture Association, 2003; Tajamul Haque, "Impact of Land Leasing Restrictions on Agricultural Efficiency and Equity in India" (paper presented at Annual World Bank Conference on Land and Poverty, Washington, D.C., April 23–26, 2012.

41. *Economist*, "When Others Are Grabbing Their Land," May 5, 2011.

42. In Ghana, for example, three-quarters of all land is held by villages, with individuals as secondary holders; Joseph Blocher, "Building on Custom: Land Tenure Policy and Economic Development in Ghana," *Yale Human Rights and Development Law Journal* 9 (2006): 166–202.

   The South African government has extended the control of tribal chiefs over land rights since the end of apartheid; Greg Nicolson, "South Africa: Who Controls the Land Anyway?" *Daily Maverick*, April 12, 2012.

43. Blocher, "Building on Custom."

44. World Bank, *Agriculture for Development*, *World Development Report* 2008.

45. Alain de Janvry, Kyle Emerick, Marco Gonzalez-Navarro, and Elisabeth Sadoulet, "Delinking Land Rights from Land Use: Certification and Migration in Mexico," Society for Economic Dynamics, *2014 Meeting Papers* 138, June 27, 2013.

46. Pierre Boulanger, Patrick Jomini, Xiao-guang Zhang, Catherine Costa, and Michelle Osborne, "An Economic Assessment of Removing the Most Distortive Instruments of the Common Agricultural Policy (CAP)" (paper presented at 12th Annual ETSG Conference, Lausanne, Switzerland, September 9–11 2010.

47. David Hallam, "Foreign Investment in Developing Country Agriculture: Issues, Policy Implications, and International Response," OECD Global Forum on International Investment (December 2009).

48. Ira Glass, "Retracting 'Mr. Daisey and the Apple Factory," *This American Life* (blog), March 16, 2012. www.thisamericanlife.org.

49. Keith Bradsher and Charles Duhigg, "Signs of Changes Taking Hold in Electronics Factories in China," *New York Times*, December 12, 2012. The entire series can be found at www.nytimes.com/interactive/business/ieconomy.html.

50. Mikey Campbell, "Apple Terminates Contract with Supplier After Audit Finds Underage Labor Violations," *Apple Insider*, posted January 24, 2013. www.appleinsider.com; China Labour Bulletin, "From Shanxi to Dongguan, Slave Labour Is Still in Business," posted May 21, 2008. www.clb.org.hk.

51. *Want China Times*, "High Staff Turnover a Problem for Most Chinese Firms: Poll," posted February 6, 2013. www.wantchinatimes.com.

52. There is some controversy surrounding South Africa's unemployment figures, but the academic literature has put it in the vicinity of 25 percent since 1999. Broad unemployment, which includes workforce dropout, is closer to 40 percent; Abhijit Banerjee, Sebastian Galiani, Jim Levinsohn, and Ingrid Woolard, "Why Has Unemployment Risen in the New South Africa?," *Economics of Transition* 16, no. 4 (October 2008): 715–40; Nir Klein, "Real Wage, Labor Productivity, and Employment Trends in South Africa: A Closer Look," *IMF Working Paper* 12/92, April 2012.

53. *Economist*, "Unions v Jobs," May 26, 2005; Banjeree, Galiani, Levinson, and Woolard, "Why Has Unemployment Risen?," 2008.

54. Patrick Craven, "COSATU Is Shocked by the Latest Unemployment Figures," press release, Congress of South African Trade Unions, May 8, 2013.

55. Johann Van Eeden and Taku Fundira, "South African Quotas on Chinese Clothing and Textiles: 18-Month Economic Review," *TRALAC Working Paper* No. 08/2008 (November 2008); Johann Van Eeden, "South African Quotas on Chinese Clothing and Textiles Economic Evidence," *Econex Research* Note 9, March 2009; Joshua Wolmarans, "The Impact of Trade Policies on the South African Clothing and Textile Industry: A Focus on Import Quotas on Chinese Goods," Thesis, University of Stellenbosch, South Africa, 2011 SUNScholar Research Respoto, Stellenbosch University Library and Information Services. http://hdl.handle.net/10019.1/8544.

56. Devon Maylie, and Jenny Gross, "South Africa Textile Firms in Tatters," *Wall Street Journal*, August 9, 2011.

57. Bhim Udas, "A Roadmap for Rebuilding," *Kathmandu Post*, May 31, 2015; Chandan Sapkota, "Imprudent Unions and Weak Industries of Nepal," *Republica*, August 27, 2011.

58. Clemens, "Economics and Emigration."

59. Mary A. O'Grady, "How to Break Open the Mexican Piñata" *Wall Street Journal*, May 12, 2006.

60. Boulanger, Jomini, Zhang, Costa, and Osborne, "Economic Assessment."

61. United States Census Bureau. "QuickFacts: United States." http://www.census.gov/quickfacts/table/IPE120214/.

62. Rent trend data in Sacramento, CA, www.rentjungle.com. Accessed Aug 7, 2016.

63. Jenny Pisillo, "Still Better to Rent than Buy, Unless You're Looking in the East Bay," *San Francisco Chronicle*, *On the Block* (blog), March 23, 2012.

64. Unlike the healthcare sector, there has not been significant wage inflation in the technology sector, indicating a fairly loose labor market. See Robert N. Charette, "The STEM Crisis Is a Myth," *IEEE Spectrum*, August 30, 2013.

65. Kim-Mai Cutler, "How Burrowing Owls Lead to Vomiting Anarchists (or SF's Housing Crisis Explained)," *Techcrunch*, posted April 14, 2014. techcrunch.com.

66. Yukon Huang, "Urbanisation Is Key to Why India Is So Far in China's Wake," *Financial Times*, June 8, 2015.

67. Manuel Melis Maynar, the chief executive officer of Metro Madrid, provided a convenient list of rules for a successful subway expansion in a note from April 2003, the best of which was this: "The author believes that we are here to meet our dates and our costs. If we have to explain why we have failed, we should leave engineering management, and shift our activities to other fields where we might find more appreciation, say in opera composing or ballet dancing"; Manuel Melis Maynar, "Madrid Metro and Railway Infrastructure 1995–2003," *Metrosur: Commuting in the 21th century,* (Devon, England: Tunnelbuilder, 2003); See also Scott Beyer, "7 Reasons U.S. Infrastructure Projects Cost Way More Than They Should," *CityLab*, April 7, 2014.

68. PricewaterhouseCoopers, "Public-Private Partnerships: The US perspective," June 2010.

69. Ibid.

70. B. S. Tang, Y. H. Chiang, A. N. Baldwin, and C. W. Yeung, *Study of the Integrated Rail-Property Development Model in Hong Kong*, Hong Kong: Hong Kong Polytechnic University, 2004; Neil Padukone, "The Unique Genius of Hong Kong's Public Transport System," *Atlantic*, September 10, 2013.

71. Banjeree, Galiani, Levinson, and Woolard, "Why Has Unemployment Risen?"

72. OECD, *International Migration Outlook 2013*, Paris: OECD Publishing, 2013.

73. Thomas Paine, "Agrarian Justice," 1797. www.ssa.gov/history/.

74. Matt Zwolinski, "The Libertarian Case for a Basic Income," December 5, 2013. libertarianism.org; Megan McArdle, "Four Reasons a Guaranteed Income Won't Work," *Bloomberg View*, December 4, 2013.

75. U.S. Department of State, "Report of the Visa Office, 2015."

76. Thomas Friedman, "Invent, Invent, Invent," *New York Times*, June 27, 2009.

77. Madeline Zavodny, "Immigration and Its Contribution to Our Economic Strength," testimony before the Joint Economic Committee, May 8, 2013. www.aei.org.

78. George Borjas, *Heaven's Door: Immigration Policy and the American Economy*, Princeton, NJ: Princeton University Press, 1999.

Bibliography

Allen, Bill. "House Subcommittee Holds Hearing on the Need for Visas for High-Skilled Employees." *Washington Labor & Employment Wire*, June 12, 2008.

Allen, Robert. "Pessimism Preserved: Real Wages in the British Industrial Revolution." *Oxford University Department of Economics Working Paper 314*, 2007.

Anderlini, Jamil. "Rural Investment Pays Off in China." *Financial Times*, September 11, 2012.

Anderlini, Jamil, and Vincent Boland. "China Car Group Sues Fiat in Copying Case." *Financial Times*, October 20, 2009.

Anderson, Jonathan. "Five Persistent Myths About China's Banking System." *Cato Journal* 26, no. 2 (Spring/Summer 2006).

———. "Hurray for Ghost Cities." Client note, Emerging Advisors Group (2013).

———. "If You're Thinking About Capital Efficiency . . . Think Again." *UBS Investment Research*, November 8, 2011.

———. "Is China Export-Led?" *UBS Investment Research*, September 27, 2007.

———. "Settling Another Old Debate on Chinese (and Argentine) Inflation." *UBS Investment Research*, January 24, 2011.

Andres, Peter, *Smuggler Nation: How Illicit Trade Made America*. New York: Oxford University Press, 2013.

Banerjee, Abhijit, Sebastian Galiani, Jim Levinsohn, and Ingrid Woolard. "Why Has Unemployment Risen in the New South Africa." *Economics of Transition* 16, no. 4 (October 2008): 715–40.

Barber, Sarah, and Lan Yao. "Health Insurance Systems in China: A Briefing Note." *Background Paper 37, World Health Report*. World Health Organization, 2010.

Barth, James R., and Gerard Caprio Jr. "China's Changing Financial System: Can It Catch Up with, or Even Drive, Growth?" Policy Brief 2007-PB05. Networks Financial Institute at Indiana State University (March 2007).

Barth, James R., Michael Lea, and Tong Li. "China's Housing Market: Is a Bubble About to Burst?" Milken Institute Report, December 2012.

Batson, Andrew. "The SOE Irritant in U.S.-China Relations." *Wall Street Journal*, July 7, 2013.

———. "Treat Different SOEs Differently." *Caixin*, January 14, 2014.

BBC News. "Convicted Chinese Businesswoman Wu Ying Given Reprieve." May 12, 2012.

Beyer, Scott. "7 Reasons U.S. Infrastructure Projects Cost Way More Than They Should." *CityLab*, April 7, 2014.

Bildner, Eli. "Ordos: A Ghost Town That Isn't." *The Atlantic*, April 8, 2013.

Blocher, Joseph, "Building on Custom: Land Tenure Policy and Economic Development in Ghana." *Yale Human Rights and Development Law Journal* 9 (2006): 166–202.

Bloomberg News. "China Lets Local Authorities Convert Debt into Muni Bonds." *Bloomberg*, March 9, 2015.

Bloomberg News, with Henry Sanderson. "China Scraps Trial of Local Government Bonds, Studies Risks." *Bloomberg*, June 26, 2012.

Bloomberg News. "Chinese Zombies Emerging After Years of Solar Subsidies." *Bloomberg*, September 8, 2013.

Bonifazi, C., F. Heins, S. Strozza, and M. Vitiello. "Italy: The Italian Transition from an Emigration to Immigration Country." *IDEA Working Papers* 5, March 2009.

Borjas, George, *Heaven's Door: Immigration Policy and the American Economy*. Princeton, NJ: Princeton University Press, 1999.

Borst, Nicholas. "China's Carefully Managed Local Government Bond Issuance." Peterson Institute for International Economics, *China Economic Watch* (blog), November 30, 2011. blogs.piie.com.

Boulanger, Pierre, Patrick Jomini, Xiao-guang Zhang, Catherine Costa, and Michelle Osborne. "An Economic Assessment of Removing the Most Distortive Instruments of the Common Agricultural Policy (CAP)." Paper presented at 12th Annual ETSG Conference, Lausanne, Switzerland, September 9–11 2010.

Boxun. "Jiǎ língmǐn zìshù: Shíbā dà qíjiān bèi bǎngjià, ōudǎ hé qiújìn de jīngguò" [Jia Lingmin: While the Eighteenth Congress of the Communist Party was happening, I was kidnapped, beaten and imprisoned]. November 14, 2012.

———. "Zhèngzhōu duō rén bèi rēng ní gōu hòu fāxiàn fángwū yǐ bèi qiángchāi" [After being thrown in a ditch, Zhengzhou people return to find their houses destroyed]. October 25, 2010.

———. "Zhùmíng wéiquán rén jiǎ língmǐn, liú de wěi fēnbié bèi pàn 4 nián hé 1 nián bàn qíng kàn bóxùn rèdiǎn: Qiángxíng chāiqiān" [Well-known activists, Jia Lingmin, Liu Dewei, sentenced to four and a half years]. November 6, 2015.

Bradsher, Keith. "Chinese Solar Panel Giant Is Tainted by Bankruptcy." *New York Times*, March 20, 2013.

Bradsher, Keith, and Charles Duhigg. "Signs of Changes Taking Hold in Electronics Factories in China." *New York Times*, December 12, 2012.

Bramall, Chris. "Chinese Land Reform in Long-Run Perspective and in the Wider East Asian Context." *Journal of Agrarian Change* 4 (2004): 107–41.

Brandt, Loren, Chang-tai Hsieh, and Xiaodong Zhu. "Growth and Structural Transformation in China." In *China's Great Economic Transformation*, edited by Loren Brandt and Thomas G. Rawski, 683–728. Cambridge, UK: Cambridge University Press, 2008.

Brandt, Loren, Scott Rozelle, and Guo Li. "Tenure, Land Rights, and Farmer Investment Incentives in China." *Agricultural Economics* (1998): 63–71.

Branigan, Tania. "China Becomes an Urban Nation at Breakneck Speed." *Guardian*, October 2, 2011.

Brodsgaard, Kjeld Erik. "Foreign Direct Investment in China: Origin, Distribution, and Impact on the Economy." In *China: Business Opportunities in a Globalizing Economy*, edited by Verner Worm, 43–62. Copenhagen: Copenhagen Business School, 2008.

Burdekin, Richard C. K., and Ran Tao. "China's State-Owned Banks' Lending Practices, 1994–2005: Empirical Tests and Policy Implications." *Open Economics Journal* 1 (2008): 14–24.

Burn-Callander, Rebecca. "Migrant Entrepreneurs Driving Job Creation Across Britain, Study Shows." *Telegraph*, March 4, 2014.

Bush, George W. *Decision Points*. New York: Crown, 2010.

Cai, Fang, and Wang Dewen. "Impacts of Internal Migration on Economic Growth and Urban Development in China." In *Migration and Development Within and Across Borders: Research and Policy Perspectives on Internal and International Migration*, edited by J. DeWind and J. Holdaway, 245–72. New York: International Organization for Migration and the Social Science Research Council, 2008.

———. "The Sustainability of China's Economic Growth and Labor Contribution." *Journal of Economic Research* 10 (1999): 62–68.

Campbell, Mikey. "Apple Terminates Contract with Supplier After Audit Finds Underage Labor Violations." *Apple Insider*, January 24, 2013.

Cao, Bonnie. "China's Developers Face Shakeout as Easy Money Ends: Mortgages." *Bloomberg News*, March 28, 2014.

Cao, Kang H., and Javier A. Birchenall. "Agricultural Productivity, Structural Change, and Economic Growth in Post-Reform China." *Journal of Development Economics* 104 (2013): 165–80.

Cary, Eve. "Reforming China's State Owned Enterprises." *Diplomat*, June 19, 2013.

CCTV. "Party and Government Organs at All Levels Have Introduced Countermeasures." December 15, 2003.

Cassel, Susie Lan. *The Chinese in America: A History from Gold Mountain to the New Millennium.* Walnut Creek, CA: AltaMira Press, 2002.

Chan, Kam Wing. "A Road Map for Reforming China's Hukou System." *China Dialogue,* October 22, 2013. www.chinadialogue.com.

Chan, Kam Wing, and Will Buckingham. "Is China Abolishing the Hukou System?" *China Quarterly* 195 (September 2008): 582–606.

Chan, Melissa. "China's Empty City." *Al Jazeera,* November 10, 2009. www.aljazeera.com.

Chan, Vinicy. "Chinese Shoppers Overtake U.S. as Top Luxury Buyers." *Bloomberg,* December 11, 2012.

Chang, Leslie. *Factory Girls: From Village to City in a Changing China.* New York: Spiegel & Grau, 2009.

Charette, Robert N. "The STEM Crisis Is a Myth." *IEEE Spectrum,* August 30, 2013.

Chen, Jiajian, Robert Retherford, Minja Kim Choe, Li Xiru, and Cui Hongyan. "Population Policy, Economic Reform, and Fertility Decline in Guangdong Province, China." *East-West Center Working Papers* 120, May 2009.

Cheng, Edwin, and Tsan-Ming Choi, eds. *Innovative Quick Response Programs in Logistics and Supply Chain Management.* Berlin: Springer, 2010.

Cheng, Tiejun, and Mark Selden. "The Origins and Social Consequences of China's Hukou System." *China Quarterly* 139 (1994): 644–68.

Chiang, Langi. "Anhui Tests Land Reform in Wake of Plenum Vow on Rural Property Rights." *South China Morning Post,* November 13, 2013.

China Daily. "Banking Goes Underground on Tightening." December 28, 2010.

———. "Illegal Land Development Zones Cut." June 26, 2004.

———. "Sun Zhigang's Brutal Killers Sentenced." June 10, 2003.

The China Development Research Foundation. *China's New Urbanization Strategy.* New York: Routledge, 2013.

China Labour Bulletin. "From Shanxi to Dongguan, Slave Labour Is Still in Business." May 21, 2008. www.clb.org.hk.

China News Weekly. "Zhèngzhōu hùjí gǎigé shòucuò fǎnsī wénjiàn hòu xū shēnkè zhìdù biàngé" [Zhengzhou household registration setback reflects the need for profound institutional change]. April 23, 2007.

China Real Time Report (blog). "What Worker Shortage? The Real Story of China's Migrants." *Wall Street Journal,* January 4, 2013.

Choate, Allen. "Local Governance in China: An Assessment of Villagers Committees." *Asia Foundation Working Paper Series,* February 1997.

———. "Local Governance in China II: An Assessment of Urban Residents Committees and Municipal Community Development." *Asia Foundation Working Paper Series,* November 1998.

Choi, Chang kon. "The Employment Effect of Economic Growth: Identifying Determinants of Employment Elasticity." 2007. http://faculty.washington.edu/karyiu/confer/busan07/papers/choi.pdf.

Clemens, Michael. "Economics and Emigration: Trillion-Dollar Bills on the Sidewalk?" *Journal of Economic Perspectives*. Volume 25, no. 3 (Summer 2011): 83–106.

———. "Migration Is a Spectacularly Good Investment for Most: New Study from Bangladesh." Center for Global Development, *Views from the Center* (blog), May 21, 2010.

———. "Skill Flow: A Fundamental Reconsideration of Skilled-Worker Mobility and Development." Center for Global Development, *Working Papers* 180, August 2009.

Coase, Ronald, and Ning Wang. *How China Became Capitalist*. London: Palgrave Macmillan, 2012.

Collins, Timothy L. "Rent Regulation Prior to the Establishment of the Board." In *An Introduction to the New York City Rent Guidelines Board and the Rent Stabilization System*, 15–20. New York City Rent Guidelines Board. *Rent Regulation Prior to the Establishment of the Board*. Revised February 2016.

Craven, Patrick. "COSATU Is Shocked by the Latest Unemployment Figures." Press release. Congress of South African Trade Unions, May 8, 2013.

CRI Online. "Zhōngguó tiělù chūnyùn 40tiān fāsòng lǚkè 2.4yì réncì" [China's trains saw 240 million passengers during the 40 days around the Spring Festival]. March 10, 2013.

Cross, Eddie. "The Cost of Zimbabwe's Continuing Farm Invasions." *Economic Development Bulletin* No. 12. Cato Institute, May 18, 2009.

Cutler, Kim-Mai. "How Burrowing Owls Lead to Vomiting Anarchists (Or SF's Housing Crisis Explained)." *Techcrunch*, April 14, 2014.

Daily Alta California, "Anti-Chinese Crusade," February 12, 1886.

Das, Mitali, and Papa N'Diaye. "Chronicle of a Decline Foretold: Has China Reached the Lewis Turning Point?" *IMF Working Paper* 13/26, January 2013.

Davis, Bob. "Chinese College Graduates Play It Safe and Lose Out." *Wall Street Journal*, March 25, 2013.

de Janvry, Alain, Kyle Emerick, Marco Gonzalez-Navarro, and Elisabeth Sadoulet. "Delinking Land Rights from Land Use: Certification and Migration in Mexico." Society for Economic Dynamics, *2014 Meeting Papers* 138, June 27, 2013.

Dean, Robin, and Tobias Damm-Luhr. "A Current Review of Chinese Land-Use Law and Policy: A 'Breakthrough' in Rural Reform?" *Pacific Rim Law and Policy Journal* 19, no. 1 (2010): 121–59.

Dearie, John, and Courtney Geduldig. "More Immigration Means More Jobs for Americans." *Wall Street Journal*, December 29, 2013.

Deng, F. Frederic, and Youqin Huang. "Uneven Land Reform and Urban Sprawl in China: The Case of Beijing." *Progress in Planning* 61 (2004): 211–36.

Deng, Gang. *The Premodern Chinese Economy: Structural Equilibrium and Capitalist Sterility*. London: Routledge, 1999.

Deng, Haiyan, John Haltiwanger, Robert McGuckin, Jianyi Xu, Yaodong Liu, and Yuqi Liu. "The Contribution of Restructuring and Reallocation to China's Productivity and Growth." The Conference Board, *Economics Program Working Papers* 07-04, December 2007.

Deshpande, R. S. "Current Land Policy Issues in India." *Land Reform* 3, Food and Agriculture Association, 2003.

Docquier, Frederic B., Lindsay Lowell, and Abdeslam Marfouk. "A Gendered Assessment of the Brain Drain." *IZA Discussion Paper* 3235, Institute for the Study of Labor (Bonn, Germany), 2007.

Dykstra, Sarah, Charles Kenny, and Justin Sandefur. "Global Poverty Fell by Almost Half on Saturday." Center for Global Development, *Views from the Center* (blog), May 2, 2014.

Easterly, William, *The White Man's Burden: Why the West's Efforts to Aid the Rest Have Done So Much Ill and So Little Good*. New York: Penguin, 2006.

Economic Observer, "Chéngzhèn huà de zhàcài zhǐshù." [Urbanization's mustard index]. August 10, 2013.

Economist. "Counting Ghosts." January 4, 2014.

———. "Daily Bread." October 26, 2013.

———. "Feeling Your Pain." April 27, 2013.

———. "Good Tidings from the South." December 3, 2011.

———. "Moving on Up." March 22, 2014.

———. "Not Always with Us." June 1, 2013.

———. "Peace, Land, and Bread." November 24, 2012.

———. "Peak Toil." January 26, 2013.

———. "School's Out." September 3, 2011.

———. "Seeds of Change." From the print edition: Special report. June 20, 2013.

———. "This Land Is Anti-capitalist Land." April 26, 2007.

———. "Unions v Jobs." May 26, 2005.

———. "When Others Are Grabbing Their Land." May 5, 2011.

———. "Made in China," March 14, 2015.

Economist Intelligence Unit. "China's Solar Storms." *Access China*. December 6, 2012.

———. "Hebei." *Access China* (February 2014).

———. "Zhejiang." *Access China* (February 2014).

———. "Zhengzhou." *Access China* (February 2014).

Eggleston, Karen. "Health Care for 1.3 Billion: An Overview of China's Health System." *Stanford University Working Paper Series on Health and Demographic Change in the Asia-Pacific*, January 9, 2012.

Eickmeier, Sandra, and Markus Kuhnlenz. "China's Role in Global Inflation Dynamics." *Deutsche Bundesbank Discussion Paper* No. 07/2013, April 2, 2013.

England, Andrew. "South Africa's Black Farmers Struggle with Land Reform." *Financial Times*, December 5, 2013.

Fairlie, Robert W. "Immigrant Entrepreneurs and Small Business Owners and Their Financial Capital." United States Small Business Administration/Office of Advocacy. Report No. 396, May 2012.

Fauna [psued.]. "Anti-Mainlander Hong Kong Ad Parodied, Becomes Internet Meme." *Chinasmack*. February 4, 2012. www.chinasmack.com.

Fewsmith, Joseph. "Chambers of Commerce in Wenzhou and the Potential Limits of 'Civil Society' in China." *China Leadership Monitor* 16, Stanford University (2005).

Fibre2Fashion. "US, Japan lead in China's Textile Exports: CCCT." January 20, 2014.

Flannery, Russell. "Where's China's Growth? Textile Industry Is Weaving Expansion." *Forbes*, September 2, 2013.

Fleming, Chris. "U.S. Health Spending Projected to Grow 5.8 Percent Annually." *Health Affairs, Health Affairs* (blog), July 28, 2011.

Forsythe, Michael. "China Eclipses U.S. as Biggest Trading Nation." *Bloomberg*, February 10, 2013.

Friedman, Thomas. "Invent, Invent, Invent." *New York Times*, June 27, 2009.

Gallagher, Kevin. *The Dragon in the Room: China and the Future of Latin American Industrialization*. Stanford, CA: Stanford University Press, 2010.

Gao Xu. "Are Chinese Statistics Manipulated?" World Bank, *East Asia & Pacific On the Rise* (blog), March 23, 2010.

———. "State-Owned Enterprises in China: How Profitable Are They?" World Bank, *East Asia & Pacific On the Rise* (blog), March 2, 2010.

Gao Yuan. "China Now World's Biggest Smartphone Market." *China Daily*, November 6, 2013.

Gardner, Bradley. "China's Black Market City." *Reason*, December 2011.

———. *Renminbi Rising: Onshore and Offshore Perspectives on Chinese Financial Liberalisation*. Economist Intelligence Unit Report Commissioned by State Street, 2014.

Gillet, Kit. "Zhang Xin." *China International Business*, January 2010.

Glaeser, Edward. "Urban Colossus: Why Is New York America's Largest City?" *Economic Policy Review* 11 (2005): 7–24.

Glass, Ira. "Retracting 'Mr. Daisey and the Apple Factory." *This American Life* (blog), March 16, 2012.

Global Entrepreneur. "Guōtáimíng wú jiě nántí: Fùshìkāng chāojí dà gōngchǎng de sǐjié" [Guo Taiming has no answers for the difficult problems of Foxconn factories]. November 5, 2012.

Global Times. "When the Ordos Bubble Burst." July 12, 2013.

Goldstein, Jacob. "So You Think You Can Be a Hair Braider?" *New York Times,* June 12, 2012.

Grant, Madison. "America for the Americans." *The Forum,* September 1925.

Gurr, Ted Robert. "Historical Trends in Violent Crime: Europe and the United States." In *Violence in America—Volume 1: The History of Crime,* edited by Ted Robert Gurr, 21–54, Newbury Park, CA: Sage, 1989.

Hallam, David. "Foreign Investment in Developing Country Agriculture: Issues, Policy Implications and International Response." Paper prepared for OECD Global Forum on International Investment VIII, Paris, December 7–8, 2009.

Haltmaier, Jane. "Challenges for the Future of Chinese Economic Growth." *Board of Governors of the Federal Reserve System International Finance Discussion Papers* 1072 (January 2013).

Hamlin, Kevin. "China's Desert Ghost City Shows Property 'Madness' Persists." *Bloomberg,* June 23, 2010.

Haque, Tajamul. "Impact of Land Leasing Restrictions on Agricultural Efficiency and Equity in India." Paper presented at Annual World Bank Conference on Land and Poverty, Washington, D.C., April 23–26, 2012.

Hatton, Timothy J., "International Migration and World Development: A Historical Perspective." *Historical Paper* 41, National Bureau of Economic Research, September 1992.

Hess, Chester Newten. "What California Means to Its Oldest Living Chinese." *Westways* 26, no. 3 (March 1934).

Hille, Kathrin. "Hebei Steel Merger Prompts Doubts." *Financial Times,* December 30, 2008.

Hines, Tony. "Globalization: An Introduction to Fashion Markets and Fashion Marketing." In *Fashion Marketing: Contemporary Issues,* edited by Tony Hines and Margaret Bruce, 1–24. Oxford: Butterworth Heinemann, 2001.

Horn, John, Vivien Singer, and Jonathan Woetzel. "A Truer Picture of China's Export Machine." *McKinsey Quarterly,* September 2010.

Horton, Carol A. *Race and the Making of Modern Liberalism.* New York: Oxford University Press, 2005.

Hu Yuanyuan. "Down Payment for Second-Home Buyers to Hit 70%." *China Daily,* April 8, 2013.

Huang, Haizhou, and Shuilin Wang. "Exchange Rate Regimes: China's Experience and Choices." *China Economic Review* 15 (2004): 336–42.

Huang, Yanzhong. *Governing Health in Contemporary China.* China Policy Series. New York: Routledge, 2013.

———. "What Money Failed to Buy: The Limits of China's Healthcare Reform." *Forbes*, March 4, 2014.

Huang, Yasheng. *Capitalism with Chinese Characteristics.* Cambridge, UK: Cambridge University Press, 2008.

———. "The China Boom: Rural China in the 1980s." *The China Boom Project*, The Asia Society Center on US-China Relations, June 1, 2010.

Huang, Yeqing, and Neng Wan. "Dynamic Changes of Labour Market and Employment Opportunities of Migrant Workers in Transitional China: Evidence from Three Metropolises." Paper presented at the Global Development Network's 13th Annual Global Development Conference, Budapest, June 16–18, 2012.

Huang, Yukon. "Urbanisation Is Key to Why India Is So Far in China's Wake." *Financial Times*, June 8, 2015.

Hussain, Zahid. "New Evidence Reaffirms that Migration Is Costly but Still Worthwhile for Bangladeshis." World Bank, *End Poverty in South Asia*, May 15, 2010.

Jager-Waldau, Arnulf. *PV Status Report 2013.* European Commission, JRC Scientific and Policy Report, September 2013.

Jewish Women's Archive. "Pauline Newman Organizes Influential New York Rent Strike." n.d.

Jin, Jing, and Heng-fu Zou. "Soft-Budget Constraint on Local Government in China." In *Fiscal Decentralization and the Challenge of Hard Budget Constraints*, edited by J. Rodden, G.Eskeland, and J. Litvak, 289–324. Cambridge, MA: MIT Press, 2003.

Jinrong jiewang. "Yínjiānhuì jìxù qiánghuà róngzī píngtái xìndài jiānguǎn chéng tóu zhài bǎochí jiào dà fā háng guīmó" [CBRC supervision of credit financing platform to continue to strengthen]. March 28, 2013. http://bond.jrj.com .cn/2013/03/28141915183909.shtml.

Johnson, Ian. "China's Great Uprooting: Moving 250 Million into Cities." *New York Times*, June 15, 2013.

———. "China Releases Plan to Incorporate Farmers into Cities." *New York Times*, March 17, 2014.

Juan, Du. "Steel Companies See Profits Drop." *China Daily*, December 23, 2012.

Klein, Nir. "Real Wage, Labor Productivity, and Employment Trends in South Africa: A Closer Look." *IMF Working Paper* 12/92, April 2012.

KPMG Huazhen. *Zhengzhou Zhengdong New District, Investment Environment Study 2009.* Advisory Report, 2009.

Kujis, Louis, and Tao Wang. "China's Pattern of Growth: Moving to Sustainability and Reducing Inequality." *World Bank Policy Research Working Paper* 3767, November 2005.

Kung, James Kai-sing, Chenggang Xu, and Feizhou Zhou. "From Industrialization to Urbanization: The Social Consequences of Changing Fiscal Incentives on Local Government Behavior." In *Law and Economics with Chinese Characteristics: Institutions for Promoting Development in the Twenty-First Century,* edited by David Kennedy and Joseph E. Stiglitz, 491–510. Oxford: Oxford University Press, 2013.

Landwehr, Lynn. "The Ah Louis Store," *History in San Luis Obispo County.* 2004. http://www.historyinslocounty.org/Ah%20Louis%20Store.htm.

Lardy, Nicholas R. "China's State-Owned Enterprises: Transformation of State Firms' Role Likely to Accelerate." *Bloomberg Brief: China's Reform Plan*, November 2013.

Le Deu, Franck, Rajesh Parekh, Fangning Zhang, and Gaobo Zhou. *Health Care in China: Entering 'Uncharted Waters.'* McKinsey & Company, November 2012.

Lee, Il Houng, Murtaza Syed, and Liu Xueyan. "Is China Over-Investing and Does It Matter." *IMF Working Paper* 12/277, 2012.

Lee, Jungah, and Jason Folkmanis. "Samsung Shifts Plants from China to Protect Margins." *Bloomberg*, December 11, 2013.

Leke, Acha, Susan Lund, Charles Roxburgh, and Arend Van Wamelen. "What's Driving Africa's Growth?" McKinsey & Company, June 2010.

Ley, A. J. *A History of Building Control in England & Wales 1840–1990.* Coventry, UK: RICS Business Services, 2000.

Li, Haizheng, Yunling Liang, Barbara M. Fraumeni, Zhiqiang Liu, and Xiaojun Wang. "Human Capital in China." Paper presented at 31st General Conference of the International Association for Research in Income and Wealth, St. Gallen, Switzerland, August 22–28, 2010.

Li, Lixing. "Land Titling in China: Chengdu Experiment and its Consequences." *China Economic Journal* 5, no.1 (February 2012): 47–64.

Li, Minghuan. "'To Get Rich Quickly in Europe!' Reflections on Migration Motivation in Wenzhou." In *Internal and International Migration: Chinese Perspectives*, edited by Frank N. Pieke and Hein Mallee, 181–99. Richmond, UK: Curzon, 1999.

Li, Ping. "Rural Land Tenure Reforms in China: Issues, Regulations, and Prospects for Additional Reform." In *Land Reform: Land Settlement and Cooperatives.* Special edition, 59–72. Food and Agriculture Organization of the United Nations, 2003.

Li, Shuzhuo. "Imbalanced Sex Ratio at Birth and Comprehensive Intervention in China." Paper presented at 4th Asia Pacific Conference on Reproductive and

Sexual Health and Rights, UN Population Fund, Hyderabad, India, October 29–31, 2007.

Liang Dongmei, Yang Binbin, Fu Yanyan, and Wang Duan. "How Manufacturing's Mockingbird Sings." *Caixin*, February 10, 2010.

Lin, Ling. "Guǎngdōng tóuzī jìn 2 wàn yì gōulè lùlù jiāotōng yòu rén qiánjǐng" [Guangdong to invest Rmb2 trillion to upgrade transportation infrastructure]. *Yancheng Evening News*, November 15, 2012.

Lin, W. "'Shanzhai Culture' and Its Cultural Value Identification with Adolescents" [in Chinese]. *Journal of China Youth University for Political Sciences* 5 (2009): 46–50.

Lindsay, Greg. "China's Cell Phone Pirates Are Bringing Down Middle Eastern Governments." *Fast Company*, June 14, 2011.

Los Angeles Herald. "Chinese Laundrymen Boycotting San Luis Obispo," April 6, 1887.

Lu, Ming, Jianyong Fan, Shejian Liu, and Yan Yan. "Employment Restructuring During China's Economic Transition." Bureau of Labor Statistics, *Monthly Labor Review* (August 2002): 25–32.

Lu, Yinqiu, and Tao Sun. "Local Government Financing Platforms in China." *IMF Working Paper* 13/243, October 2013.

Ly, Son-Thierry, and Patrick Weil. "The Antiracist Origin of the Quota System." *Social Research* 77, no. 1 (Spring 2010): 45–79.

Mann, Charles C. "Renewables Aren't Enough. Clean Coal Is the Future." *Wired*, March 25, 2014.

Maylie, Devon, and Jenny Gross. "South Africa Textile Firms in Tatters." *Wall Street Journal*, August 9, 2011.

Maynar, Manuel Melis. "Introduction: Madrid Metro and Railway Infrastructure 1995–2003." In *Metrosur: Commuting in the 21st Century*, 2–6. Tunnelbuilder, 2003.

McArdle, Megan. "Four Reasons a Guaranteed Income Won't Work." *Bloomberg View*, December 4, 2013.

McCabe, Kristen. "Chinese Immigrants in the United States." *Migration Information Source*, January 18, 2012.

McGrath, Dylan, "China Cracking Down on Gray-Market Handsets." *EE Times*, July 11, 2010.

McMahon, Dinny, Esther Fung, and James T. Areddy. "China Housing Prices Decline." *Wall Street Journal*, November 8, 2011.

Melander A., and K. Pelikanova. "Reform of the Hukou System: A Litmus Test of the New Leadership." *ECFIN Economic Brief* 26, July 2013.

Miller, Tom. *China's Urban Billion*, London: Zed Books, 2012.

———. "Time for a Reality Check on China's Ghost Cities." *China Dialogue*, August 10, 2013. www.chinadialogue.net.

Milholland, John. "Immigration Hysteria in Congress." *Forum*, January 1921, 104–16.

Ming, Holly H. *The Education of Migrant Children and China's Future: The Urban Left Behind*. New York: Routledge, 2014.

Ministry of Education of the People's Republic of China. "Outline of China's National Plan for Medium- and Long-Term Education Reform and Development (2010–2020)." October 12, 2010.

Ministry of Finance of the People's Republic of China. "Guānyú yìnfā '2013 nián dìfāng zhèngfǔ zìxíng fā zhài shìdiǎn bànfǎ' de tōngzhī" [On the issuance of 'The approach to the launch of 2013 local government bonds']. July 2013. gks .mof.gov.cn.

Miroff, Nick. "Latin American Equality: Free Markets or a Left-Wing Success?" *Global Post,* December 1, 2012.

Moses, Jonathon W., and Bjørn Letnes. "If People Were Money: Estimating the Gains and Scope of Free Migration." In *Poverty, International Migration, and Asylum*, edited by George J. Borjas and Jeff Crisp, 188–210. New York: Palgrave Macmillan, 2005.

Moyo, Dambisa, *Dead Aid: Why Aid is Not Working and How There is a Better Way for Africa*. New York: Farrar, Straus and Grioux, 2010.

Murphy, Rachel, "Domestic Migrant Remittances in China: Distribution, Channels and Livelihoods," International Organization of Migration, *MRS 24* (2006).

National Development and Reform Commission. "Zhèngzhōu hángkōnggǎng jīngjì zònghé shíyàn qū fāzhǎn guīhuà (2013–2025)" [Zhengzhou's airport economic zone development planning (2013–2025)]. April 2013.

Nicolson, Greg. "South Africa: Who Controls the Land Anyway?" *Daily Maverick*, April 12, 2012.

O'Brien, Kevin J., and Lianjiang Li. "'Accommodating Democracy' in a One-Party State: Introducing Village Elections in China." *China Quarterly* 162 (June 2000): 465–89.

O'Grady, Mary A. "How to Break Open the Mexican Piñata." *Wall Street Journal*, May 12, 2006.

OECD, based on work by Junyeop Lee. "State-Owned Enterprises in China: Reviewing the Evidence." OECD Occasional Paper. January 26, 2009.

———. *OECD Rural Policy Reviews: China 2009*. Paris: OECD Publishing, 2009.

———. *International Migration Outlook 2013*. Paris: OECD Publishing, 2013.

———. *OECD-FAO Agricultural Outlook 2013–2022*. 2013. https://stats.oecd.org /Index.aspx?DataSetCode=HIGH_AGLINK_2013.

Ona, Enrique T. "Universal Health Care in the Philippines: Gains and Challenges." Powerpoint, November 12, 2013. csis.org.

Oncology Nursing Society. "Oncology Nursing Society Position on the Impact of the National Nursing Shortage on Quality Cancer Care." *ONS Positions*, January 2013.

Ottaviano, Gianmarco I. P., Giovanni Peri, and Greg C. Wright. "Immigration, Offshoring, and American Jobs." *Working Paper* 16439, National Bureau of Economic Research, October 2010.

Overseas Research Department, Japan External Trade Organization. "The 22nd Survey of Investment-Related Costs in Asia and Oceana." April 2012.

Padukone, Neil. "The Unique Genius of Hong Kong's Public Transport System." *Atlantic*, September 10, 2013.

Paine, Thomas. "Agrarian Justice," 1797. www.ssa.gov/history/.

Philippine Daily Inquirer. "What Went Before: Glut of Nursing Graduates." July 9, 2013.

Pisillo, Jenny. "Still Better to Rent than Buy, Unless You're Looking in the East Bay." *San Francisco Chronicle*, On the Block (blog), March 23, 2012.

Pomeranz, Kenneth. "Land Markets in Late Imperial and Republican China." *Continuity and Change* 23 (2008): 101–50.

Porter, Eduardo. "China's Vanishing Trade Imbalance." *New York Times*, May 1, 2012.

Pozen, Robert. "Tackling the Chinese Pension System." *Paulson Policy Memorandum*, The Paulson Institute, July 2013.

PricewaterhouseCoopers. "Public-Private Partnerships: The US Perspective." Report, June 2010.

Pritchett, Lant. "Does Learning to Add Up Add Up? The Returns to Schooling in Aggregate Data." In *Handbook of the Economics of Education*, edited by Eric A. Hanushek and Finish Welch, 635–696. New York: Elsevier, 2006.

Qi, Liyan. "China to Create Unified Pension System." *Wall Street Journal*, February 7, 2014.

Qin, Duo, and Haiyan Song. "Sources of Investment Inefficiency: The Case of Fixed-Asset Investment in China." *Journal of Development Economics* 90, no. 1 (September 2009): 94–105.

Qu Hongbin, Sun Junwei, Paul Mackel, and Wang Ju. "The Rise of the Redback II." HSBC Global Research. Report, March 2013.

Que Aimin, and Yin Jiangyong. "Hùjí xīnzhèng jiào tíng zhèngzhōu míngquè biǎoshì hū hùjí gǎigé bù huì zhǐbù" [Though the new policy has halted, Zhengzhou has shown the *hukou* system needs reform]. *Henan Newspaper*, September 22, 2004.

Rabinovitch, Simon. "Strong Demand for China Local Bond Sale." *Financial Times*, November 15, 2011.

Rathod, Chandni, and Gus Lubin. "And Now Presenting: Amazing Satellite Images of the Ghost Cities of China." *Business Insider,* December 14, 2010.

Roane, Debra, Rebecca Zhang, Katie Chen, and David Rubinoff. "What's Ahead for Local Government Bond Market in China." *Moody's Investor Service,* July 17, 2013.

Roberts, Dexter. "China Gambles on Affordable Housing." *Bloomberg Businessweek,* April 26, 2012.

———. "To Fix Overproduction, China Wants to Supersize Industries." *Bloomberg Businessweek,* January 23, 2013.

———. "Why Factories Are Leaving China." *Bloomberg Businessweek,* May 13, 2010.

Ruhs, Martin, and Carlos Vargas-Silva. "Briefing: The Labour Market Effects of Immigration." The Migration Observatory, March 5, 2014.

Russo, Bill, Tao Ke, and Edward Tse. "An Inorganic Approach to Globalization: The Marriage of Geely and Volvo." Booz & Company, 2009.

Rutkowski, Ryan. "Will Municipal Bonds Save China's Urbanization Plan." Peterson Institute for International Economics. *China Economic Watch* (blog), February 19, 2013.

Sandmeyer, Elmer Clarence. *The Anti-Chinese Movement in California.* Champaign, IL: Illini, 1973.

Sapkota, Chandan. "Imprudent Unions & Weak Industries of Nepal." *Republica,* August 27, 2011.

Saville, John. *Rural Depopulation in England and Wales.* Abingdon, UK: Routledge, 1957.

Shanghai Railway Bureau. "Chūnjié huángjīnzhōu shànghǎi tiělùjú sòngkè 569.6 Wàn rén" [Shanghai Railway Bureau: During the Spring festival 5.696 million people travelled]. February 16, 2013.

———. "Shànghǎi tiělùjú chūnyùn 40tiān ānquán sòng kè 4113wàn rén" [Shanghai Railway Bureau: in 40 days around spring festival 41.13 million people travelled safely]. March 7, 2013.

———. "Shànghǎi tiělùjú tíqián zuò hǎo chūnyùn chēliàng zhǔnbèi gōngzuò." [Shanghai Railway Bureau prepares for the Spring Festival]. December 27, 2012.

Shen, Chunli, Jing Jin, and Heng-fu Zou. "Fiscal Decentralization in China: History, Impact, Challenges, and Next Steps." *Annals of Economics and Finance* 13, no. 1 (2012): 1–51.

Shi Baoyin. "Nation's First Airport Economic Zone Taking Off." *China Daily,* May 18, 2013.

Shi, Lu, and Bernard Ganne. "Understanding the Zhejiang Industrial Clusters: Questions and Re-Evalutations." Paper presented at International Workshop Asian Industrial Clusters, Lyon, France, November 29–December 1, 2006.

Shi, Tianjin. "Village Committee Elections in China: Institutionalist Tactics for Democracy." *World Politics* 51, no. 3 (April 1999): 385–412.

Shih, Toh Han. "Hebei Iron Resignation Reveals Firm in Crisis." *South China Morning Post*, December 14, 2013.

Smith, Graham. "Where Is Everyone? The Derelict Majesty of Chinese Ghost Town Built to House One Million but with Less than 30,000 Residents." *Daily Mail*, July 24, 2012.

Snyder, Jim, and Christopher Martin. "Obama Team Backed $535 Million Solyndra Aid as Auditor Warned on Finances." *Bloomberg*, September 12, 2011.

Song Fuli, and Hu Dan. "Build It and They Will Come." *Economic Observer*, March 25, 2013.

Stanway, David. "China Ditches Steel Industry Consolidation Targets in New Plan." *Reuters*, March 25, 2014.

Steel Orbis. "Hebei Steel Co.'s Net Profit Down 92 Percent in 2012." April 15, 2013.

Stoney, Sierra, and Jeanne Batalova. "Mexican Immigrants in the United States." *Migration Information Source*, February 28, 2013.

Strauss, Valerie. "China's 10 New and Surprising School Reform Rules." *Washington Post*, *Answer Sheet* (blog), October 30, 2013.

Studwell, Joe. *How Asia Works.* New York: Profile, 2013.

Szreter, Simon, and Graham Mooney. "Urbanization, Mortality, and the Standard of Living Debate: New Estimates of the Expectation of Life at Birth in Nineteenth-Century British Cities." *Economic History Review* 51, no. 1 (1998): 84–112.

Tang, B. S., Y. H. Chiang, A. N. Baldwin, and C. W. Yeung. *Study of the Integrated Rail-Property Development Model in Hong Kong.* Hong Kong: Hong Kong Polytechnic University, 2004.

Tang Xiangyang, and Ruoji Tang. "Considered Opinion: The Wu Ying Case." *Economic Observer*, April 19, 2011.

Terrazas, Aaron, and Jeanne Batalova. "Filipino Migrants in the United States." *Migration Information Source*, April 7, 2010.

Tian, Ying. "China Ends U.S.'s Reign as Largest Auto Market." *Bloomberg News*, January 11, 2010.

Tsai, Kellee. *Back-Alley Banking: Private Entrepreneurs in China.* Ithaca, NY: Cornell, 2002.

Udas, Bhim. "A Roadmap for Rebuilding." *Kathmandu Post*, May 31, 2015.

Ulrich, Jing. "China's Housing Imbalance: Is Affordable Housing the Cure?" JP Morgan, *Hands-on China Report*, September 7, 2010.

United Nations. *The Millennium Development Goals Report 2015.* New York: United Nations, 2015.

Van Eeden, Johann, and Taku Fundira. "South African Quotas on Chinese Clothing and Textiles: 18 Month Economic Review." *TRALAC Working Paper* No. 08 /2008, November 2008.

Van Eeden, Johann. "South African Quotas on Chinese Clothing and Textiles Economic Evidence." Econex. Research Note 9, March 2009.

Vogel, Ezra. *Deng Xiaoping and the Transformation of China.* Cambridge, MA: Harvard University Press, 2010.

Wagstaff, Adam, Magnus Lindelow, Shiyong Wang, and Shuo Zhang. *Reforming China's Rural Health System.* Washington, DC: World Bank, 2009.

Walter, Carl, and Fraser Howie. *Red Capitalism: The Fragile Financial Foundation of China's Extraordinary* Rise. Singapore: Wiley Asia, 2011.

Wang, Hongyi. "Aging Population May Be Catalyst for Change." *China Daily*, June 24, 2010.

Wang, Kaihao. "Kangbashi Thrives Despite Perceptions." *China Daily*, December 24, 2012.

Wang, Tao. "Bubble or No Bubble? The Great Chinese Property Debate." *UBS Investment Research*, March 25, 2011.

———. "China Unveils Local Government Debt Solutions." *UBS Investment Research*, October 7, 2014.

———. "Something Positive from the SOE Reform Plan." *UBS Investment Research*, September 21, 2015.

Wang, Xinye. "Migrant Workers in Shortage After Spring Festival Holiday." *CCTV*, February 19, 2013. http://english.cntv.cn/.

Want China Times. "Foxconn Expanding into China's Third- and Fourth-Tier Cities." December 10, 2013. www.wantchinatimes.com.

———. "High Staff Turnover a Problem for Most Chinese Firms: Poll." February 6, 2013. www.wantchinatimes.com.

Watts, Jonathan. "The Tiger's Teeth." *Guardian*, May 24, 2005.

Wei, Lingling, "China Unveils Overhaul of Bloated State Sector." *Wall Street Journal*, September 13, 2015.

Whalley, John, and Xiliang Zhao. "The Contribution of Human Capital to China's Economic Growth." *China Economic Policy Review* 2, no. 1 (2013): 1–22.

Whatley, Monica, and Jeanne Batalova. "Indian Immigrants in the United States." *Migration Information Source*, August 21, 2013. www.migrationpolicy.org.

Wildau, Gabriel. "China's State-Owned Enterprise Reform Plans Face Compromise." *Financial Times*, September 14, 2015.

Wolmarans, Joshua. "The Impact of Trade Policies on the South African Clothing and Textile Industry: A Focus on Import Quotas on Chinese Goods." Thesis, University of Stellenbosch, South Africa, 2011. SUNScholar Research Respoto,

Stellenbosch University Library and Information Services. http://hdl.handle
.net/10019.1/8544.

World Bank. *Agriculture for Development*. World Development Report, 2008.

———. "Integration of National Product and Factor Markets: Economic Benefits
and Policy Recommendations." Report No. 31973-CHA, June 13, 2005.

World Bank and the Development Research Center of the State Council. *China
2030: Building a Modern, Harmonious, and Creative Society*. Washington, DC:
World Bank, 2013.

Worstall, Tim. "Now Apple's Manufacturing Is Leaving China," *Forbes*, August
24, 2013.

Wu, Bin, and Valter Zanin. "Exploring Links Between International Migration and
Wenzhou's Development." *Discussion Paper* 25, University of Nottingham China
Policy Institute, November 2007.

Xiaoxiang Morning News. "Zhùle 700duōtiān dìsān gè wōpéng yòu bèi chāi" [After
living there for 700 days, Jia Lingmin's third shack is destroyed]. August 23, 2012.

Xinhua. "Beijing to Complete Land-Use Rights Registration by 2018." December
27, 2013.

———. "China Allows 2 More Local Gov'ts to Issue Bonds." July 5, 2013.

———. "China Expected to Bolster Rice Import." October 18, 2013.

———. "China Seeks Unified Pension Scheme Before 2020." February 2, 2014.

———. "China to Become World's Largest Consumer Market in 2015: Commerce
Minister." May 28, 2012.

———. "China Vows Sufficiency in Grain Production." January 22, 2013.

———. "Guójiā xīnxíng chéngzhèn huà guīhuà (2014–2020 nián)." March 16, 2014.

———. "More Regions to Reform Migrant Education System." January 4, 2013.

———. "Overcapacity Poses Major Risk to China's Economy." November 30, 2013.

———. "Rural Land Reform Means Bigger Profits for China's Farmers." February 2, 2014.

———. "2013 Nián wǒguó jìn chūkǒu zǒng zhí zēngzhǎng 7.6% Shǒu pò 4 wàn yì
měiyuán guānkǒu" [In 2013 China's export value grew 7.6% broke the $ 4 trillion
mark for the first time]. January 10, 2014.

———. "Zài hù nóngmín gōng tóng zhù zǐnǚ míngnián jiāng quánbù miǎnfèi
jiēshòu yìwù jiàoyù" [All children of migrant workers living in Shanghai will
get free compulsory education next year]. December 18, 2009.

Xu, Jin. "Quánguó 2yì yóukè chūnjié chūxíng shànghǎi shìmín xuǎnzé chūjìng yóu
zhàn bǐwéi 39.85%" [Across the country 200 million people travelled during the
spring festival, including 39.85% of Shanghai residents]. *Eastday*, February 19,
2013.

Xu, Ke Priyanka Saksena, Xie Zhe, Huang Fu, Haichao Lei, Ningshan Chen, and Guy Carrin. "Health Care Financing in Rural China: New Rural Cooperative Medical Scheme." *Technical Briefs for Policy-Makers* 3, World Health Organization, 2009.

Yang, Jass, and Chenyan Liu. "Turnover Rates at Chinese Factories." CSR Asia, November 8, 2005. www.csr-asia.com.

Yang Jisheng. *Tombstone: The Great Chinese Famine 1958–1962*. New York: Farrar, Straus and Giroux, 2012.

Zhengzhou Evening News. "Zhèngzhōu píngjūn měitiān chūshēng 300 rén 2020 nián rénkǒu jiāng dá 1500 wàn" [In Zhengzhou, 300 people are born per day, population will reach 15 million by 2020]. November 27, 2012.

Zhengzhou Urban and Rural Planning Bureau, "Zhèngzhōu shì chéngshì guǐdào jiāotōng xiàn wǎng guīhuà xiū biān" [Zhengzhou City Rail Transit Network Planning Revision (2015–2050). March 8, 2016.

Zhou, Kate. *China's Long March to Freedom: Grassroots Modernization*. New Brunswick, New Jersey: Transaction, 2009.

Zhu Keliang, and Roy Prosterman. "Securing Land Rights for Chinese Farmers: A Leap Forward for Stability and Growth." Cato Institute: Center for Liberty and Prosperity. Development Policy Analysis 3, October 15, 2007.

Zuo, Xuejin. "Designing Fiscally Sustainable and Equitable Pension Systems in China." In *Designing Fiscally Sustainable and Equitable Pension Systems in Asia in the Post Crisis World* (Powerpoint), January 9, 2013. www.imf.org.

Zwolinski, Matt. "The Libertarian Case for a Basic Income." December 5, 2013. libertarianism.org.

Index

About the Author

BRADLEY M. GARDNER is a Research Fellow at the Independent Institute and a Foreign Service Officer with the U.S. Department of State. Prior to joining the Foreign Service, he worked as a Research Analyst with the China office of The Economist Intelligence Unit, covering regional economics, finance-sector reforms, and international trade. He has also worked as Managing Editor of *China International Business* and Editor-in-Chief for *China Offshore/Invest In* at Mx Media, as well as covering the financial sector and economic policy for the *Czech Business Weekly* in Prague, Czech Republic.

Bradley holds an M.A. in humanities from the University of Chicago and a B.A. in Chinese from the University of Southern California. In rare moments between travels, he and his family live in California.

The views expressed in this book are the author's alone and not necessarily those of the U.S. government.

Independent Institute Studies in Political Economy

For further information:

510-632-1366 • orders@independent.org • http://www.independent.org/publications/books/